Beneath a Single Moon

Beneath a Single Moon

Buddhism in Contemporary American Poetry

Edited by Kent Johnson *&* Craig Paulenich

Introduction by Gary Snyder

SHAMBHALA
BOSTON & LONDON
1991

Shambhala Publications, Inc.
Horticultural Hall
300 Massachusetts Avenue
Boston, Massachusetts 02115

Shambhala Publications, Inc.
Random Century House
20 Vauxhall Bridge Road
London SW1V 2SA

9 8 7 6 5 4 3 2 1

First Edition
Printed in the United States of America on acid-free paper
Distributed in the United States by Random House, Inc., and in Canada by Random House of Canada Ltd
Distributed in the United Kingdom by Random Century Group

Pages 344–350 constitute an extension of this copyright page.

Library of Congress Cataloging-in-Publication Data
Beneath a single moon: Buddhism in contemporary American
   poetry / edited by Kent Johnson and Craig Paulenich; introduction
   by Gary Snyder.—1st ed.
        p.   cm.
      ISBN 0-87773-535-2 (pbk.)
        1. American poetry—20th century—History and criticism.
   2. Buddhist poetry, American—History and criticism. 3. American
   poetry—Buddhist influences. 4. Buddhism in literature.
   I. Johnson, Kent. II. Paulenich, Craig.
   PS310.B83B46 1991   89-43311
   811'.509382—dc20   CIP

Four temple gates
four ways
beneath a single moon

—MATSUO BASHO

Contents

Philip Whalen 328
About Writing and Meditation

John Wolff 338

Preface

THE HAIKU BY BASHO that serves as the epigraph to this book reaches to the core of our experience in assembling this anthology of essays and poems. The book has its genesis in our long standing interest in Buddhism and in our awareness, at the outset of the project, of the role it had played and was actively playing in the work of a dozen or so well-known American poets. We had begun this project wanting to compose an anthology that would depart from the regional or generational parameters that define most anthologies of poetry, and offer, instead, a collection defined on the basis of a chosen spiritual discipline. This, we thought, would provide for an interesting and unusual, if relatively modest, collection of work. But as responses to our letters of inquiry returned from around the country, more and more poets with a serious involvement in Buddhism were drawn to our attention. Many of these were poets with whose work we were acquainted, but whose association with Buddhism was unknown to us. Others were, for us, new faces. Nearly all shared a background of committed Buddhist practice.

As their numbers grew, we were delighted to find that what we had perceived as a significant "sub-genre" was, in fact, considerably more than that. What had begun to take shape was far more extensive—and intensive—than an esoteric influence or trend. Nor was it anything one could, in the usual sense of the word, call a current or movement, for the broad affinities of program or style often associated with such terms were simply not present. Instead, the manifestations of spiritual engagement and the aesthetics of the different poets revealed a diversity that, at least at first glance, seemed more paradoxical than clarifying. What *was* certain, however, was that the variousness of the work stood very much at odds with the fairly common notion of American "Zen" poetry as a literary remnant of the sixties, with derivative, and generally identifiable, "Eastern" criteria. It was even more immediately at odds, perhaps, with the well-diffused perception—at least in the West—of Buddhism as collectivizing and inimical to individual spirit.

As we searched for a means of expressing what we had found, we thought of Basho's poem. Here, beneath the single moon of a great spiritual tradition, were multiple manifestations of form and intent—not only at the level of poetic styles, but also in how the essays we had received revealed a richness of alternatives for *thinking through* the intersections of writing and spiritual practice.[1] The multiplicity of what came together in the anthology was, we saw, a kind of embodiment of Basho's haiku; the appearance of difference in oneness was not so much a paradox to be puzzled as a given interpenetration consistent with the very teachings of Buddhism.

And so in many ways this book is much more a gathering of unsuspected accretions than a product of editorial insight and will. If such an admission seems an unusual one for anthology editors to make, it is not intended to suggest some special quality of modesty on our part—nor, for that matter, an undervaluing of our labors. It's to say, simply, that this collection was *ready* to happen in uncommonly tangible ways. When it did, it seemed to do so in a manner parallel to those moments in poetry itself when things make themselves manifest beyond compositional intent. The result, we believe, is a document that reflects a significant and insufficiently recognized textural field—albeit an unfolding one—in American poetry.[2]

As Rick Fields reveals in his important book *How the Swans Came to the Lake: A Narrative History of Buddhism in America,* there has been, since the arrival of D. T. Suzuki in San Francisco in 1897, a patient and persistent continuity and growth of Buddhist practice in the United States. If Buddhism cannot quite yet claim to have erased the aura of otherness that surrounds it in the West, this collection is certainly partial evidence that its influence in American culture has become much greater than first sight would reveal. In fact, in terms of American letters at least, Buddhism has arguably come to be the most vital spiritual influence in poetry today.

But it is not only in recent years that Buddhism has made itself felt in American literature. The varied infusions of Eastern religion in the work of Emerson, Thoreau, and Whitman have been the subject of a number of studies, which have identified compelling affinities between Indian Vedanta, Zen, and Transcendentalist philosophy. And while discussions of the influence of Buddhism on American writing in this century have almost exclusively centered on the Beat writers coming to prominence in the 1950s, the development of much American poetry since the early work of Ezra Pound has followed lines of aesthetic investigation that bear more than coincidental affinities with age-old forms of Buddhist expression. In fact, the very beginnings of the modernist revolution in Anglo-American poetry, with its calls for "direct treatment of the thing," and formulations of "superpositional" techniques, is largely sparked by the influence of haiku on Pound and the Imagist movement he founded shortly before the First World War.[3]

Nearly concurrently, the Chinese *shih*[4] contained in the manuscripts of Ernest Fenollosa—himself one of the first American Buddhists—were to give Pound the basis for his formulations of Vorticism and his elaboration of the "ideogrammic" method in the *Cantos,* arguably the single most influential English language poem of the century. As with haiku, a vital impulse of the prosodic and semantic tensions of T'ang dynasty verse lay in Taoist and Ch'an (Zen) principles. While the elisions and juxtapositions of the *shih* are facilitated by Chinese grammatic structures, they are also profoundly architectonic, measured to unsettle the dependent and linear categories of normative thought. Form and content in the *shih* are mutually and dynamically inscribed, and it is precisely this conjoining that is transmitted into a central current of American writing. As Pound put it, "We have here not a bare philological discussion, but a study of the fundamentals of all aesthetics. In his search through unknown art, Fenollosa, coming upon unknown motives and principles unrecognized in the West, was already led into the many modes of thought since fruitful in 'new' Western painting and poetry."[5] Indeed, a whole poetic tradition, from William Carlos Williams and the Objectivists, through Charles Olson, Robert Duncan, Robert Creeley, Allen Ginsberg, Gary Snyder, and recent poets like Michael Palmer and Rachel Blau Du Plessis, can be traced back to the central role the paratactic energies of the haiku and *shih* played in the formation of Pound's poetics.[6] While most central figures of the ideogrammic stream (including, most saliently, Pound himself) have had little if any personal relation to Buddhism, one can identify, through their poetry and theoretical writings, a tradition of poetic stance that bears marked affinities with Buddhist principles of interpenetration and the identity of subject and object, meaning and form.

But because the specific articulation of these principles has varied so significantly in Buddhist artistic expression, the affinity must be regarded as a relative one. It is only necessary in this regard to compare the delicacy and detail in the art of Zen painters like Sesshu or Gakuo with the explosive boldness and abstraction of the *zenga* brushwork of Sengai, Jiun, or the contemporary Korean artist Jung Kwang, who has been called the Jackson Pollock of Zen. In poetry, the gentle narratives of the eighteenth-century monk Ryokan could hardly seem to come from the same source as the wildness and velocity of image informing the work of the modern master Shinkichi Takahashi. The possible contrasts are many, and they exemplify how the Buddhist tradition is actually *without* any single, unified body of aesthetic principles or techniques. Indeed, the reification of any particular form as the most appropriate vehicle of insight would be quite contrary to the Buddhist spirit, in its Zen, tantric, or Theravada Buddhist expressions. In part, this volume demonstrates the wide diversity of options at hand within a rich and complex spiritual tradition, and it dispenses, one hopes, with the fairly common notion that "Zen poetry" belongs only to the province of transcendent experience. What many of the writers eloquently argue in these essays and poems is that poetry in the Buddhist tradition, like meditation, is a most practical activity: part of the "real work" that is embedded into—and acts upon—spiritual praxis.

In Dogen Zenji's great *Shobogenzo,* a gathering of philosophical meditations that engage the interpenetration of language, being, and emptiness, the Zen master notes:

> There are indeed a number of ways to study the flowers of emptiness: seeing by dim eyesight and seeing by clear eyesight; seeing by a buddha's eyesight and seeing by a patriarch's eyesight; seeing by the Way's eyesight and seeing by the blind's eyesight; seeing by three thousand years and seeing by eight hundred years; seeing by a hundred kalpa's and seeing by immeasurable kalpa's. Though each of these ways sees the "flowers of emptiness," the emptiness is always variegated, and the "flowers" are also manifold.[7]

For Dogen, there is no one form or "way" of expression that is necessarily privileged over others. As T. P. Kasulis explains, commenting on Dogen's views on language, "The Buddha's truth is communicated at times discursively in ordinary words that can be rationally understood and at other times esoterically in 'intimate words' that must be grasped immediately without discursive thinking. Dogen believes that both are equally legitimate means of transmitting the correct Dharma."[8]

Dogen's perspective might help contextualize the diversity of "seeings" in this book. In various instances, poems herein are centered in a speaking voice, exploring matters of emotion or recollection within "realist," narrative frames. Such discursive strategies may seem contradictory in light of Buddhism's rejection of the self and the causal hierarchies of language and thought that structure daily consciousness. Yet Buddhism also affirms the givenness and primacy of *samsara*—the immediate realm of human experience and suffering. It is Nagarjuna, in fact, the second-century founder of Madhyamika Buddhism and the philosopher to whom the Mahayana Buddhist tradition owes the doctrine of the Middle Way, who in the very process of dismantling the referential

assumptions of language argues against the nihilistic rejection of conceptual experience. Like Ryokan, the ground engaged by poets such as
Lucien Stryk, Sam Hamill, Jim Harrison, Jane Hirshfield, or Susan Griffin is, in a sense, one that is meant to be broken through and returned to
in compassion.

On the other hand, writers such as Alan Davies, Charles Stein, Leslie
Scalapino, Norman Fischer, or Armand Schwerner work from compositional modes that share strong affinities with strategies that might be
regarded as "avant-garde" or "postmodern." While many readers may
find few if any reference points in Zen poetry for such work, it is possible
to see this writing as expanding the Buddhist aesthetic tradition into
dimensions that are expressively contiguous with the Nagarjunian deconstruction of referential thought. In these poems, language itself at
times seems to beckon—in its lack of ultimate ground—toward the emptiness of *shunyata*. In such writing, the dissolution of conventional distinctions (noumena/phenomena, reading/writing, language/world) is
projected through radical moves to break the temporal and spatial hege-
monies of narrative. The reader is confronted with the "thusness" of the
language field—not as something impenetrable, but as a realm of open
possibility.

John Cage and Jackson Mac Low, two of this century's masters of
textual experiment, push such gestures even further, into territory where
our usual assumptions of what is meant by poetry and poet must completely give way. Largely composing by chance-generated procedures,
their texts are nearly emptied of any authorial presence and are often
meant to be completed through the active interventions of readers and
performers. Subjectless (or more accurately, perhaps, with a multitude
of subjects), these works partake from, and speak of, the prereflective
and nonintentional realm that underlies being. For both Mac Low and
Cage, composition lies at the heart of their practice. And as if writing and
meditation had fully penetrated each other, words in these "poems" offer
themselves out of emptiness.

Of course, such cataloguing can only be a provisional and very tentative mapping of infinitely rich and shifting terrain. As Shinkichi Takahashi puts it in his brief poem "Potato": "Inside of one potato / there
are mountains and rivers"—a delightful expression, it might be said, of
the *Heart Sutra*'s teaching, that "form is emptiness, emptiness is form."
Such capaciousness of spirit harbors worlds of the possible; there is perhaps no richer ground for its enactment than the variousness of American
poetry.

The writing presented in this anthology speaks to that mutual richness
and demonstrates that the openness and vitality at Buddhism's heart is as

much at home here as in any other place or time. As Gary Snyder puts it in his introduction to this collection, the nature of the Buddha's teaching, which is indivisible from its practice, is as "common as grass," and has been here as long. One could predict that its spirit and our poetry will be interwoven for a long time to come. This book is offered as a strand in the actualizing of that fabric.

Notes

1. It had been our original intention to include an essay by each poet; regretfully, the constraints of space made this impossible. (Some of the poets had also preferred not to include essays.)

2. There are, of course, many other poets whose work is centrally indebted to Buddhism who might have also been included in this anthology. We have, in fact, a list of more than thirty names of widely published poets who, for the most part, were not considered for inclusion here because we were too late in finding out about their involvement with Buddhism. In any case, to begin naming them would be unfair to those many other poets we are still unaware of. It is relevant to point out, however, that among late figures of the last three decades whose relationship to Buddhism was much more than "literary," and whose importance to American literature is central, are Jack Kerouac, Lew Welch, Kenneth Rexroth, and Robert Duncan.

3. Most of the leading Japanese haiku poets were Zennists, and the form's origin and development is interwoven with the history and ontology of Zen. In an important essay, Jody Norton observes that the haiku is structured so that "mind is thus led toward an intuitive recognition of Mind—the Buddha-nature as undifferentiated Oneness—through the fusion of two ontologically equivalent yet manifestly diverse images, across the thought pause, into a powerful, aesthetically complete moment." ("The Importance of Nothing: Absence and Its Origins in the Poetry of Gary Snyder," *Contemporary Literature* 28, no. 1 [1987]).

4. *Shih,* meaning "song," is a relatively short form (usually eight to twelve lines) dominant during the T'ang dynasty of the eighth and ninth centuries, the era of such great poets as Tu Fu, Wang Wei, Po Chu-i, and Li Po. Most of the transcriptions in Fenollosa's manuscripts, as well as most of Pound's later versions in his book *Cathay* are from the poems of Li Po, a devout Taoist.

5. Ernest Fenollosa and Ezra Pound, *The Chinese Written Character as a Medium for Poetry,* first published in installments in *The Little Review* (September, 1919), cited in Rick Fields, *How the Swans Came to the Lake: A Narrative History of Buddhism in America* (Boston: Shambhala Publications, 1981).

6. Laszlo Gefin eloquently argues the centrality of the Fenollosa-Pound encounter in his *Ideogram: History of a Poetic Method,* (Austin: University of Texas Press, 1982).

7. Quoted in Hee-Jin Kim, "The Reason of Words and Letters: Dogen and Koan Language," in *Dogen Studies,* ed. William LaFleur (Honolulu: University of Hawaii Press, 1985).

8. Thomas P. Kasulis, "The Incomparable Philosopher: Dogen on How to Read the Shobogenzo," in *Dogen Studies,* ed. William LaFleur (Honolulu: University of Hawaii Press, 1985).

Acknowledgments

A PROJECT of this size and duration cannot, by necessity, be the product of its editors alone. We would like to acknowledge the following people for their roles in its actualization.

For affording us the opportunity to undertake this project as we simultaneously pursued our dissertations at Bowling Green State University, we would like to thank Dr. Bruce Edwards, in whose class the work first began to take shape, and Professor Howard McCord, the chair of both of our dissertation committees. Dr. Les Barber, Chair of the English Department, Professor Michael Mott and Dr. Gerard Smith have all provided wisdom and encouragement along the way. Thanks also to Phil O'Connor, Director of the Creative Writing Program at BGSU, who made program resources available to us on a number of occasions, and to Mary McGowan, the program secretary, for many gestures of helpfulness. Dean James Cooney, of Kent State University, Salem campus, kindly made resources available as we prepared the manuscript for final copy.

The poets who appear herein have been wonderfully supportive. We wish especially to express our gratitude to Gary Snyder and Lucien Stryk, who since the project's inception have supported, encouraged, and, when necessary, challenged us. Without their guidance, this project would have remained little more than a promising idea. The caring advice and counsel of Armand Schwerner, too, has been invaluable. Other contributors whose input has been instrumental—in numerous and diverse ways—include Stephen Berg, Norman Fischer, Sam Hamill, Nathaniel Tarn, and Anne Waldman. Although we regret that he declined to contribute to this book, we also send thanks to W. S. Merwin, whose warm correspondence was gratefully received. Surely any subsequent accounting of the role of Buddhism in American poetry will need to address his significant contributions.

The publishing houses through which much of this work has previously appeared could not have been more cooperative and gracious. The staff members at Shambhala Publications were all we could have hoped for, and we cannot imagine a more helpful project editor than Peter Turner.

For giving us our introduction to meditational practice, we are deeply indebted to the Venerable Samu Sunim and Sukha Murray of the Ann Arbor Zen Buddhist Temple. The challenges and fulfillments of those weeks of first practice will always be remembered with gratitude.

And we wish to thank our respective spouses, Deborah Elzinga and Karla Krodel, who both know that this book is also of their making. In these essays and poems the unsaid thank-yous will be found.

Beneath a Single Moon

Introduction

IN THIS WORLD of onrushing events the act of meditation—even just a "one-breath" meditation—straightening the back, clearing the mind for a moment—is a refreshing island in the stream. Although the term *meditation* has mystical and religious connotations for many people, it is a simple and plain activity. Attention; deliberate stillness and silence. As anyone who has practiced sitting knows, the quieted mind has many paths, most of them tedious and ordinary. Then, right in the midst of meditation, totally unexpected images or feelings may sometimes erupt, and there is a way into a vivid transparency. But whatever comes up, sitting is always instructive. There is ample testimony that a practice of meditation pursued over months and years brings some degree of self-understanding, serenity, focus, and self-confidence to the person who stays with it. There is also a deep gratitude that one comes to feel for this world of beings, teachers, and teachings.

No one—guru or roshi or priest—can program for long what a person might think or feel in private reflection. We learn that we cannot in any literal sense control our mind. Meditation cannot serve an ideology. A meditation teacher can only help a student understand the phenomena that rise from his or her own inner world—after the fact—and give tips on directions to go. A meditation teacher can be a check or guide for the wayfarer to measure herself against, and like any experienced guide, can give good warning of brushy paths and dead-end canyons from personal experience. The teacher provides questions, not answers. Within a traditional Buddhist framework of ethical values and psychological insight, the mind essentially reveals itself.

Meditation is not just a rest or retreat from the turmoil of the stream or the impurity of the world. It is a way of *being* the stream, so that one can be at home in both the white water and the eddies. Meditation may take one out of the world, but it also puts one totally into it. Poems are a bit like this too. The experience of a poem gives both distance and involvement: one is closer and farther at the same time.

Traditions of deliberate attention to consciousness, and of making poems, are as old as humankind. Meditation looks inward, poetry holds forth. One is private, the other is out in the world. One enters the moment, the other shares it. But in practice it is never entirely clear which is doing which. In any case, we do know that in spite of the contemporary public perception of meditation and poetry as special, exotic, and difficult, they are both as old and as common as grass. The one goes back to essential moments of stillness and deep inwardness, and the other to the fundamental impulse of expression and presentation.

People often confuse meditation with prayer, devotion, or vision. They are not the same. Meditation as a practice does not address itself to a deity or present itself as an opportunity for revelation. This is not to say that people who are meditating do not occasionally think they have received a revelation or experienced visions. They do. But to those for whom meditation is their central practice, a vision or a revelation is seen as just another phenomenon of consciousness and as such is not to be taken as exceptional. The meditator would simply experience the ground of consciousness, and in doing so avoid excluding or excessively elevating any thought or feeling. To do this one must release all sense of the "I" as experiencer, even the "I" that might think it is privileged to communicate with the divine. It is in sensitive areas such as these that a teacher can be a great help. This is mostly a description of the Buddhist meditation tradition, which has hewed consistently to a nontheistic practice over the centuries.

Poetry has also been part of Buddhism from early on. From the 2,500-year-old songs of forest-dwelling monks and nuns of India to the vivid colloquial poems of Kenji Miyazawa in 1930s Japan, there is a continuous thread. Poetry has had a primary place of respect in Chinese literary culture, and many of the best-known poems of the Chinese canon are touched with Ch'an and Taoist insight. Some of the finest poets of China were even acknowledged Ch'an adepts—Po Chu-i and Su Tung-p'o, to name just two.

Although the Chinese Ch'an masters liked to say, "The lowest class of monk is the one who indulges in literature," we have to remember that blame is often praise in the Ch'an world. The Ch'an training halls, with their unconventional dharma discourses and vivid mimed exchanges, and the tradition of the Chinese lyric poems, *shih*, with their lucid and allusive brevity, were clearly shaping each other by the early T'ang dynasty.

Ch'an teachers and students have always written their own sort of in-house poems as well. In formal *gung-an* (koan) study a student is often called upon to present a few lines of poetry from the Chinese canon as a proof of the completeness of his or her understanding—an exercise called *cho-yu*, "capping verses" (*jakugo* in Japanese). Such exchanges have been described in the book *A Zen Forest* by Soiku Shigematsu, a Japanese Rinzai Zen priest. Shigematsu Osho has handily translated hundreds of the couplets as borrowed from Chinese poetry and proverb. They are intense:

> Words, words, words—fluttering drizzle and snow.
> Silence, silence, silence—a roaring thunderbolt.
>
> Bring back the dead!
> Kill the living!
>
> This tune, another tune—no one understands.
> Rain has passed, leaving the pond brimming in the autumn light.
>
> The fire of catastrophe has burned out all
> Millions of miles no mist, not a grain of dust!
>
> One phrase after another
> Each moment refreshing.

These bits of poems are not simply bandied about between Zen students as some kind of in-group wisdom or slangy shorthand for larger meanings. They are used sparingly, in interviews with the teacher, as a mode of reaching even deeper than a "personal" answer to a problem, as a way of confirming that one has touched base with a larger Mind. They are valued not for the literary metaphor but for the challenge presented by the exercise of physically actualizing the metaphor in the present. They help the student bring symbols and abstractions back to earth, into the body. Zen exquisitely develops this possibility—yet it's not far from the natural work of poems and proverbs anyway.

The Buddhist world has produced numerous poets and singers of the Dharma whose works are still admired and loved. Milarepa, whose songs are known by heart among Tibetans, and Basho, whose haiku are read worldwide, are perhaps the most famous.

I started writing poetry in my adolescence, to give voice to some powerful experiences that I had while doing snowpeak mountaineering in the Pacific Northwest. At first I wrote "directly as I felt." Then I discovered the work of Robinson Jeffers and D. H. Lawrence. Aha, I thought, there is more to poetry. I became aware of poetry as a craft—a matter of working with materials and tools—that has a history, with different applications and strategies all over the world over tens of thousands of years. I came to understand poetry as a furthering of language.

(Language is not something you learn in school, it is a world you're born into. It is part of the wildness of Mind. You master your home tongue without conscious effort by the age of five. Language with its sinuous syntax is not unlike the thermal dynamics of weather systems, or energy exchanges in the food chain—completely natural and vital, part of what and who we are. Poetry is the leap off of—or into—that.)

I ran into a poem by Gerard Manley Hopkins with the lines

> O the mind, mind has mountains; cliffs of fall
> Frightful, sheer, no-man-fathomed. Hold them cheap
> May who ne'er hung there. Nor does long our small
> Durance deal with that steep or deep.

This helped me realize that literal mountains were not the only place to climb. I was recovering at the time from a little frostbite suffered on a winter ascent of Mount Hood. (It should be said that mountaineering is not simply some sort of challenging quest. It has that aspect, but for dedicated climbers the strategy, the companionship, and the cooperation is what makes climbing the game it is.) Climbing also opened me up to the impermanence, the total scariness, the literal voidness under my feet, the *exposure* as we say, of consciousness itself. What deep and soulful thoughts that witnessing the gulf below can give you.

My interest in writing brought me to the twentieth-century modernists and Chinese poetry; and my thoughts on nature and wilderness brought me to Taoism and then to Zen. This growing awareness of Zen was also interwoven with the discovery of Chinese landscape painting. I studied classical Chinese with Peter Boodberg and Shih-hsiang Chen at Berkeley. I learned of the poet Han-shan in seminars with Professor Chen and began a little translating of my own. I came to see that some of the finest of the Chinese poems had a mysteriously plain quality, and I wanted to understand where that came from. I started doing sitting meditation, zazen, by myself at home. These various strands got laid together in the summer of 1955 when I was a trail-crew worker in the High Sierra of California. I started writing poems out of the labor on the trails that echoed the crispness of classical Chinese poems and also had the flavor of my nightly meditations up on the cliffs. On those clear nights in the High Sierra I saw the stars as further rocks and trails leading onward and out. Although I had written dozens of poems before, these were the first I could acknowledge as entirely my own. They are in the collection *Riprap*. I made plans to travel to Japan, to learn more of meditation.

A year or so later, in Kyoto, I asked my teacher Oda Sesso Roshi, "Sometimes I write poetry. Is that all right?" He laughed and said, "It's all right as long as it comes out of your true self." He also said, "You know, poets have to play a lot, *asobi*." That seemed an odd thing to say, because the word *asobi* has an implication of wandering the bars and pleasure quarters, the behavior of a decadent wastrel. I knew he didn't mean that. For many years while doing Zen practice around Kyoto, I virtually quit writing poetry. It didn't bother me. My thought was, Zen is serious, poetry is not serious. In any case, you have to be completely serious when you do Zen practice. So I tried to be serious and I didn't write many poems. I studied with him for six years.

In 1966, just before Oda Roshi died, I had a talk with him in the hospital. I said, "Roshi! So it's Zen is serious, poetry is not serious." He said, "No, no—poetry is serious! Zen is not serious." I had it all wrong! I don't know if it was by accident or if it was a gift he gave me, but I started writing more, and maybe I did a little less sitting too. I think I had come to understand something about play: to be truly serious you have to play. That's on the side of poetry, and of meditation, too. In fact, play is essential to everything we do—working on cars, cooking, raising children, running corporations—and poetry is nothing special. Language is no big deal. Mind is no big deal. Meaning or no-meaning, it's perfectly okay. We take what's given us, with gratitude.

The poet in us can be seen at both the beginning and the end of a life. Everybody knows a child can come up with a rhyme, a song, a poem that will delight us. At the same time, the old priest on his deathbed will write a poem, his last act. The most refined and accomplished people will express their deepest understanding in a poem—and the absolute beginner will not hesitate to try to express a transient transcendent moment. There is no sure way to predict which poem will be better than the other.

Poetry is democratic, Zen is elite. No! Zen is democratic, poetry is elite. Which is it? Everybody can do zazen, but only a few do poetry. Everybody can do poetry but only a few can really do zazen. Poetry (and the literary world) has sometimes been perceived as dangerous to the spiritual career, but also poems have been called upon to express the most delicate and profound spiritual understanding.

We can appreciate Ikkyu's probing poem "Ridiculing Literature":

> Humans are as stupid
>   as cows and horses.
>   Poetry, literature—
>   works out of hell.
>   Self-pride, perverse pride,
>   the misery of the passions—
>   We can sigh for those
>   traveling so intimately with demons.

Ikkyu, a fifteenth-century Japanese Zen master and a fine (and strikingly fearless) poet himself, laughingly ridiculed his fellow poets, knowing as he did the distractions and temptations that might come with literary aspirations. His "intimacy with demons" is not to be seen in the light of the occidental romance with alienation, however. In Japanese art, demons are funny little guys, as solid as horses and cows, who gnash their fangs and cross their eyes. Poetry is a way of celebrating the actuality of a nondual universe in all its facets. Its risk is that it declines to exclude demons. Buddhism offers demons a hand then tries to teach them to sit. But there are tricky little poetry/ego demons that do come along, tempting us with suffering or with insight, with success or failure. There are demons practicing meditation and writing poetry in the same room with the rest of us, and we are all indeed intimate. It didn't really trouble Ikkyu.

For a gathering of poetry yogins and yoginis at Green Gulch Zen Center near San Francisco I wrote:

> We have to appreciate the Mind that floats our many selves, gives shelter to our hard-won information and word hoards, and yet remains a sea of surprises. (Whatever made people think Mind isn't rocks, fences, clouds, or houses?—Dogen's ingenuous question.) Meditation is the problematic art of deliberately staying open as the myriad things experience themselves. Another one of the ways that phenomena "experience themselves" is in poetry. Poetry steers between nonverbal states of mind and the intricacies of our gift of language (a wild system born with us). When I practice zazen, poetry never occurs to me, I just do zazen. Yet one cannot deny the connection.

On seeing Ikkyu's poem (and these comments) my friend Doc wrote me from his fish camp:

> Ikkyu says, "Humans are endowed with the stupidity of horses and
> cattle."
> I think Ikkyu is full of shit.
> Humans are endowed with a stupidity all their own.
> Horses and cattle know what to do.
> They do it well.
> He is right about poetry as a work out of hell.
> We ought to know.
> Phenomena experience themselves as themselves.
> They don't need poetry.
> We are looking at a mystery here.
> How do these things have such an obstinancy
> and yet are dependent on my consciousness?

When I practice fishing with two teenagers
poetry never occurs to me.
But later it does.
I can go over the whole day.
Hooray! That's what being human is all about.
It is just as much a weakness as a strength.
You say language is (a wild system born with us.)
I agree.
It is wilder than wild.
If we were just wild we wouldn't need language.
Maybe we are beyond wild.
That makes me feel better.

Doc Dachtler
Kanaka Creek

Beyond wild. This can indeed include language. Poetry is how language experiences itself. It's not that the deepest spiritual insights cannot be expressed in words (they can, in fact) but that *words* cannot be expressed in words. So our poems are full of *real presences.* "Save a ghost," you might be asked by your teacher—or an owl, or a rainforest, or a demon. Walking that through and then putting a poem to it is a step on the way toward realization. But the path has many switchbacks, and a spiritual journey is strewn with almost as many land mines as a poet's path. Let us all be careful (and loose as a goose) together.

I will enlarge on that a little further: Being careful, being organized, structuring your work, will help you get a lot done. But being deliberate does not guarantee the advent of a poem or insight that *surprises* you. In writing, one can search things out, track them, stalk them, and *get* them. We do that a lot in prose. The other case is the one where something is eerily standing just behind your shoulder breathing on your neck, and then suddenly you are being carried off. Of the two, being chosen is by far the most amazing, certainly in terms of the poems that come forth. In *both* cases—the cultivation of formal mastery and the attitude of availability—meditation helps. Meditation helps one be open, and also it makes one capable of (spiritually) striking when the time is right.

Spending time with your own mind is humbling and broadening. One finds that there's no one in charge, and is reminded that no thought lasts for long. The marks of the Buddhist teachings are impermanence, no-self, the inevitability of suffering, interconnectedness, emptiness, the vastness of mind, and the provision of a Way to realization. An accomplished poem, like an exemplary life, is a brief presentation, a uniqueness in the oneness, a complete expression, and a kind of gift exchange in the mind-energy webs. In the *No* play *Basho* (Banana Plant) it is said that "all poetry and art is offerings to the Buddha." These various Buddhist ideas in play with the ancient Chinese sense of poetry is part of the weave that produces an elegant plainness, which we name the Zen aesthetic.

What about the poets of this anthology? As contemporary American poets, they have no set forms and strategies that would mark them as a group, and as far as poetic affiliations go, they could be said to represent several current streams of writing. But diverse as they are, there are some qualities I think they share. They are unsentimental, not overly abstract, on the way toward selflessness, not particularly self-indulgent, wholehearted, nonutopian, fluid (that is, able to shift shapes), on the dry side, kindhearted, unembarrassed, free of spiritual rhetoric and pretense of magic, and deeply concerned with the questions of knowing—"how knowing gets itself known," as Steve Benson says. They have come up with sophisticated questions rather that simpleminded answers. There is a rich, shrewd prose commentary in this gathering too.

Diane di Prima provides a bit of history: "What then appeared to us to be a Zen point of view was soon taken for granted as the natural—one might say axiomatic—mind-set of the artist. A kind of clear seeing, combined with a very light touch, and a faith in *what one came up with* in the work: a sense, as Robert Duncan phrased it years later, that 'consciousness itself is shapely.' A kind of disattachment goes with this aesthetic: 'you'—that is, your conscious controlling self—didn't 'make' the work, you may or may not understand it, and in a curious way you have nothing to lose: *you don't have to make it into your definition of 'good art.'* A vast relief."

Allen Ginsberg: "Express yourself courageously—be outrageous to yourself."

Jim Harrison: "The kapok in the zafu beneath your ass is without nationality." [Jim Harrison's poem "Walking" an unresisting, unhesitating passage through all conditions, all the edges of awareness open—]

S. J. Marks: "Suffering warms the coldness of life."

Jed Rasula: "Waves are the practice of water. Writing is the practice of language." [Although I would like, in respect to the countless poets of our long past who did quite well without writing systems, to change "writing" to "writing?"]

Andrew Schelling: "Gautama Buddha was contemporary with Panini, the world's first, probably the world's greatest, linguist. Coincidence? Who's kidding whom? Something big was going on, these simultaneous inquiries into Mind and Language, twenty-five hundred years ago."

Charles Stein: "I think I want my mind to be loose. Precise, but loose."

Tu Fu said, "The ideas of a poet should be noble and simple." In Ch'an circles it has been said, "Unformed people delight in the gaudy and in novelty. Cooked people delight in the ordinary." This plainness, this ordinary actuality is what Buddhists call thusness, or *tathata*. There is nothing special about actuality because it is all right here. There's no need to call attention to it, to bring it up vividly and display it. Therefore the ultimate subject matter of a "mystical" Buddhist poetry is profoundly ordinary. This elusive, ordinary actuality that is so touching and refreshing, all rolled together in imagination and language, is the work of all the arts. (The really fine poems are maybe the invisible ones, that show no special insight, no remarkable beauty. But no one has ever really written a great poem that had perfectly no insight, instructive unfolding, syntactic deliciousness—it is only a distant ideal.)

So there will never be some one sort of identifiable "meditation poetry." In spite of the elegant and somewhat decadent Plain Zen ideal, gaudiness and novelty and enthusiastic vulgarity are also fully real. Bulging eyeballs, big lolling tongues, stomping feet, cackles and howls—all are there in the tradition of practice. "I like my garden to appear full, luscious, disheveled, blasting / Out of its borders spilling into the copse beyond the form," writes Norman Fischer. And there will never be— one devoutly hopes—one final and exclusive style of Buddhism. I keep looking for poems that see the moment, that play freely with what's given,

Teasing the demonic
Wrestling the wrathful
Laughing with the lustful
Seducing the shy
Wiping dirty noses and sewing torn shirts
Sending philosophers home to their wives in time for dinner
Dousing bureaucrats in rivers
Taking mothers mountain climbing
Eating the ordinary

appreciating that so much can be done on this precious planet of samsara.

Gary Snyder

Jane Augustine

Jane Augustine is a poet, fiction writer, and mixed-media artist. Winner of two fellowships in poetry from the New York State Council on the Arts, she teaches at Pratt Institute in Brooklyn and in the M.F.A. Summer Writing Program at the Naropa Institute in Boulder, Colorado. She has two chapbooks, *Lit By the Earth's Dark Blood* (Perishable Press, 1977), and *Journeys* (Pig Press, U.K., 1985).

Beginningless Beginning

I grew up in the Berkeley hills in a rather plain California stucco house with a triple-terraced garden steeply sloping up behind it and a view of San Francisco Bay from every front window as well as from a stone bench under an apricot tree at the top of that garden. As a child, in summer I could creep in under Shasta daisy bushes to make a snug hideout and when tired of being pensively enclosed leap up and stand on the bench with Berkeley and Oakland and the whole blue bay below to look at. For a moment I'd think I'd like to be a bird and be carried by the wind even higher, if it weren't so scary. But the oriental principle of beauty and balance—heaven, earth, and man—prevailed in my universe from the beginningless beginning, so it naturally came about that I was drawn to poetry, sung or read to me, before I could read or write.

Poems intensify the beauty of things, and longing for that intensity made me start writing poems when I was about six years old. I read Wordsworth's poem on a "host of golden daffodils" dancing in the wind, and I saw that the words referred to the big yellow star-and-trumpet daffodils that bloomed in our garden, next to starry white narcissus, indescribably sweet-smelling. I wanted to shape the words into some equivalence of that ineffable odor.

11

"Accept the challenge things offer to words," says Francis Ponge, at the beginning of his poem "The Carnation," and continues: "I won't give up until I have put together a few words that will make anyone reading or hearing them say: this has to do with something like a carnation." From the beginning that effort has been mine too. It doesn't imply mimesis, representation, or "realism," particularly. It's just that the world we live in makes the words live. A poem therefore must be the living thing, not a bouquet of artificial flowers decoratively painted to look like real ones, an interior designer's cultural artifact.

Sitting meditation is really just doing nothing, so it can't be artificial either—there's no way to fake it, or make it look like something impressive. I began sitting after many not very sane years in which I couldn't write or do much except fight my own mind. Words and my experience were walled off from each other. In this state I began to go to hear talks by Chögyam Trungpa Rinpoche. He was not a fake, not a manipulator; I woke up enough to be able to hear him, really, when he said: "The situation is workable." He gave me a very great gift: after telling me to sit, he left me alone—alone in both senses: I was not advised or meddled with in any way, and I was on my own, genuinely responsible for finding my own path.

Living by myself for a while in a cabin in the Sangre de Cristo range of southern Colorado, where I hiked actual rocky paths up to the high lakes, I began to write again and found my subject, central image, or "objective correlative"—the mountains. I still go every summer to live where 13,000-foot peaks rise behind the cabin and ponderosa pine spreads down to the valley below—another union of heaven, earth, and man. So "Cloud, Rock, Scroll" becomes the title and motif of a poem on H.D. (Hilda Doolittle), whose Imagist poems established the "new" verse forms in English of the early twentieth century. She conveyed a vision of the sky and sea islands of ideal Greece in words resembling those of the Chinese T'ang masters Li Po and Tu Fu, but the images began with the pear tree and roses of her childhood garden in Pennsylvania.

Concentration on the image—direct presentation of the thing—is the source of the similarity between the Chinese, whom I never stop reading, and the modern woman writer. One seldom needs to add comment to the image, since, as Robert Frost said, "Anything more than the truth would be too much." Images clearly seen reveal how things are symbolic of themselves, an idea expressed in the teachings of *mahamudra,* but already manifest long ago in the daffodils.

Rules for oneself may be unbuddhistic, but I have some:

1. Don't write what anyone could call Buddhist poetry. If this category existed, it would have to be as corrupt as Christian or Communist poetry, or Catholic mathematics—a propaganda tool for an institution or a sectarian point of view.

2. Avoid Buddhist terms whenever possible. Readers don't know what they mean, and often get the impression that the poet is showing off his mysticism or "higher levels" of achievement, which strikes a wrong note and defeats the poem.

Still, when writing on my father's death I used lines from *The Tibetan Book of the Dead* because I said them for him then, but even so, now I question this seeming inevitability of word choice. It was probably a mistake—too high-sounding, as if I were religious when I'm not.

Death, grief—these are the real incentives to Buddhist practice. "Kill the Buddha," say the Zen teachers, meaning, "Don't be religious; don't design yourself fancy ideas of being a special person, a mystic, a big deal," and meaning also, "Don't rely on an external saviour; nothing and no one outside you will save you." This fact—that one has only oneself to work with—connects back to being alone. I'm just alone, fundamentally, not propped up by any external religion or politics.

So poems can't be propped up either, or made to look good according to some fashion of the moment, or slanted to fit the purported taste of some imaginary external judge of good poetry—the theistic or eternalist view. And they can't be crazily vomited out because anything goes—the nihilist view is wrong too. Words have power. Things have power. They are what they are, and the poem is a conduit between them, one hopes, if the poet is sane—that is, remembers death.

Two stories stay in my mind. One is told of Prajapati, the aunt of Shakyamuni. She walked from village to village talking to mothers whose babies had died at birth or in infancy, because those women especially had need of the Buddha's teachings.

Another is told of Lakshminkara, the "crazy princess," an eighth-century *mahasiddha* (great master). Sent as a betrothed child bride to a non-Buddhist prince, she watched him and his retinue ride in from the hunt with animal carcasses slung across their saddles and understood what her future married life would be like. She fainted and then went mad, gave away her money and jewels to her servants, tore off her silks, smeared her body with dung, and hurled objects at whoever came to talk to her. She wandered off, eating food thrown out for the dogs and living for many years in cremation grounds, among stench and corpses. Cut off from the conventions of upper-class Indian life, she found the way to live. When the prince encountered her again, by accident, and understood her accomplishment, he asked her to teach him, but she told him that one of his latrine sweepers was to be his teacher. When he asked which of his many sweepers, she said, "Put your trust in the man who feeds the people after finishing his work."

William Carlos Williams wrote:

> It is hard to get the news
> from poems, yet men die every day
> for lack of what is found there

These lines are from his elegy and apologia written not long before his death, "Of Asphodel, That Greeny Flower." A garden encyclopedia says that the asphodel with its long, leafless stem belongs to the lily family, whereas the Chinese sacred lily is related to the Amaryllidaceae, along with the narcissus and daffodils. A dictionary adds that the "asphodel" of ancient Greek poetry is usually narcissus. In the mountains, the rare sego lily is called mariposa, butterfly—the mind released from the cocoon— and looks like pale white wings. These facts are useful for poems, as Marianne Moore said of baseball fans, a wild horse taking a roll, and the "immovable critic twitching his skin." Poems report news, the news that is in things, most of which eludes the poem—hence the vision and workability of writing.

From Cloud, Rock, Scroll

(from the Colorado mountains, meditating on H.D., mythmaker and inspirer of mythmaking, in her sea garden, speaking as a dead priestess, and as Helen in Egypt—"she is the writing herself.")

(i)
ROCK ROSE

Wild roses among rocks
in sun-blanched grasses
twine the cabin's split steps.

Petals infold
concealing gold stamens.
Drought crumples them.

Night frost will surely
scatter them—
yet more at morning
bloom among boulders.

Your peony-pink
is stitched on green leaf-brocade
sprung from dust.
How has desert thrust you up?
You are foreigners
born here.

Your silk spins from a harsh worm.
You flare in high wind.
Do your roots reach
down to a hidden river?

> *At sundown mountains darken.*
> *The sky fills with rose-fire clouds.*

(ii)
ROCK LILY

Lily of the rocks,
lily of aspen shadows,
rare mariposa, your ivory petal-cup

streaked with subtlest purple
bends to the meadow
on a single stalk

as a wise woman averts her eyes
not needing praise.

> *Delia of Miletus, priestess,*
> *healer, speaks after death as one*
> *who 'stood apart,*
> *and 'sang a secret song.'*

Lily of willow springs
lily of mountain mist
you are rooted far
from white sand
or temple column—

an offering
without shrine

(iii)

WRAITHS

(*on a trail to treeline*)

Fog hides the peaks.
Scarves of mist drift among pines.
The dark boughs drip.

No laurels in these woods,
no spirit's scented flower-breath.
The stream runs cold

and rough. It speaks
of nothing beyond itself. It eats away
the trail beside it.

Deeper woods.
                An old mine
shaft—human remnant—fills with dirt
under a fallen fir-trunk—

after that no trace
of construct or precursor.
                        Harder rain.

Wet trees stand
in the path, wraiths black but veiled.
I fade into their landscape, insubstantial,

present by absence.
No deity, shrine nor scripture,
crucible nor angel
but her seeking mind remembered

and these shape-shifters, pale
behind cracked branches, draw me on—

> *Rock creates the fall of water,*
> *air its dispersion,*
> *earth its catch-basin.*

> *Formless runnels*
> *form cross-trails.*
> *Mud hollows hold*
> *a momentary silver,*

> *sky-mirror*
> *light-giver,*
>
> *incessant*
> *reformation of water.*

(iv)
SKY

Blue sky of emptiness:
deepest blue   intensest
blue of amethyst, of lapis,

of turquoise buried
under most ancient rock   blue
of transient lupine,

drooping harebell at
lake's rim two miles high in blue
air where fossil shells

imprint the granite—
blue   o blue over these peaks
once sea-bottom, your height

depth endless, 'nothing
whatever yet everything
comes of it.'   Water

in blue tarns above
treeline covers pearly stones
that sink from sight as

mountains rise to hide
in clouds that lie on those blue
mirrors. Sky, water,

rock self-existing,
twined in utter difference,
open mystery

—'not why it is but
that it is'—that mind can see
as word and woman

in one hieroglyph:
she is the writing herself

—and light to read it.

A Bracelet of Turquoise From Aguilar

On my arm, three small oceans
anchored on two silver equators,

their green-blue brilliant as mountain noon,
ecstatic hue, shimmer of a glacial lake

two thousand feet below the climber
who walks the highest ledge over sheer drop

not perfectly steady but facing
both heights and depths, luminous herself

in that blue luminosity.
Turquoise from Aquilar contains black matrix;
a heavy continent upthrust blots out the blue,

outlines it.
                    I walk, in a nightmare, a tunnel
or half-blind street, searching how to

'clean up my act.' A woman friend is angry:
you were rude, you were reading when you should

have been watching the actors—her eyes
are light blue.
                    I wake to strange knowledge.
In waking life she likes me, especially for
not hiding how I build myself up, how I strive

for those heights and expansions. In this waking
the man who loves me holds me in his arms.

That dark weight I call my 'self' heaves up
rough-edged into turquoise air, the opening day.

The dream-self fades, the day-self won't resume,
too tentative, yet both are lingering—

On my arm, the weight of this rock: blue
waters, black islands sand-polished to luster,

poise in the grip of harsh metal that's hammered
and beaten and molded.
                    The sky
opens endlessly outward but never
fails to encircle the planet.

Steve Benson

Steve Benson has worked in retail book selling in the region of San Francisco Bay and has published several books of poetry. He has been an actor, and a freelance proofreader at a corporate law firm, has done volunteer counseling, and has collaborated in intermedia performance work. His most recent books are *Blue Book* (The Figures, 1989) and *Reverse Order* (Potes & Poets, 1990).

Disconstitution

My poetry has tended to begin again persistently as an inquiry into what I am and what mental and verbal processes can do to demonstrate, effect, and obfuscate such a subject and such an inquiry. I have not tried to use my writing to flesh out theories of my own or any typical psychology. Composition processes constructed like experimental conditions both encourage and channel associations that may be as impetuous as they are constrained. The qualities or values demonstrated are more ethical and aesthetic, I think, than matters of theory or fact. The kinds of attention that go into reading and writing my poetry depend on an exercise of even hovering as well as license for diverse spontaneous and compulsive interventions. I always have a sense of the poetry as an engagement, an occasion for reflection, a study mutual to myself and any reader.

I wrote the paragraph above about a week ago for an application to a graduate program in clinical psychology. What's written below will be inevitably a sort of rewriting of the above—in other words, at another time—a translation into, if not another language, another circumstance. The chronic and repetitive are as native to any one of us as breathing; the presumption to think the next thought, as though that might be separate or distinctly other than the one before, is one of these chronic and repetitive tics that measure one's persistence over against the rising and the fading light and the exuberant and the restive body that would be claimed to ground the self.

As I rewrite, the page gets shorter. To determine what is essential seems to require that I read into it. Then shall I toss away what appears to me to be essential? It is certain that I cannot keep it. If it remains anywhere, it remains in the writing, yet I may not see it there another time.

I have all the pages I've ever written before. Many, it would seem, might pertain to the subject of the relation of Zen study to my work, and yet none of them are of any use to me. I refuse to look at them. I want to know what I think now—under the pressure of this set of circumstances. Now it's up to me, or . . . The delusion that I haven't a thought in my head is a furious outpouring of resistance, anger, guilt, and fear. I don't have anything (worthwhile) to say and I will be shown up as a fraud (that is, nonexistent). That illusion of nonexistence is cheap; it gets me nowhere.

Did I say (again and again) that my writing originated in an insecurity about the nature and actuality of my existence? I expected, having written and so being able to have my writing (a trace of my actual existence in whatever respects could obtain in that) read (by others, or by myself at another time), to be able to identify who or what or how I am by the comparison writing might afford to such an other. Comparison: not with an objective "standard," but as though the writing were a shadow left deliberately behind, that could then be compared to another shadow (the reader's, cast down next to it, or across it, on the page).

There are a million things wrong with this formulation—perhaps including, to my personal regret, its factual accuracy. Is this just a tale I've made up, when I was off my guard, dreaming excuses, constructing defenses? Researching through my back pages might tell, but I don't trust to any particular objectivity or stability of vantage for interpreting the data I would find. So what? The theory exercises a semblance of authority that affords a nudge, to get the impulse over the hump of self-absorptive complaint and into an inertia that exerts consideration toward effects and toward their complementary failures.

The model here (the idea of the "shadow") sort of presupposes the possibility of translation, through a membrane (I keep writing "membrance," by mistake, then shortening it), as though one thing, albeit having suffered some sea change, corresponds in whole and parts to some other, the way a film ("*n.* 1. A thin skin or membranous coating") forms a shadow on the field light throws through a strip of celluloid onto a white screen, analogous to the form of that film itself, if *seen* in two dimensions, and also to that image a camera aimed at some time ago.

Writing leaves these black marks. The reader projects through them the light of a fantastic, wayward, riffling regard, and interprets the play of surfaces that appears to generate itself before that reader's imagination (but actually *in* it?) as though that play of surfaces were *something* to be known, as though there were beyond it a ground one could assume, as though that *were* that reader, *what* she or he knows. The reader assumes this interpretation or activity could match what I found myself knowing.

This is what I mean by translation: there is no real or true translation; there is only the fantasy that there might be—that you might know or imagine what I do, that one's self-knowledge might be replicated in another person (or in the same person, another moment). This ridiculous, quixotic, futile chimera has been a source of persistent fascination with me (due to my resentfully dissatisfied narcissistic neediness?). It's colored my pervasive sense of any poetics as tragicomic, without hope of stability or resolution.

The very materiality and the consequent ephemerality of this membrane (nitrite on the strip of celluloid, ink on the paper) constitute or overdetermine the writing (the movie, the shadow, the translation) as two-faced from its inception. And then every other value or function that, with utmost civilization and circumspection, we may attribute to it or cultivate in it will propagate this duplicity. In willing collusion, the reader will make something of it, as instinctively and willingly as a dog will fetch a bone thrown out into the field, as though snatching it from the borderline of oblivion and returning it to the pertinent intentionality and valuation of the agency that threw it out there. It's this aspect of enhanced significance ("It counts. You count."), so peculiarly foregrounded and lit up in *art* but with which we typically attempt to ground the world to us anyway, that the reader scurries in and out of and in aftereffect, which may also permeate a reading of the poem, bathes in luxuriously.

> I am interested in the dynamics and discoveries of "wandering mind" or inattention, and assume this attribute on the part of listeners and readers, including as it does that reversion to the self-discipline of a concentrated, purposive attention. The "level" or valency of significance of any particular set of particles of text being up for grabs, not specifically preconditioned by the material preceding it, the reader is asking repeatedly, "What is it?" The discipline of attention is rhythmically refreshed and reinforced with the discipline of inattention, just as understanding is always in an active and shifting relationship to misunderstanding and unwillingness to understand.

"Not taking anything for granted." This goes for genres and codes (and credos), as well as for styles and techniques. It means the purpose and rationale of anything is up for question. (When I'm feeling moralistic or comparative, it means it all *should* be up for question. "Should" is, of course, up for question too, when I remember.) This means too that the writing doesn't take responsibility for proving or convincing.

> The realization of inquiry as an instable performative event is more central to my intentions than the derivation of any conclusions or the beauty or balance of an overall statement or poem. Consequently, the written work survives and adjusts itself to publication in a posture of compromise between its role as documentation and its occasion as a ground for further research and reflection. I have the feeling this two-faced-ness isn't peculiar to my work but is endemic to writing that alerts the imagination and that it quickens the pulsation of tension and release, of reciprocal discovery and transformation, that lets the work seem to "live" with a stimulating presence "of its own." Writing, like meditation, serves me as a means of checking and challenging myself, of stopping myself in my preoccupations by derailing their devices, inviting me to begin again, to plow under, to acknowledge what I can't control or articulate comprehensively by naming.

It's not that nothing matters or that everything is relative, so much as that everything has the considerate, selective urgency of experiment: the artwork is a separate yet equally vital and impenetrable occasion, the constraints of which sector off this field for a set of investigations into how knowing gets itself known and what it might *mean* by doing so. (What does it think it's up to? Does it know anything about itself at all?) I notice that, the way I put it, I seem to assume that knowing may have some intentionality, some plans or purposes.

January 10, 1989

from The Stand-in Under Duress

A sense of linearity defined against
the confetti made of everything what sense matters contains
Speak of or for things: 2 ways to speak in relationship
    either   trying to speak from their position
    or   trying to speak about them
    To speak of/about things/circumstances acknowledges their
resonance, they— In other words, if you're trying to describe
a thing, that flower there, it's red and has this green thing
        hanging down that's a support system for it
        they— Things echo back, distort or challenge, answer

what's said
Mute resistance or susceptibility
In other words, it either fights, which is not exactly— or
it just appears to take it.

The 'loose' translation torn from its assignation.
The bare wall treated as space.
(In other words, suppose you're given this loose translation,
like, "well, it's red and it's got this green thing coming off
the bottom," then what are the properties of

A picture held up as for display, a New Image painting of
a man, you're confronting this person in the picture head over
heels, literally, his hands on his feet and his feet in the air
trying to make this strange adjustment in order to meet you eye
to eye. The perspective of this vision very closely parallels
your own.

The image is of a page in the middle, a man standing on his
hands in it, stuck under his feet and the typewriter ribbon
streaming through them; he can't meet them, he can't move, or
else the feet are in the air on the blank page head twisted
against reasonably to look right at you, sky-light behind—
Through a freaky twist he sees what we can't, the aimless
rummage of the ribbon through the expectation everything will
comment on one another, maybe not quite soon, blow up in smoke
like a balloon leaving shock everywhere, dispelling confusion
licensing mind to start, a handicap in effect.

I had a vision as a ribbon, sheer continuity of imagery
seeming to maintain such contact in the midst of imminent
explosion within which we're sitting assuredly as possible.
Shock everywhere, etc. There are still more streams stuck
through that, like tracks explorers hypothetically take,
wondering what will get them into scrapes and which a surer
chance of survival and furthering the means. Survive in the
face of death, extend one's life through all that threatens
it, to survive I mean as an intention, rather than just a fact
of being one has happened to lapse into. To survive purpose-
fully, go through circumstances of being, floating sometimes
pounding at the pavement with your fist, feet, experiments in
timbre, focusing the mind like a hot sword or the detail of
a break.

Many of my images seem to be of penetrating, as though to
live were to get through some thick seamy— but the temperature
is different, of a different kind. I was going to talk about

an idea of writing that wants to go every which way, rub every parameter, and only by the macrocosmic presumption of the omniscient— not the narrator obviously, but— and who for all I know might not be a writer either— in fact, this authority is a fictive extension of the technology of writing into the hunger and fatality of one's own mind. Does it make any kind of persistent sense, but, tautologically, by demanding a gestalt horizon, practicing over and over codes to resurrect that gasp that catches in the throat hesitating to be described until some other starts to materialize?

Imagine a man like so, then, or a woman, though a mean tangled man is easier for me. He enters the bookstore head first, slams his hand down on the counter, and says, hip shoved against the newspapers, "What do you have for my daughter? She's ten, she's in third grade." I'd taken an orange from the cooler before coming on the shift, so managed to meet the thermometer in case the background register too purposely decided anyway. "Everyone thinks for him or her self" in this society, which is impossible anyway. We all govern each other's needs as we see fit, perhaps because the language, like all researches, is communal and coordinated; I can't say business unless someone comes in and buys something. It's easy to listen to someone who's listening to you, whether or not you're speaking: when they're trying to find out who or what you are, or what the difference is— But what is it like to listen to someone not even consciously pointing attention towards their own potential difference but just running on ahead? Who knows what they may be thinking? The cash register then drops open and white snakes wriggle out to redeem the moment of explosive expectation. Of course words do something; many seem to do the same, whether tactfully compassionate or cavalierly torquing the charade, may pick a pocket of so far indefinite understanding and substitute some token of exchange, ironically spinning person as plural to a no-man's-land of lolling insecurity, a suspended gray plate miles above some food.

Fiction

The inadequacy of the case was good at keeping it together.
Allegiance; tact. I was always writing it in my mind.
   (Time almost over.) The neighborhood ball. Defection
     to a side. ("Come over, Red Rover!")
The eagle—or the gull—on the pavement, doesn't have to do with
  this.

They can't embrace.
The cerebral judgment learning to spell a language of choice from
   the fragments of devices sentences plan across the yard.
   Adults quarrel among themselves, supposedly being
   childish, public toilets within sight.

The world relative to some beyond, on which may be fixed a lever.

Translate the accessible into the inaccessible and back.

   Going to be, going away.

   Clouding the surface, numbered by webs, a dark murmur
   tries to break through dawn's tension. Thought
   boils over as I rush to get it. You
   face someone. Sitting on a toilet, I turn
   suddenly right, thinking I'd seen a sign there,
   paper, pasted, probably warning, something
   to be read in any event, but nothing's there
   but the stall wall, hospital green flecking
   a pale salmon, an otherwise undifferentiated field
   seen as relief projection of a color blindness test.
   The superficial resemblance of overlapping borders
muddles one's sense of circumstances. One knows they
aren't exactly there but may fall trampled in their pattern
any second without realizing. World events ooze further
on, are scarcely what they seem. Hands stick in the shake.
The experimental phase still legendary.

What's unknown, one claims for one's own, illuminating the
windowpane with an eye of fixed grace. But we distinguish
an alienated and stereotypical application of ethics. This
all needs, it says here, to be reduced to something too,
standing for something potentially posed as use. Revising
it in perspective, register the concentration foreshortening
effects. Certain key pits eliminated. But passages? The
lamp spreads intensity and edges. Cut half to expose the
necessary tissues. I can't beat what I did, can't respond
that way again.

Let's try to repeat all the things we tried to say today, but for some
   reason weren't able to.
Alright. But we still won't be able to.
That's okay. Let's see what we say.
Okay. After thinking all day of things I wanted to do, I can't think
   of anything to do.
Okay. After thinking of things all day, I wanted to do, I think of
   you, my darling, my honey.
That's terrible. You're doing it completely wrong— you're not
   even— you're doing something else.
I know. What else were you going to say?
Nothing . . . I was going to say, I am the other half of your brain.
Why do you think I'm only a half?
That's not what you were supposed to say. You're supposed to say,
   That's what they say.
Or, I don't know.
Then— then what?
Are you okay? Is this going okay?
I don't know. Actually, I really don't think things have another side.
You think they only have the side facing towards us?
That *appears* to— No, let me say, Did you ever notice that 'have'
   and 'halve' have the same sound, are the same words, almost? I
   almost confused them, when you—
My equipment is in my pocket, and I'm suddenly thinking about it.
   I've got to do something to it, with it.
I was thinking, when I was on the way home, walking, how stul-
   tifying it is, or was, seemed to be, there's nothing left but just to
   go ahead and *do* it, whatever, whether one is in the mood or not,
   I mean what other mood can there be, except of frustration, but
   I was still walking home, and since I was thinking of something
   I couldn't do until I got here, I wasn't able to see that that kind of
   absolute either/or fatalism, about doing it or not doing it, is exactly the good thing about it, I mean that it's nothing but a relief
   to do it.
You really think that?
But instead I thought, at the time, and there was nobody to say it to,
   that it was going to be terribly difficult, and I'd be just faced with
   a mess of tangential possibility, and I'd just have to move forward
   through it inexorably, like dragged by time, mainly, and trying to
   effect an intention or two while mainly I'm damaging, thwarting
   and wasting all these possibilities—
That's interesting, to think of giving yourself to things as wasting
   them— I don't think there's any alternative.

Except to see only what you intentionally mean.

I guess so.

Now what'll we do?

Are we finished?

Well, I managed to say what I could remember wanting to say, I can't think of anything else I've saved up, that I wanted to say.

How about all the things that, say when you were reading, and things came into your mind, that weren't on the page, half-thought-of?

I wonder what's the difference between them and thinking of something else when I'm talking to someone. I think there is a difference, sometimes. Some things in conversation get syntactically finished and I just don't want to say them. But the things you mentioned were only— mostly kinds of sensory— formulated as an image, in the sense of, a soundless, or a subvocal word image, sensory like a word, like a small animal, in a context, or contextualizing in some way, a carrier of the other, so that immaterial as it is, actually slightly hallucinatory, in effect, there's always the sense of something underneath it, or else behind it, however you look at it, however you—

Like you always look forward to it, and you always look back to it, but you never . . .

What?

What was I going to say? I was going to say something before, but—

About "a soundless word image"? "Contextualizing"? "Carrier of the other"? "Immaterial as it is"?

Oh yes!, what was interesting was that you almost immediately forgot whatever it is, the thing itself, that you wanted to say, that wasn't really there anyway, but just the occasion to say it, but I don't think that was really there then, either, so . . .

Stephen Berg

Stephen Berg is founder and coeditor of the *American Poetry Review*. Poet, essayist, translator and anthologist, he is the recipient of Guggenheim, National Endowment for the Acts, and Ford Foundation Translation fellowships, and has been awarded the Frank O'Hara Memorial prize and Columbia University Translation prize. His books of poetry include *Grief* (Viking, 1975), *With Akhmatova at the Black Gates* (University of Illinois Press, 1981), *In It* (University of Illinois Press, 1986), and *New and Selected Poems* (Copper Canyon Press, 1991). His translation of the poetry of the fifteenth-century Zen master Ikkyu, *Crow with No Mouth* (1989), was published by Copper Canyon Press. *Sleeping Woman,* a public artwork involving words in collaboration with painter Tom Chimes (commissioned by the Fairmount Part Art Association), has recently been installed along the Schuylkill River in Philadelphia.

Oblivion

I

I thought the Greek root would tell me something I didn't
    know
but there is no Greek root—ME, MF, fr. L. oblivion-,
    oblivio
and then to forget, perhaps fr. ob- *in the way* + *levis*
    smooth—
an act or instance of forgetting . . . but I thought it meant
    something like where we go
after death, i.e. "to oblivion," the future of us, the true,
inescapable condition of existence without consciousness,
human consciousness. So it's being forgotten more than
    anything
that hurts us, and immortality is—to be remembered?
What it really means is what someone said to me a few
    months ago

when I said "I've always thought of you as immortal, I
    guess,
but now I know you're not." "Yes, I am. I'm in your
    mind," he replied.
It's that "in your mind" that has a kind of murderous
    tenderness,
it's like saying someone *let* himself be part of you, to help
    you, yes,
but also because he trusted he could not be destroyed by
    your mind,
just as a mother takes up a screaming baby into her arms
and croons to it and pats it over and over Now Now Now
    she whispers and presses
the helplessly small body to her breast and it
calms, whimpers, calms fully and falls asleep there.

2

The elephant-gray elms bathed in overcast light glow.
Cobalt-blue sky peeps through hills of shaggy clouds.
Windy and cold, 30 on the thermometer outside my
    window,
chirpings off to my right from behind Jim Wilson's house,
branches stripped clean, bouncing and waving, the day
    bright, brighter,
then darkening under speeding clouds, everything held,
accepted, in an order, the mind and world one
forgetting in which only this moment has meaning. It's
    much much clearer now.
All's changed color: the lime-freckled salmon brick of Jim's
    house,
for example, suddenly flares crimson, fists of ailanthus
    pods
and stuccoed housewalls seem the same bleached tan,
    even the copper cross
(lived here ten years and never noticed it) perched on the
    church tower
a block northeast is greener, complete because of the light.
But it's the jumble of stacked, rusting
tricycles and two-wheelers leaning against the side of a
    house on the backyard shed roof
and the oval yellow plastic wading pool tilted on edge
next to them and the cement bucket, white, left on
    the shed and, most, the homemade red

white and blue doghouse planted a few feet from the
    shed
that give this life its fullness, for now—
the miniature, peaked, green tarpaper roof and doorless
    door look kind,
a gift of absent hands, or animals taken in, fed.

Big Mood

The people who came here first
from Puerto Rico's calm, crisp air,
their lighted plastic Christs and tin window decorations—
roses, Virgins, scenes of the Nativity—
gutted, half-rehabed, finished shells,
the gleam of fresh paint on a door,
on a sunny day this
"It is enough to be here
I accept things as they are"
makes being a man
miraculous, sane,
makes the plain act of standing here
on my front steps
considering loose bricks tamped lengthwise
into the dirt bordering our bent young cherry
complete, like being what I see, like air.

No Word

Inside each of us
there's a mammoth dome of light
like the one sheltering me
when I walked out that night
alone in the middle of pines
in Maine, near the ocean.
Black wherever I looked,
even my arms and hands.
I reached out and grabbed a spray of needles,
then tried to see down the path
I knew went in front of me
through elms and brush to water.
Nothing. So I looked up
and found it, flowing in its white fires above my face,
with no word for what it is,
as when a face turns toward you

on the street and you recognize
someone you do not know.

To the Being We Are

Nobody's
with me this time.
Gray sky smeared over the gray trees and water.
Nothing's in it.
Each word the sages use to describe God
disgusts me.
Who cares what exists?
Driving. The river on my left.
Long floors of shale cling to the hillsides,
yellow weeds jut right out of the stone,
cars, the road, distance,
they don't stop anywhere
I'm not here so I see everything,
listen and see,
hands perched on the black shiny wheel
so lightly it steers by itself.
I park and step onto one of the dirt paths
leading to the water and stretch out
by the side of the river and stare into the
cloudless sky until
that's all there is. Not even
my heart. I can't feel anything
except the vast moist breath of the unnamable thing
we live in, someone's mouth close to my skin . . .
forget it.
I know the spirit doesn't exist.
What dies is hatred, and love, too.
And you can call anything anything then.
Today the river didn't move, or the leaves,
or anything except us, bodies tossed anywhere,
held anywhere. Listen, I was trying to
see God, touch God. I laid my cheek on the grass.
I could hear that nation I will be joining under me
celebrating itself, at peace with itself,
chewing things.
I stuck my fingertips into the gritty mouth
of the earth.
I pissed in the bushes.

Bob Boldman

Bob Boldman has lived in Dayton, Ohio, all his life, though he has
traveled to study meditation. A Zen Buddhist, he was, for a time, a teacher
of kundalini yoga. He has worked in hospitals as a clerk, emergency room
technician, orthopedic technician, and, as of late, a respiratory therapist.

Zen, Art, and Paradox

When I first read of Zen I was in college, studying fine arts. I began with
Essays in Zen Buddhism by D. T. Suzuki. As time passed, usually as I
worked at my easel, I began having spontaneous experiences of the
empty mind. And at times, beyond that a Void. Shortly thereafter I had
a "death experience." I had been working at a hospital, in the evenings
and late at night, and had been contemplating for days the matter of the
first death I had witnessed when I passed into a "shining, blissful Void."
After that I began reading, studying, meditating, and the primary interest in my life was no longer art. I still sketched, painted, sculpted, but my
works became a reflection of my meditation. The Void permeated my
drawings, and objects began to fade, recede into the space around them.
I continued to read and to practice. And I traveled. But I found essays
difficult, and the essence of practice often eluded me, and though experiences came, it was always when I was least expecting them—not when
I was seeking or wishing for them. I found translations of the Zen classics
to be unrewarding, and the elements of Japanese culture uninviting. It
was not until I happened upon a book in a used bookshop entitled *Zen
Poems of China and Japan* that it seemed I had extracted the essence from
Zen. On the pages were words pointing beyond words, to the Zen mind.
To experience. On that day it seemed as though even the heavens had
moved. Relatively late in life I turned from painting to writing. Poetry
became my link to Zen, whereas others that had begun with me had
found their link in zazen, or in translations or essays. I did not attempt to

publish, for the poems I wrote were an element of my Zen practice—
usually outdated in weeks, always pointing away, at a wordless state
where forms merged with other forms and form merged with nothingness. In this way I practiced (and wrote) for many years. And it was
many years later that I found another book, in a discard bin, entitled *The
Haiku Anthology*. I was impressed, but was not really affected until I was
loaned another book, *Modern Japanese Haiku,* translated by Makoto Ueda.
As before, when I had read *Zen Poems,* each poem endeavored to point
away from itself, to awaken even the page it was on.

As a result I began writing haiku and, from the beginning, publishing
in the small presses. This was because I found writing haiku difficult, and
it was only by submitting to publishers that I could be critiqued. Gradually haiku became wedded to my Zen practices and I became widely
published. To me haiku had become the voice of paradox, for I had
found that within the Zen-Void-Suchness, paradox was not resolved but
embraced. And when I wrote a haiku I could live with, I could embrace,
it was paradox.

the priest
his shadow caught
on a nail.

This was the first haiku I wrote that I felt contained Zen-spirit. It
speaks of tangible events, but also leans away from them, into the Void,
beyond sense, and into paradox.

To me Zen art *is* Zen practice, and therefore does not seek to develop
a remedy for paradox, to take sides with good or evil, dark or light, form
or nothingness. It must embrace both, and therefore exist upon the
vanishing edge, in between abstraction and experience, in between form
and its absence. Each experience we have is in conflict with others, every
thought contradicts others. Within this art I attempt to express that Zen
practice is not to retreat into the Void but to bring the Void forward into
experience and thought.

lark song
down to
its bones

Zen art forms, practices, essays, are unlike any other because they
must evolve into paradox. Paradox cannot be plainly understood or
explained, but can be experienced. The content of Zen art is irrelevant,
as is the form. For it is my opinion that Zen art exists not to exemplify
or exalt Zen but to move away from itself, away from Zen, Buddhism,
Buddha, into an understanding that is paradox.

A few years ago I wrote a poem that reflected my state of understanding. I was meditating on the Void, and it had assumed my nature.

Awakened!
The wind returns the sky
to the burial site of Buddha

Because I am nothing,
nothing can be done for me.

Recently my understanding became that of paradox, Void and form coinciding. Upon this occasion I wrote a poem.

Awakened!
In the wind are the ashes
of Buddha.

As I return from the Void,
and put a shoulder to the wheel
of birth and death.

In a few years my understanding may have changed. I will at least have another poem that begins:

Awakened!

dawn
loosened
leaf by leaf

walking with the river
the waters does my thinking

in the pines
my spine
straightens

writing this
the dandelions ache
in my fingers

turning in my sleep
the skeleton
key

mist,
panties on the line

a firefly
on the web
lit

zazen
growing
from my shadow

dark
moths moving
the distant mountain

lilies open
the lonely
hand

at night i find them
the plants from the garden
entering my dreams

Olga Broumas

Olga Broumas was born in Syros, in the Cyclades Islands of Greece. She is the author of six collections of poetry in English, among them *Beginning With O* (Yale University Press, 1977), a Yale Younger Poets selection, and two books of translations from the Greek of Odysseas Elytis. A recipient of fellowships from the National Endowment for the Arts and the Guggenheim Foundation, she makes her home in Provincetown, Massachusetts, where she is a licensed massage therapist.

I came across Phillip Kapleau's *The Three Pillars of Zen* the summer of my twenty-first year, just after graduating from architecture school. I was a resident advisor at the dorms for incoming "disadvantaged students" and worked two shifts a day at the local upscale restaurant to make graduate school tuition. I had given myself a year, earlier that spring, to get out from under a terrible depression that centered, or seemed to, on the emotional difficulty of being deeply attached to my father, an orphan who had loved me consistently and deeply as his first and only blood kin the length of my life, and being appalled by his decision to remain in the army in the context of the military junta that had seized power in Greece a few months before I left to study in Philadelphia, a junta that was, each day, torturing friends of my friends and dividing, once again, my country. I had vowed to myself that if I could not find some joy in living at the end of that year, I would kill myself. It was a calm decision, unlike other of my histrionic attempts at resolving inner conflict.

My most significant religious influence to that date, apart from the generic and mostly cultural Greek Orthodoxy I was raised in along with almost all other Greeks since the Nazis had pared down our populace, had been the Hassidic concept of serving God through joy, through acts of a whole and integrated self, with sin defined as any act of divided intention. I felt completely divided and, in that division, completely fallen from the grace that constituted, for me, a deity. I read *The Three Pillars of Zen* and began sitting zazen. I either did not read, or failed to retain, instructions about limiting sittings to a half hour twice a day. I sat for almost all my free time, hours on end when I had them. Soon I began to lose my sense of continuous self, to go for walks and become what I looked at, to find myself in strange parts of town without memory of how I arrived there. I was frightened—the university was in a dangerous part of Philadelphia—and also thrilled. As a child, my dearest solace had been to look at something, usually the sea, until I became it for a spell, however brief. A stillness began its hold on me.

I moved to Oregon for graduate school, found the courage to drop out of architecture—my family's and culture's choice of an acceptable profession for a well-brought-up girl: one could practice at home, among the family—and spent a year working the heavy limestones in the lithography studios until I found that I could study formally what I had done privately since childhood: write. I read more on Zen. I sat as best I could. I heard of Gary Snyder and his statement, graduating Reed College when he had been my age, that the most difficult discipline is that of following your own desires. I read W. S. Merwin, whose directness, depth, and simplicity seemed to me unimpeded utterance from innermost song to God's ear. In us all. I heard they both practiced zazen. I had company. Since then I have deepened daily my attempt to "sweep the garden, any size," to practice what I may conjure as belief and keep the words about it as closely limited to song as I can. I don't trust words that are not linked, through the music of poetry, to both sides of the brain, to heart and soul.

My most active desire, having been carried in the womb in the bloody aftermath of the Second World War, having been raised in one room while the adults told and retold the forced marches, the missing frost-bitten digits, limbs, the humans missing from our fold, the executions carried out by the jagged tops of tin cans opened with those old-fashioned implements still found on Swiss army knives so "it took longer"—I was maybe three when I heard that in the soft and bitter murmuring in the circle of light around the table just beyond my crib—my most active desire is for peace. As best as I can define that, challenged by a workshop on Nuclear Despair and Empowerment where most of us came up with static definitions hinging on the absence of war, is that the active state of peace is healing. My garden has become the human bodies I can touch, in love, respect, and silence, in my daily practice as a massage therapist. I sweep and sweep and am incredulously thankful it is possible to thus construct a life. Poems rise from that sweeping and are held in memory for a time, then written down. Everything else is the spirited noise of this world, this time, if I am still enough, even the dying that surrounds us

now in our small, gay, fishing village where more than a quarter of our
people may be infected by AIDS, mirroring the terrible suffering everywhere on the globe. I have no hope, nor absence of hope. I have the
sweeping. I bow.

Sweeping the Garden

for Deborah Haynes

Slowly learning again to love
ourselves working. Paul Eluard

said the body
is that part of the soul
perceptible by the five senses. To love
the body to love its work
to love the hand that praises both to praise
the body and to love the soul
that dreams and wakes us back alive
against the slothful odds: fatigue
depression loneliness
the perishable still recognition
what needs

be done. *Sweep the garden, any size*
said the roshi. Sweeping sweeping

alone as the garden grows
large or small. Any song
sung working the garden brings
up from sand gravel soil through
straw bamboo wood and less
tangible elements Power
song for the hands Healing
song for the senses what can
and cannot be perceived
of the soul.

from Lumens

> *There are no secrets.*
> *It's just we thought that they said dead*
> *When they said bread.*
> > —John Cage

BRIDGE

A song unhinges bitterness easy enough from sorrow
Some vowel litany with stops to pass until
The most ordinary is not

AFTER YES

To build the chair
To build the chair
To build the chair
To sit
To sit
Witness the mystery
World

EACH LOVE

Parallel
Infinite
Unequal

TEACUP

Flared at the lip like clematis
One swallow
Raised bottom where the sugar sleeps

PRIMITIVE

The heart leaps the heart opens the heart
Closes the heart grieves

It blames it sinks
Into your hand it heals

Prayer With Martial Stance

Days of eyes
nights of velocities
of insects planets soundwaves
of the brain
days and nights without interruption
green days of chlorophyl light and lungs
water and silence streaming
where no logger trucks
no biker rides I camp
here imagining this
daily discipline
of silence
Silence

Break in praise

Avoid causes of complaint

Change what you can't avoid

In this be

Ruthless

Wedding Song

Our mound of earth dug up
  for a new bedroom
is as graceful as the dunes we drive to see.
  The seen
dwarfs our scale, we feel it
  tugging at our brow

and bow
  like guests in it yet we
for bending are allowed to
  sing

some blond dune's surface.
　We believe what we see

through the image is the song
　at its source
and so assume the world,
　love, shares our intelligence
of heart, the natural
　hug, the quick kiss overturned. The smug

like their smiles more than what makes them
　smile:
white cows in November meadows,
　in the galactic ravines.
Venus enters the bull at birth and again at will.
　A door shuts, twice.

The twelve rings of the night, outposts
　reefs, pockets of great abandon, what
we expected poetry to be
　as children, yield. As women
we are beautiful for remembering
　how to relax all force

in an unmeasured field.
　The moment heals. Out
past where the shale you think is
　going to hold and doesn't
silver fish leap from the water.
　Tears are worlds not seen.

Mercy

Out in the harbor, breaths of smoke
are rising from the water, sea-smoke
some call it or breath of souls,

the air so cold the great salt mass
shivers and, underlit, unfurls the ghosts
transfigured in its fathoms, some

having died there, most aslant
the packed earth to this lassitude,
this liquid recollection

of god's eternal mood. All afternoon
my friend counts from her window
the swaths like larkspur in a field of land

as if she could absorb their emanations
and sorting through them find the one
so recent to my grief, which keeps,

she knows, my eyes turned from the beach.
She doesn't say this, only, have you seen
the sea-smoke on the water, a voice absorbed

by eyes and eyes by those
so close to home, so ready to resume
the lunge of a desire, rested and clear of debris

they leave, like waking angels rising
on a hint of wind, visible or unseen, a print,
a wrinkle on the water.

John Cage

John Cage has published numerous books, musical compositions, and
graphic works. He has received a Guggenheim Fellowship and an award
from the National Academy of Arts and Letters for having extended the
boundaries of music. He has been elected to the American Academy of Arts
and Sciences and the American Academy of Arts and Letters. He is musical
advisor for the Merce Cunningham Dance Company and was the 1988–89
Charles Eliot Norton Professor of Poetry at Harvard University.

from *Where'm'Now*

When I was young and still writing an unstructured music, albeit me-
thodical and not improvised, one of my teachers, Adolph Weiss, used to
complain that no sooner had I started a piece than I brought it to an end.
I introduced silence. I was a ground, so to speak, in which emptiness
could grow.

At college I had given up high school thoughts about devoting my life
to religion. But after dropping out and traveling to Europe I became
interested in modern music and painting, listening-looking and making,
finally devoting myself to writing music, which twenty years later, becoming graphic, returned me now and then for visits to painting (prints,
drawings, watercolors, the costumes and decors for *Europeras 1 & 2*).

In the late 1930s I heard a lecture by Nancy Wilson Ross on Dada and
Zen. I mentioned this in my foreword to *Silence,* then adding that I did
not want my work blamed on Zen, though I felt that Zen changes in
different times and places, and what it has become here and now, I am
not certain. Whatever it is it gives me delight and most recently by means
of Stephen Addiss's book *The Art of Zen.* I had the good fortune to attend
Daisetz Suzuki's classes in the philosophy of Zen Buddhism that he gave
at Columbia University in the late 1940s. And I visited him twice in
Japan. I have never practiced sitting cross-legged nor do I meditate. My

work is what I do and always involves writing materials, chairs, and tables. Before I get to it, I do some exercises for my back and I water the plants, of which I have around two hundred.

In the late 1940s I found out by experiment (I went into the anechoic chamber at Harvard University) that silence is not acoustic. It is a change of mind, a turning around. I devoted my music to it. My work became an exploration of nonintention. To carry it out faithfully I have developed a complicated composing means using *I Ching* chance operations, asking questions instead of making choices.

The Buddhist texts to which I often return are the *Huang-Po Doctrine of Universal Mind* (in Chu Ch'an's first translation, published by the London Buddhist Society in 1947), *Neti Neti* by L. C. Beckett, of which (as I say in the introduction to my Norton lectures at Harvard) my life could be described as an illustration, and the *Ten Oxherding Pictures* (in the version that ends with the return to the village bearing gifts of a smiling and somewhat heavy monk, one who had experienced Nothingness). Apart from Buddhism and earlier I had read the *Gospel of Sri Ramakrishna*. Ramakrishna it was who said all religions are the same, like a lake to which people who are thirsty come from different directions, calling its water by different names. Furthermore this water has many different tastes. The taste of Zen for me comes from the admixture of humor, intransigence, and detachment. It makes me think of Marcel Duchamp, though for him we would have to add the erotic.

As part of the source material for my Norton lectures I thought of Buddhist texts. I remembered hearing of an Indian philosopher who was very uncompromising. I asked Dick Higgins, "Who is the Malevich of Buddhist philosophy?" He laughed. Reading *Emptiness: A Study in Religious Meaning* by Frederick J. Streng, I found out. He is Nagarjuna. But since I finished writing the lectures before I found out, I included, instead of Nagarjuna, Ludwig Wittgenstein, the corpus, subjected to chance operations. And there is another good book, *Wittgenstein and Buddhism*, by Chris Gudmunsen, which I shall be reading off and on into the future.

from Themes & Variations

Mesostics on the name of David Tudor

we Don't know
At dawn
and Valley
thIngs
to Do

whaT we're doing

zen becomes confUsing
south sea islanD

mOuntain

mountain bReeze

Desert

lAke

to leaVe no traces
nothIng in between
no neeD

before stuDying
whAt
we'll haVe
zen Is zen

while stuDying
excepT

bUt
after stuDying

mOuntain

mountain bReeze

we Don't know
At dawn
what i haVe

zen Is zen

all i neeD

mounTain
for yoU

south sea islanD
Of
mountain bReeze

sounDs of birds

A way
and Valley

zen Is zen

herDed ox

we Don't
mountAin
we'll haVe
when we fInish
to Do
whaT we're doing
for yoU
Duality

they fly abOve
mountain bReeze

Desert
lAke

whereVer they're
a lIttle value

Difference

the white birDs
reheArse together
they haVe

zen Is zen
while stuDying

sTill am

tUt
Duality
Odd
River

"There Is Not Much Difference Between the Two." (Suzuki Daisetz)

iT
is A long time
i don't Know how long
sInce
we were in a room toGether   now i hear
that yoU are dead   but when i think of
now as now i have the Clear impression
tHat
tenderly smIling you're alive as ever

Toyama 1982

deaTh is
At all times
liKe
lIfe
now that you are aGhost
yoU are as you were
a Center among centers
world-Honored
world-honorIng
late yeSterday evening
tHe moon in los angeles
low in the east not fUll
do you see suZuki daisetz
give him my lOve

Alan Davies

Alan Davies conducts his business in New York City. His recent books include *Name* and *Signage*.

Zen?   *Who Knows?*
or
A Small Statement of Disbelief for Norman Fischer

What doesn't signify? Walking down the street you might see red hair passing. At that moment of recognition, the red hair is a signifier, signifying its signified, the word *red*.

There is nothing arbitrary about the sign. When we think that there is we are noticing our own confusion about the arbitrary way, and our own arbitrariness about the confusing way, in which we have assigned it to a place or to places in our mind, in our uses of it, in the world, and so on.

In fact, what is interesting is the act of recognition.

The Zen master says to you: "When sitting, just sit." Then, as if not wanting you to be bored, he gives you a koan upon which to concentrate as you sit. Perhaps we have learned to delineate: When sitting, just sit; when doing koan, just do koan; when sitting and working on koan, just sit and work on koan.

I would not try to define koan practice. And yet to say what I would say, that koan practice is its own definition, is already also my definition of it. In fact, just: koan practice.

But I will admit that as I understood and used koan practice at one time, it was that very solipsistic nature of it, or which I ascribed to it, which perhaps was that about it which most appealed to me. This solipsism, which I would define by referring to its tautological tendencies, was at that time congruent with, or at least in metonymic accord with, other circular tendencies of thought, feeling, action, and the circulating tendency to separate them. This is something which I think we all understand. We all live, were educated, and think, in the so-called West, in Western ways. We have all shared in the production of oppositions, definitions, delineations, and dialectics.

Perhaps we have all done too much without having done enough. Perhaps we have all made the mistake of doing that, of thinking that, of calling that a mistake, and so on.

What is the relationship between koan study and writing?

Neither of them can be described, neither of them makes any sense, and maybe we should leave it at that.

One can talk about them, but *describe* them? and be done with it? And the longer they're talked about, the less sense either makes, or is it, perhaps, that the more sense either makes the less necessity is attached to the doing of either? Let's do one or the other, or both, and a few other things too, and, yes, leave them all at that.

Zen. Who knows?

It is frequently asserted that discovery is a process of redefinition, and frequently it is explained that growth also is a matter of redefining values and the like. But seldom is this understood, and more seldom yet for what it really is.

First, it is important to leave the definitions alone. They're too sluggish for words. If we must imagine it this way at all, think of the dictionary page, then leave the definitions alone and move the words around. In this way, courage is attainable, for instance, rigor will achieve a new value, simplicity will get its due, and an alert life of pleasure will be possible. These are examples from my experience. You know what you need.

And last, we might do well to leave the definitions, as they say, behind. Entirely behind.

The dialectical thinker stands a step back
from the nondialectical thinker but they're
both looking in the same direction.

Those many pines
are read as people
and it warps the scale.

So this is where people are who take drugs all the time:
kind of off to the side.

The mother. The daughter.
She's been talking to her for a long time.
It's beautiful.

It's too simple, you see,

too above-board.

It may be just what we want.

Desire, —affection with an occasion, really.
Desire, affection
with a location.
You strung an incredible tent across an abyss.
There is no connection between a cardinal and the infinite number;
I want to habituate the filthy poor of this and every other world
for no reason;
I love you.
The world is lewd with your little street tragedies.
You always make me think of licking the back of the neck of the
    proletariat.
We'll see if you can get by with half of what you think you need.
It's lust. We'll call it lust.
Her poignant breasts. —here damaged by description.
A vulva.
Along the top of the hill the row of shining teepees were one by one
    set light to.
Emboldened by love so to speak;
we came away in her hands.

REALITY REARS ITS UGLY HEAD

I always liked the sound of other voices.

Just this is the ground of all being.

Dicktion is male.

We can fecundate ourselves without reasons
like this plant next to me,
crepuscularly sending power where it is needed.

Deny the problem.

Deny the solution.

Literature, so boyish
really, and a little silly.

This leaf is death.
It's not nothing.
It's an illusion.
And in your case it's trapped in a thought.

Loose your tongues,
the marvelous clear eyes of destiny
are shooting down the track.

But reality is after all a personifiable reality
and so it contracts
into the young stalks of our children
that prevent it from being so.

How perfectly simple that this
is all there is.

Diane di Prima

Diane di Prima lived and wrote in Manhattan for many years, where she became a significant figure in the Beat movement. She later moved upstate to participate in Timothy Leary's psychedelic community at Millbrook. For the past twenty-five years she has lived and worked in northern California, where she took part in the activities of the Diggers, lived in a late-sixties commune, studied Zen Buddhism, Sanskrit, and alchemy, and raised five children. She is currently based in San Francisco, where she is one of the cofounders and teachers of the San Francisco Institute of Magical and Healing Arts. Her current works in progress include an autobiographical memoir, *Recollections of My Life as a Woman.*

As it did for many other artists of my generation, Buddhism first came into my life in the mid-1950s by way of D. T. Suzuki's essays on Zen. What then appeared to us to be a Zen point of view was soon taken for granted as the natural—one might say axiomatic—mind-set of the artist. A kind of clear seeing, combined with a very light touch, and a faith in *what one came up with* in the work: a sense, as Robert Duncan phrased it years later, that "consciousness itself is shapely." A kind of disattachment goes with this aesthetic: "you"—that is, your conscious controlling self—didn't "make" the work, you may or may not understand it, and in a curious way you have nothing to lose: *you don't have to make it into your definition of "good art."* A vast relief.

In 1962 I came to the West Coast and encountered Shunryu Suzuki Roshi, who had recently begun the San Francisco Zen Center. Meeting Suzuki Roshi for the first time I met some rockbottom place in myself. I have often said that if Suzuki had been an apple picker or a welder, I would have promptly taken up either of those arts. I sat because he sat. To know his mind. It was the first time in my twenty-eight years that I had encountered another human being and felt trust. It blew my tough, sophisticated young-artist's mind.

When I returned to New York I brought a zafu back with me. Sitting alone in New York was not the same as sitting at Soko-ji, but I stuck with it and wrote to Suzuki once or twice a year through Richard Baker, who passed Roshi's comments back to me. And whenever I found myself in San Francisco on poetry business, 5:00 A.M. would find me hitchhiking up Bush Street to zazen.

Finally, after five or six years of this, I moved to San Francisco with my four kids. One of my main motives was to be close to my teacher; the other was to do my share of the work of the "revolution." It was 1968. My days were filled with distributing free food, writing poems for guerilla theatre, hosting the Diggers and the Living Theatre, and sitting zazen. For a while four of the fourteen adults in my commune sat, and we could be seen daily pushing my blue VW bus with its broken starter up Oak Street in the predawn light.

Suzuki Roshi sat with us every morning in the old Japanese temple on Bush Street while the birds and the city slowly came awake, and after the chants he would stand at the door and bow individually to each of us, scrutinizing us keenly but gently as we left. I felt that nothing escaped him, and that the manner of our bows, the hesitation, self-consciousness, or bluff we presented as we set out, told him everything about where we were "at."

I learned much more than I know—even now—from Shunryu Suzuki Roshi in the few years that I studied with him. At the last lay ordination ceremony in 1971 I received a name from him, which I treasure to this day: Kenkai Banto means, I am told, both "Inkstone Ocean, Ten Thousand Waves," and "Inkstone Mother, Ten Thousand Children" (in that *ocean* and *wave* in this particular relation also stand for *mother* and *child*). My friend and teacher Katagiri Roshi also laughingly translated it as "Ocean (or Tempest) in an Inkstone, Ten Thousand Poems."

After my teacher's death I found the differences I had with Zen Center to be more than I knew how to deal with: my anarchism was at odds with their probably necessary organization. I continued to sit on my own, and to rely on brief visits with various teachers when I was "on the road" to further my practice. In particular, I sought out Katagiri Roshi in Minneapolis, Chögyam Trungpa Rinpoche at Naropa Institute in Boulder, and other friends: Kwong Roshi and Kobun Chino Roshi when I could.

After eleven years on my own, during which I was also studying, working in, and teaching some of the Western spiritual practices we call Magick, I came to the end of where I could go without a teacher. It became clear that I needed a tradition of Magick that was unbroken, dharmic, and explicit, and a master and *sangha* I could connect with. The Tibetan tradition, growing as it does out of *Bönpo,* is the Buddhism that most explicitly addresses the juxtaposition of the magickal view of the world and the dharma. In 1983 I went to see Chögyam Trungpa Rinpoche, whom I had known since his first visit to Tassajara in 1970 and had worked with for ten years at Naropa Institute, told him of my dilemma, and was accepted as his student. At this time I am studying and practicing the Vajrayana—with, I suspect, something of my own Zen flavor.

I cannot really pin down the influence of Buddhism in my work or my life—I have written very few explicitly "Buddhist poems." What I feel is that Buddhism has permeated my way of seeing the world and of being in it. For me, the basic dharmic teachings are simply axiomatic: emptiness, interdependence. They describe the actual *structure* of the world. Put another way, the dharma is the warp of the world on which the colors are woven.

But more than that: whether we are aware of it or not, something of Buddhism pervades American consciousness. When Bodhidharma came from India to China with the Buddhism that was to become Ch'an and later Zen, his answer to the Chinese emperor's request for "the holy teachings" was "VASTNESS, NO HOLINESS!" This seems to me to be at the very core of who we are, what we are doing in the world at this time, as a nation and as a species, as we move out of time into space. It's a big risk and, as the dharma reminds us, there are no answers—but consciousness *is* shapely, and we do know more than we know.

Tassajara, 1969

Even Buddha is lost in this land
the immensity
takes us all with it, pulverizes, & takes us in

Bodhidharma came from the west.
Coyote met him

I Ching

for Cecil Taylor

                                :mountain & lake
the breakup
                        of configurations.
all the persian rugs in the world
                        are doing a dance,
or conversely smoke.

outside my window the hoods are shouting
                        about Ty Cobb
on Friday nite it was girls
                        & they were drunk.
But the white car stays the same
                        that they lean against.

Trajectory

suffering, sd the Lama, is the greatest blessing
because it reminds us
to seek the disciplines, like:
I don't drink coffee 'cause I once
had an ulcer; and of the four
"continents" of humans, this, the South
Continent (planet Earth) he says
is best because hardest. So this
1970 must be
an excellent time
when even the telephone poles scream in agony
when the streets are fire beneath
all our windows,
when even the Bodhisattvas stop their ears.

as if they could.
as if we could, we sit
zazen, retreat to the woods
fast, pray, remember bardos
unwritten, even in Tibet.
they come again.
they have us by the throat.

we break before the image of the future

now no more blood runs
from the wounded Earth. our hope
lies in the giant squid that Melville saw, that was
acres across. our hope
lies in the insect world, that the rustling
Buddha of locusts, of ants, tarantulas
of scorpions & spiders
teaching crustacean compassion might extend it
to our species.
(the Hopi say that it's been done before
and plant their last corn before coal mines
destroy the water table)   a child of mine
waits to be born in this.   *Tristesse. Tristesse.*

Dolor. Now is no star seen
as it was seen by our fathers
now is no color on the hills, no brightness
in the bay. Now do sea creatures rot
with oily fur
with oily feathers choke on black sand.
the hungry ghosts like a wind
descend on us.

Letter to Jeanne (at Tassajara)

dry heat of the Tassajara canyon
moist warmth of San Francisco summer
bright fog reflecting sunrise as you
step out of September zendo
heart of your warmth, my girl, as you step out
into your vajra pathway, glinting
like your eyes turned sideways at us
your high knowing 13-year-old
wench-smile, flicking your thin
ankles you trot toward Adventure
all sizes & shapes, O may it be various
for you as for me it was, sparkle
like dustmotes at dawn in the back
of grey stores, like the shooting stars
over the Hudson, wind in the Berkshire pines

O you have landscapes dramatic like mine
never was, uncounted caves
to mate in, my scorpio, bright love

like fire light up your beauty years
on these new, jagged hills

Visit to Katagiri Roshi

A pleasure.
We talk of here & there
gossip about the folks in San Francisco
laugh a lot. I try
to tell him (to tell someone)
what my life is like:
the hungry people, the trying
   to sit zazen in motels;
the need in America like a sponge
   sucking up
whatever prana & courage
"Pray to the Bodhisattvas" sez
   Katagiri Roshi.

I tell him
that sometimes, traveling, I am
too restless to sit still, wiggle &
   itch. "Sit
only ten minutes, five minutes
at a time" he sez—first time
it has occurred to me that this
wd be OK.

As I talk, it becomes OK
there becomes some continuity
in my life; I even understand
   (or remember)
why I'm on the road.

As we talk a continuity, a
   transfer of energy
takes place.
It is *darshan,* a blessing,
transmission of some basic joy
some way of seeing.
LIKE A TANGIBLE GIFT IN THE HAND
   In the heart.
It stays with me.

Patricia Donegan

Patricia Donegan is the author of *Without Warning, Bone Poems* (*Minicantos*), *Hot Haiku,* and the forthcoming titles *China Poems, Earthquake Flowers,* *"Chiyo-ni" Woman Haiku Master,* and *Replies to a Hungry Bowl: Homeless People, U.S.A.* She lived in East Asia for eight years, including one year of study with a haiku master in Japan. As a student of Chögyam Trungpa, she has practiced and taught meditation for many years. For a decade she was a teacher of Poetics at Naropa Institute in Boulder, Colorado. She is currently adjunct faculty at the California Institute of Integral Studies and College of Notre Dame and teaches in the Poets in the Schools Program in San Francisco.

from Haiku Studio

Last night lightning
this morning
the white iris.

Long walk—
cherry petals stick
to the bottoms of my shoes.

Plum rain—
the young prostitute
washes her underwear

As rain drops diminish
I hear the tapping
of the monk's wooden bell.

Winter afternoon
not one branch moves—
I listen to my bones.

Half-Open

These days
I wear my robe half-open
the purple silk parts, showing scarlet lining
the thick blue sash, a tangle on the floor,
I sway around the house easily
feel the weight of the robe
a cool breeze on my skin as I pass the window
& see no one's watching
only blue sky outlines clear-cut mountains half-clothed
& green grass tufts peek through
the cracked brown earth.

For Tu Fu's Bones

April 1987, 'Tu Fu's Cottage', Chengdu, China

Late spring afternoon
walking in & out of ancient pavilions
white butterflies between pink azaleas
dragons carved in wood
white lilies on still ponds
zither & flute music in the air
I wander into the poet's cottage
see in the glass case
all your bare bones, Tu Fu
your skull tilted back, a few yellow teeth left
your jawbone gaping open
as if you died in pain or screaming your last poem,
a sad song for the oppressed people
who pulled carts loaded with bricks
along the Yellow River
while others sat in silk robes
sipping wine, listening to
your scathing poems, 1,200 years ago.
Tu Fu, you are now all bones
yet not crumbled to dust
skin shrunken, clinging to the bone
your penis flat & withered
even your toenails intact
your bony knees big & knobby,

your bone arms & hands crossed over your rib cage.
Oh, Tu Fu, I didn't want to see you like this,
you look horrible, embarrassing, tiny, shrunken
like nothing very human
nothing like a poet
should, yet like everything
that's hidden behind the
skin, beyond the mirror,
to the place of mystery, down
to the bone, down to the very poem
you wrote, about eternally
drinking wine in the face of death.

The Perfect Dialogue

March 1987, Guilin/Yangshuo, China

The new moon sets over midnight sky's
late winter night in Chicago,
I hunch over the white paper, gaze into space
the hum of the electric typewriter like
the locusts in the flooded rice fields of Yangshuo
last spring, where a barefoot old man
in baggy blue pants crouched next to his water buffalo
pausing between centuries,
& we, too, got off our bicycles & stood together
for a moment on the dusty road
breathing with them in & out.

Down to the Bone

Not for a king or queen
  a furtive kiss
  scintillating intellect
  sense of humor
  secure home
do I love you
but for the possibility of hearts
  connecting to bone.

In my dream
I write in black ink
  on your white bones

cover them up with little words
   like the monk Hoichi's body, yet leave
   your skull untouched, pure white,
the gold tip of the pen
   scratches your bones
ink seeps into the cracks
   like the river Yangtze
   through mountains & valleys
   night & day
cracks on oracle bones,
   "poems, unspeakable, at last."

My own skull I give you
that is, if you want it
that is, if I die first
here, have it, take it,
hold in both hands as
a gift, bouquet, cup of tea
touch without fear or hesitation
explore every crack & bump of me,
feel the weight, heavy, a gold crown,
   conch shell, piece of cut glass
   yet none like the weight of the skull,
note the texture, smooth breasts, rough sand
smell the musty scent of ocean water, in between
   earth & sky,
poke your fingers gently through the hollows
   of my eyes
is it sad, frightening, ugly, awesome?

Speak to me, come on, sing a mantra,
   a song of Milarepa, or quiet hello
remember my soft kisses,
   my obsessions, the hard letting go,
let me be a reminder, each breath, each word,
   each gesture, your last,
above all, fill my skull with ink, to write
   your words, fill me with amrita
   to splash on Buddha's face above your shrine,
   & finally hold me up empty to the night
   stars or wide sunny sky of day.

Norman Fischer

Norman Fischer is a Zen priest and lineage holder in the Suzuki Roshi line of American Soto Zen. Since 1981 he has lived at the Green Gulch Farm Zen Center, just north of San Francisco, where he presently serves as Resident Teacher. He was born in Wilkes-Barre, Pennsylvania, and educated at Colgate University, the University of Iowa Writer's Workshop, and the Graduate Theological Union. He has published several books of poetry, including *Turn Left in Order to Go Right* (O Books 1990). *Here and There* a book of poetry and photographs written in collaboration with Leslie Scalapino, is forthcoming from Chax Press.

Meditation and Poetry

At their best, both of them, meditation and poetry are ways of being honest with ourselves. Only by honesty can we see anything because honesty opens the eyes or cleans them. Without it we'd see what we'd like to see, or what we think we'd like to see, or what someone else would like us to see.

Meditation is when you sit down, let's say that, and don't do anything.

Poetry is when you get up and do something.

I don't think there is any escape from these activities: all of us have to do both of them. And both of them are involved with the imagination, that human faculty that creates, envisions, or transforms a world.

Somewhere we've developed the misconception that poetry is self-expression, and that meditation is going inward. Actually, poetry has nothing to do with self-expression, it is the way to be free, finally, of self-expression, to go much deeper than that. And meditation is not a form of thought or reflection, it is a looking at or an awareness of what is there, equally inside and outside, and then it doesn't make sense anymore to mention inside or outside.

Experience, I think, is a never-ending adjustment.

Practically speaking I would say that meditation gets you used to failure and gives you great familiarity with the mind's excitement, to the point of boredom, and so much so that there is a great acceptance of all experience, and there is no wish to favor one kind of experience over another. It is all pretty remarkable. This attitude is an aid to poetry.

So you are not that interested in "poetic" experience nor in "poetic" language. These seem unnecessary exaggerations. Only that you know, as a human, that you live intimately, intensely, with language, honestly with it, in it, as it, and it is necessary to keep that up, to clarify and deepen it.

That is why some aspects of poetic form are not helpful. And that is why, with your eye on the main purpose of the poem, you feel compelled at first to challenge poetic form, and then later to simply do away with it (by which I mean to stop being concerned with it terribly). At this point you are thinking in, or thinking as, technique.

How do you do this? Practically speaking, I think meditation offers a feeling for or sense of experience, very broadly, that allows us to find a way to do this. The grip on self can very naturally loosen, the grip on meaning loosens, and there is the possibility of entering wholeheartedly into a dark or unknown territory. That, and talent (a little), familiarity with poetic form (a little more), courage, and luck. An interesting footnote is that it is not a struggle: it is the release from struggle.

I imagine that no really amusing (a word Ted Berrigan insisted on, and I understand as "from the muse") literary work was ever conceived without meditation. Without an insistent, intent, single-minded holding in the mind of a single object until it dissolves. I am convinced every poem involves this process, at least narrowly conceived. And the broader we make our meditation the more implications it has for our poetry.

Do not imagine that I am advocating a particular approach or that even worse I am suggesting a "meditative" verse modeled on the oriental or occidental poetry written in previous centuries by meditators or contemplatives. I read and learn from this poetry, but much of it I do not like very much.

No, I am talking about a life in which we can be radically simple. And out of this great simplicity or honesty one does what one can.

I think if meditation can show you that there is really no such thing as, nor would one want, a poetic voice, then it is already worthwhile.

If I am recommending one thing that can be clearly understood I suppose it must be an unerring sense of humor.

Untitled Poem #37

Always it irks me—this body not my own
Which I cannot chose to move in any supple way
Though uneasy it takes a wayward motion I call
Marxism it lopes or sputters to the Jews who
Would have longed to settle here some years ago
I do not choose to hear the sound of a bird yet do
The ear consciousness produces desires that lead to lives
Tolstoy, Ibsen, and Zola, the infamous Dreyfus case,
I bang the gate but nobody answers
This is another example of the futility of human expression
I lope but later on leap or limp I stutter or hope
To hear nor do I choose either what I feel it bursts
Forth from me I try to ride it it roars its own rails
It rails so often against me I am old I abhor
A vacuum oars of orchid wood oars of silver
There must be there is of certainty a pattern a plague
Of human events a way a fortress or press you call muse
Strike down the empty moon the set of alabaster contrition
For there is no further destiny and the Presidential race
Is not that at all my delight increased at the
Thumping of the boat I was drunk and threw off
All my predecessors in a single gulp no longer
Able to vote condign reader lurching here with me
Into the lovely house full of lovely things view of garden
Complete with ancient mossy stones by pond through picture
    window
Tibetan bells, Naziism, Poland, France, and Yugoslavia
Mann was right of course. But the cost of such integrity
At once plunging, the skill with which the dory was saved from
    destruction
The Heart Sutra humming in the background that was a mighty
    dressing down
I got these words from a bare antagonistic forecourt
God is waiting at the capital.
She came to see me.
She was home.
I like my garden to appear full, luscious, disheveled, blasting
Out of its borders spilling into the copse beyond the form
Won't contain never I do not choose the shape I am
Eyes see ears hear nose smells tongue tastes mind confuses
Words line up still alive from a year ago

I begin slowly planting
It is a joy when after two seasons there are humming birds in the
  jasmine vine
The house is painted pink and she is there, trimmed in pale green,
And she is huge there, adventurous, dangerous, lifting up and off
  the
Floor and away up into the distant air, stars without number
I won't forget you.
Time does not go from past to present rather from future to past
Or present to past to future. If you think about this it begins
To add up.
I won't forget you.
Emma Bovary's ebbing sensuality in *The Cherry Orchard*.
Sit softly and listen
To the down it is there
In the whistling of your hair
For life give
Hate all up
The rigorous first boat up-anchored and began to move
There is really no way to do this because there was never a purpose
  only to sing
In excess of joy to care because the plans were too large
And the escarpment, I am standing on the embankment, a
  detachment
Yet splashing in the stream nevertheless and it is not a single image
I taste vocabulary
Reading is writing, standing is walking, seeing is hearing,
  swimming is flying
This is a chair, this is a table, this is not a pen
At twilight fine rain was still falling
And there was mist coming from the horse's nostrils
Below the humped outline of the darkened hills all about—
The world distinctly there in all the words without the words no
  world
Just a blur and yet things exist conventionally and in
Their ultimate aspect they are not to be seen in the same way
Song sears and the self wearies of hanging
In the danger of snow. That is why there is fear
For boys to take care of them. Then they alleviate.
I remember that I was wiser. The pupils of the eyes.

The Tooting

I theorize any group of words
Yields the profound secret
If we but tax them
For thirst goes a long way
Toward night and it lasts
You and I are both incomplete
Leaving the house naked carrying nothing
So as not to lose it
Trying to keep everything a secret
That flows according to laws
Which are fixed according to plans
There are liable to be repercussions
We can't stay awake all night long
but you are clammy and insistent
Nature itself becomes an emissary
Hence place names assume importance
And counting things out carefully
Must be kept track of
Simultaneous with the best spent days
You and I only opine
Past present and future purely
As a matter of personal preference
As the mists curl around our heads
The tooting in the house goes on
And flames enwrap the cauliflower
Nature itself seems at a loss
So as not to waste any time
People become dull nitwits and boobs
Across the stream the bright area
Is another season of the year victimizes
We are never certain of what of
For there is a will and a way for
As a matter of preference you
Can go ever so slowly up that way
For the view is so much that way
Seeing all around one side and another
That way you can keep track of
The flames and their progress
Toward the house so you can know
How to act like a reflective person
Keeping strictly to the quotidian
Just a few choice words not a lot

Placed in clusters or groups
And talking quietly to one another
Because they have known each other a long time
Words are different than looks
In some identifiable ways
And you can go that way
For the view is so much that way
Can go ever so slowly up that way
Along another fissure
You and I only lose
This is where we start
To finish with that as a means
To flow according to laws
Or become too tired to quit
Exasperated by emotion and spent
Past present and future
Lengthened according to the spirit
And what can be played out
Can also be tailor-made
For the tooting is only nearness
Words are only responses
Trails are only place names
Ways are only fissures
That have come to conclusions
They do not mean to appear
To finish with that
They go ever so slowly
According to mists and how
The tooting is carefully identified
Makes all the difference in the end
Conduct is most becoming in a person
Sharing meals in silence
And coming down to the real stuff
Because our days are soon spent
Wandering right and left over the globe
A wonderful night of stars
Nature itself seems at a loss before you
Who flows according to laws into
Structures which the view suits
We share this nature and this view
The taste of bitter coffee
The travails of distant landscape
The longing for blissful secure situations
Can also be tailor-made

And can affect facades
Who organized this party?
Which explained amounts to very little
A toy I picked up on my travels in Egypt
Shutting the casement windows
Lets go on and on dancing
Lets pretend the voices are our voices
And that we make decisions
And that we speak and things change
Throw down the curtain between your selves
Or have your eyes examined weekly
Anyone can set down pretty words
But how many know whereof they speak
Solely they banter into mirrors
Or belie the devastation beyond our control
But you and I can only designate
Names for what we think or feel
We can blunder about absolutely benignly
Preening into the abyss or shadow
The season so brilliant always so short
So dearly paid for in gilded terms
The door is locked and what we keep behind it
A toy I picked up is a technique
It's a poetic turn of mind a leap
You and I make out of self defense
A wonderful taste the breath
All one could ever want or need
And a method to it form where we start
Along the way beyond the tooting
The proof is there
It's a progression that can't be denied
The duck puffs and hisses
While people work for peace
Because they've known each other a long time
So the delight is there
It can be taken only in small doses
Lightly lifted by careful fingers
And set down on the grass amid the tooting
There is still some joy left
Although the branch is withered
And think of yourself as a doctor
Not a builder or an artist
For edges sag according to severe laws

Any reflective person can notice
And keep track of
In decorated notebooks
The progression of the quotidian
Is where we start from
Just a few choice words
Which are only fissures
And conduct this force over centuries
To be in this place right now
An unexpected event
Intimate as it is effortless
A toy I picked up on my travels in Egypt
With rather a classical feeling
Ah the opening of the gate!
And the sun popping up over the hill!
Lightly it is turned
And in turning used over again
That this step is a mark
Surprises no one
Its accuracy a bliss star
So you can't get in the way
For there is no way you can get it
The flames progress toward the house
But you have a trick
It is a matter of preference
To gauge the night and examine it
Making out the glass on the stairs
Next to the family portrait
Choices are narrower the further on you go
But the breath as choice
Just gets easier all the time
Outside the names we leave like doors
Blundering about absolutely absurdly
In the freshness of foreshadowed day
Its tower pierced by its own proof
Its progression undeniable
Its ducks puffed
But you and I can only designate
What we examine and move on
We can't effect the pond
Or lay in wait for the flower to bloom
We can only laugh after the water boils
Pinning down a method from where we start

So dearly paid for in glowing terms
Lacking no warm skies
One life the equal of another
One day delight in taken
One tooting noted crushed or ruffled
Sounds like these reach our ears
Perhaps only once in a lifetime
And what seems marvelous at first
Is only outside the hands
Hence the fame of tight places
Gutters the candle and the room is dark
So dearly do we desire all things
To be with us in our pleasure
Along the way whose shelter we seek
And do find in suitable ways
Enthusiastically saddling our horse
And riding off into the shadows
For there is no way to remain
Nor is there a place to be in
There is only a garage for a bus
There is merely a shelf for a book
In this box a locked door
Is called belief
A pear tree lurks behind a simple phrase
And a child swings slowly north and south
Under a blue-green awning
Soaked with blood

On Thinking

And after you die, what then? Somewhat? Or only more of the
  same.
Spring has come; Spring is here: what profits these boots, this
  beauty?
So when a man laughs
His sleeves shake like bamboo leaves in the cold hills' folds—
Not as you'd imagined. Hence thinking takes the form
  Of plans & schemes in which you are central stage
To grand designs of projected events' passage
And their concommitant consequences: yet you worry and that is
  why

Thought churns, moves, through all those difficult passages
Somebody else's words tick. I want to find my coat since the party's
   over
   But it is not necessary to fill out a form.
Other times thinking chases itself like old foxes
   Beads of sweat appear on the brow because you can't remember
The color of your baby blanket. But as such can be
Free of thought, or free for thought, either one.
Thought is in & of the body, that is sure
And thought is a tender one more & more,
The boat which is pulling away. Thought grows to go out from the
   body
To stir all buds to make a Spring
As a line of trees first silent locks the world
And then by thought is caused to stir, unwinding,
A strand the morning hurls to frown.

Nelson Foster

Nelson Foster lived in Hawaii for twenty-five years and studied Zen there under Robert Aitken Roshi of the Diamond Sangha. Since 1984 he has been teaching in this American branch of a Soto lay lineage. A freelance editor, he now lives and does most of his work in the Sierra foothills of California. He has authored several books on political, historical, and environmental subjects. One of the founders of the Buddhist Peace Fellowship, he is active in Pacific Basin social issues.

Pieces from the Night

[1]

Out of the shut night, the mare comes
grazing into the window-light square
Pulling at the deep grass
she takes from the earth
the sound of the earth, that dark word
suggesting, after all, it's hollow
The first cypress stands up beyond
a deeper darkness on the sky
and the next and the next imagines itself
along the treeline to the road
to the hill, to the stars

The horse mutters
Suddenly no longer the man at the desk
I'm the night's white itch
what's unmoving alive
a shaking in the air and the walls

The whole blackness turns toward me
as to its sole point
or end. I don't know
how to carry this
I remember the vast world

[2]

Last thing at night, I go out
Off the backdoor steps
the first cool breath comes
a surprise, air of the great sea
blown clear into the land of sleep
Standing in the weeds I know
if I know anything at all
I'm this laughter, pissing
Under the stars' arc
in the ironwoods' sough
pissing pissing
happy to my toes, full
with something no one knows

[3]

I pass, strange to myself
through the bottom cells of night
where things I don't remember happen
things I suspect
because once I returned with words
"Rubber truncheons scatter sleep"
Perhaps I'm there always
That back room of the mind I can't use anymore
is theirs, the last hueless property
of the staggering, starved, and broken
Aren't they there? Aren't we all there
locked, mute, in terror?
Nothing carried back but one ripped sentence
by mistake or for warning, I don't know
I only guess
that when what's left of me goes
sleeping down beyond itself
it must go feeling for
what I'm always feeling for—

not solace, not peace
but answering laughter
answering rage

[4]

Waking before color
in the chill, the air uncornered
Water
stands in the riddled lettuce
Birdsong spatters the open
moment
and a thousand prisoners crest the pasture
ringing the house, to wait
hidden as light

Makawao, Maui, 1979

Lovers' Reunion
at the Cavalier Motel

It had been quiet enough
but as the formidable
energies of our reunion
subsided, suddenly
the room opened
on every other room—above, below
in all directions, it seemed
It was late
Somewhere a mother
calmed a child
A man, apparently alone
offered an impassioned soliloquy
(on the phone?) in Spanish
Someone unlatched a door
as if in a compartment of our minds
came in, threw things down
thudded out again immediately
A young couple talked through troubles
and somewhere the furniture

leapt with the rhythms of sex
Ourselves at the threshold of sleep
we smiled and went ahead
at home, uninterrupted
in the motel of the world

South San Francisco, 1988

Guessing toward Clarity

The odor of pencil shavings on your fingers
you passed your hand down, across my eyes
I went
through you, through the pungent touch
outward
Before I thought to speak
you had written it out in us, it was no one place
to be smelled or tasted
Even quiet, as our blood settled in us
you were moving, you were ceaseless and you are
ceaseless
I no longer try to imagine you
You are all imagining, and I move with you
no thoughts of my own under your dark breathing

In this fathom-length body and in yours
and between, surge hints
of things forgotten, things not yet known
Under the vault of your hair
in the rising lines and hollows of your throat
the final weight I am
is the breath held around your name
and what is
is hissing for it
from every second of the compass

I've learned not to let it go, that breath
The puny artifice of the name
doesn't work

Something added like a name
shatters in the vortex of touch

Don't be surprised, then
if I hold you off toward sight
looking for what won't yield
what won't be sucked down small into the moving
Every name that comes I feed
to the fire I need to see by

Santa Rosa Plum

If you eat this fruit
be careful, move
as if plainsong were in your mouth
Even the sourness of the skin
is not yours to mispronounce
That fierce syllable
sliced across millennia to come here
to wrap the flesh
resting in your unskilled hands
Think of the bright plum
swelling toward you all this time
until you know it's as good
as a cell of your own—
flushed, sweet and wet
and as ready to last as to vanish

Dan Gerber

Dan Gerber lives in Fremont, Montana. His most recent books are a collection of short stories, *Grass Fires* (1989), and a novel, *A Voice From the River* (1990), both published by Clark City Press. *A Last Bridge Home,* his new and selected poems, will be published by Clark City Press in January 1992.

Two Clouds

These songs
may be known
without singing

Five black crows
who steal corn

A pine forest
surrounding
individual trees

A power line leading
to an empty field

One brown apple
sweet beyond tasting

Two clouds
that pass only for clouds

from The Chinese Poems

I.

Nothing seems to get any better
I have given up waiting for more
Once we had youth on our side
full of promise
Now we are what we are
and struggle with one aging mind
to climb the wall
we no longer believe is there

22.

We always like to think
we're better now
That foolish old self
changed with the seasons
We look at old photos and smirk
at the smirk we were smirking then
We laugh and begin, "I remember . . .

34.

I thought of you
as I dropped this Grey Wulff at the base of a stump
I watched the minute dapple of water around it
I waited for some nameless creature to rise
While in the trees above, two herons were resting
a kingfisher rattled and skimmed the surface
and a turtle slid off a log
like the author of a dream
slipping into the day

35.

There are nights
I don't know what to do
with my arms
nights it would be a pleasure
to take them off
to stack them by the bed
and swim like a dolphin
through this stagnant sea

41.

A December evening and as it grows dark
the fog becomes pearly above the snow
around the black trees, between my palate and teeth
like a baleen whale I squeeze it out
half believing some magic will stick to my tongue
when next I speak
these moments between us, a thousand miles
of fog, darker with each increment of the Earth
my daughter calling and my dog drives me mad
chewing on a bone, the abrasive crackle of the fire
the unbearable stillness of these words
knowing that now this will never change

43.

Out of all this will emerge a form
contrary to what we may have thought
or what we might be thinking
there was no mold
to make our lives this way
no island from which to examine the stream
no way for the water to examine itself

The Way Back

At the edge of the woods, I take off my skis and
sit back against a tree, enjoying the midwinter
sun. The sky, a blue bowl after weeks of gray
and listless snow. All day now I've been watched,
an intruder, lumbering through the dark trees. I
look but can't see the eyes watching me. I give
myself to the warmth on my face. I close my eyes,
awaken to the blood of my eyelids and see fiery
eruptions on the surface of the sun. I am still,
and the watchers come closer, uncertain I'm not
some kind of deep-blue fungus growing on the tree.
Soon I can see through their eyes, many eyes all
together, and through the eyes of the hawk turning
above, a white spot against the sky, a blue spot
against the snow, borne away by some instinct
from this thing I have been.

Love for Instance

Voices begin to flutter
like the wings of a frantic bird,
so much to be said

the room will not hold them,
so much talk of love,
the word is finally a mouthful of dough,
love love love love love.
Now bang your head on your lover's knee,
bang bang bang bang bang,
and tell me
what's the difference.

Margaret Gibson

Margaret Gibson has published four books of poetry, all with Louisiana State University Press, the second of which, *Long Walks in the Afternoon,* was the Lamont Selection for 1982. Her most recent book is *Out in the Open* (1989). She lives in rural Connecticut and has taught in a number of colleges and universities, including the M.F.A. Program at Virginia Commonwealth University.

The Glass Globe

From where I'm sitting this morning, the rug is blue and burgundy and orange, brighter where a length of full sun from the east window falls. On the shelf of the bay window, a large glass globe, handblown, the color of the air over the shallows of the Sound on late summer evenings, rests in a manner that suggests floating. Years ago, in my aunt's house, the wide globe surrounded a candlestick and sat plumply on a table at the head of the stairs. I never saw the candle lit except at Christmas. I have taken out the candle and left the globe to fill with air and, when there is light, with light. A fit of five robins bends and bobs on the boughs of the mock cranberry bushes, their sour fruit bright red even in the aqueous shading of the glass globe. The outline of the globe frames the robins' feast.

And now the birds are gone. The cranberry branches sway from the lift of their weight into flight. This morning, glad of it, I am not going anywhere. I am glad to watch this globe fill with a simplicity of light I have not yet learned to carry with me as I leave this room and am surrounded by the tumble of events in an ordinary day, whose habitual rhythm is hurried, the rushed life within it a denial both of life and of death.

I have sometimes wanted *house* to hold me, house a genesis of sorts, a continual *let there be*. And so house gathers earth and sky around me, family and things of an elusive depth I call spirit—a fine wood table, round; my grandmother's prayer rug; a bit of broken glass washed soft by the sea. Though we hardly notice, house holds the boundless quietly near, so quietly that by earth and sky encompassed, sheltering in the family and its things, we forget how we are preparing to release ourselves, each breath in, breath out a rehearsal.

But at times, I see light and the silence of light turn wide the horizon of each leaf and sill, each facet of screen, each spoon, each cup—and I see the space that spins within things, the table now serried particles, a dance of tendencies toward light I can feel beneath my fingers.

Writing, I have the habit of working until the skin of a poem fits the object of my attention, poem the skillful means that draws and holds that person or object and whatever I am together—within the skin of the poem those two inscribed, made briefly one thing. In this way writing becomes a meditative practice, a concrete process, a way to learn how to live within a practice that allows me to leave the isolation of the single, exclusive individual, to be manifold as well as uniform— whether the poem says *I* or *she* or *he* or *you* or *we*. To find within the pronoun of the person a spaciousness, light. To find within myself sufficient emptiness.

In my living, in my writing, there are clear traces of the desire for revelation, a new light powerful enough to stand me still, turn me round, set me on a clearer way toward a more perfect self. Zen offers, by contrast, not revelation but awakening.

Accept what you are. In the Protestant tradition in which I was raised, these words meant accept myself as errant, sinful, deficient in light, in need of searing revelation. How strange then, to come upon meditation, simply sitting, a practice of concentration and a profound humility that says *accept who you are* and means I am, you are, a great being already. Just so, the cranberry bush with its sour fruit, the robins on their migration elsewhere, the yellow winter grass, the sky gathering clouds toward snow, everyone within this house and everyone beyond it—all one universe that is supportive, compassionate, cooperative, clear. How strange, how essential to try to know this, to awaken what is, rather than to wait tensely for what may be. Now I am no longer waiting for my life, but living it, feeling it live me, a tranquillity that wells and fills and spills along, traceless as air on a calm afternoon.

"Because of these intellections, flowers in the air of various kinds appear."—Dogen Zenji

The glass globe blooms in a precarious place. I have to move it aside in summer when I crank open the windows. I shift and turn it when I dust. If I am not careful, if I am near it with the awkward vacuum cleaner and my mood is angular and hard, I may knock against it.

Someone else already has—the lip of the globe has been dinged, so that a crescent of glass, fractured and scored but held in place, forms a tiny kaleidoscope as the sunlight passes through it—an imperfection that makes the globe more beautiful—in Japanese, the word is *wabi,* a compassionate beauty, a perfection that includes imperfection, beautiful because of it.

The glass globe is a made thing, and as my stepson Joshua, at eight years old, remarked, "Everything's living." He pointed specifically to the globe filled with light and an afternoon's sweep of clouds. The globe is a synthesis of sand and fire and air and muscle and lung and tool. And here it is, precarious and brief, a product of someone's having trained body and mind sufficiently, a flaring of all sorts of energies joined and transformed, beautiful because of the quality of work, the quality of attention that went into it.

To consider any made thing in this way—glass globe or poem or person—is to see the uniform that is manifold, the manifold come into single bloom. So considering, I am less likely to rush headlong past a universe making and unmaking itself constantly. So considering, I am more likely to enter that universe—or rather to realize that I am, you are, it is, we are all in this, precariously and carefully, together.

A Ripple of Deer, A Metamorphosis of Bear, A Metaphor of Mountains

I dream of mountains repeatedly,
running my fingers over maps where they spine
and cluster. Through valleys of rhododendron
and bear, wild pheasant and deer, I near them,
empty and still, leaning over my walking stick,
my breath easing out, a shrill whistle.
At night I stare at stars, cold and still, peaks
of invisible mountains in a sky steeply pitched.

As for crests, moraines and glaciers, icefalls,
seracs, cornices, spurs—they are psalms
of a wild solitude I am not brave enough to enter.

In the long journey to be other than I am,
I have struggled and not got far. Each day
I roam the fields, and I climb. I watch
from a shiver of aspen steep on a southern exposure
of cleared field. From the ridge rim of trees—
a ripple. A smooth shade of brown comes to merge
in the fern, gathering stillness and weight,
deer intent on the grass. I envy the deer.
Beyond them, the low mountains unroll. Clear nights,
I measure the cave depths of mountains
and their peaks—then in the hour between night
and dawn, the darkest, I dream into the mountain,

entering slim as a snake through cold soil
and stone, I wriggle down on my back, my soft parts
exposed, falling through caves rank as bear gut,
crooked as roots. *Accept who you are*—
of my labors the most naked and rigorous.
Mornings, I am what merges in the mists as I rise
from these depths, so attached to my ignorance,
I think I'm exalted, more rare than the seven
wise Hindu that ride in the constellation
we call the Great Bear. Then I envy the Bear.

Making Salad

after Eihei Dogen

I rub the dark hollow of the bowl
with garlic, near to the fire enough
so that fire reflects on the wood,
a reverie that holds emptiness
in high regard. I enter the complete
absence of any indicative event,
following the swirl of the grain,
following zero formal and immanent
in the wood, bringing right to
the surface of the bowl the nothing
out of which nothing springs.

I turn open the window above the sink
and see fire, reflected on the glass,
spring and catch on a branch a light
wind tosses about. Here or there,
between new leaves the Pleiades,
like jewels in the pleromatic lotus,
flash. I watch the leaves swirl
and part, gathering light fresh
from Gemini, ten millennia away, fresh
from Sirius—holding each burning
leaf, each jewel within whatever light
a speck of conscious mind can make,
unshadowed by reflection or design,

impartial. Out the tap, from a source
three hundred feet down, so close
I feel the shudder in the earth, water
spills over my hands, over the scallions
still bound in a bunch from the store.
I had thought to make salad, each element
cut to precision, tossed at random
in the turning bowl. Now I lay the knife
aside. I consider the scallions. I consider
the invisible field. Emptiness is bound
to bloom—the whole earth, a single flower.

Beginner's Mind

When I begin to see
only what I've said—
my breath in the air
a snow of blind
keyholes and braille—
I let the dogs loose
in the field, and we run.
In the dimness of trees
by the wall, they chase
memories of squirrels.
I follow the wind until
out of breath
I crouch down in blank
snow, glad of the burn
of cold air in the west,

the border of trees
black and still.
Even now the magnolia
has buds, brushtips
of branches that lift
into the open.
Overhead, slate blue,
clouds swift along east.
I wait until stars
come into the blue—
then the black
never nowhere a child
gets quietly lost in.
I race the wind home.
In the kitchen new buds
of narcissus,
paperwhites unseasonal
in their bowl of stones
on the sill, have opened.
But my eye comes to rest
on a glass cup, cobalt blue,
which once, a child,
I named first when I named
what around me in the room
was living. I lift the glass,
turn it slowly in the light,
its whole body full of light.
Suddenly I hold everything
I know, myself most of all,
in question.

In the Mountains

In the mountains, I listen—
tracing the way
mountains arch through
air without effort,
without artifice. Out here
I can almost understand
how mountains are
words said
at a height—actual
sound made manifest

as silence, a summons
I try to imitate
setting these words down,
keeping low in the power.

This morning I give
whatever slender means
I am—an eye without
self-pity, without anger—
to the lift of sun and mist
across the surface
of what seems to be repose,
to the mountains,
to the great standing still
of thought
to whose center I feel
myself drawn.

Around me, peak after peak
the mountains circle,
the air thin and clear.
Not one leans out of itself
into next week's sun.
Not one sinks
in my regard,
diminished to a stone
I can pocket
or keep in a bowl
with the rocks I collect
on the ridges as I walk.
In this pause, I ask to be turned,
circling the mountains
on a scale of wind and sun,
until I am once more
down on my knees at the lowest
rise, where the spring is,
listening, able to tell—
as the mountains flow
without flowing,
as the spring deepens
and stills
beneath its own precise
ripples and rills—
who breathes, who abides,
who rises, standing still.

Affirmations

see without looking, hear without
listening, breathe without asking
—W.H. Auden

1.

An Eskimo shaman
will take stone, and with a pebble sit quietly
for days tracing on stone a circle,
until snow and mind are one.

Gazing into the whirl of a knothole
I sit out winter. Someone mutters inside.
Just one tremor before the walls give me
another white word for snow
this wood desk shimmers, as if wind
had reached wood's spellbound
galaxies and seen
the pole star
turning.

2.

Storm coming, this sky
brews, swelters—a guttural verb.

I listen to Mahler in the darkened living room,
his tumult like birch trees, hundreds
in a limber thrashing against
black sky, light broken
from a source so electric
even the roots shake.
And in all this hear nothing
until the contralto
rises out of the swirl,
vulnerable—

and such a stillness after,
I hear water
begin to bead on the yellow sycamore outside.

3.

The word *death*
lives deep in the oddly branched vines of the lungs.
It is a wind instrument with no stops, a low

whine you ignore because conversation, or the owl's eye
yellow of the sky at dusk, or the solid crack of wood
split for the fire distract and claim you.

I am learning to breathe
without asking for breath to carry me anywhere
but here, to the split second rush before wind
strikes word, to the moment I am what I am
without knowing it.

Allen Ginsberg

Allen Ginsberg was educated at Columbia University, on the road, and in spiritual loci around the world. He is identified with the Beat movement and with the spiritual and political reawakening of America that began in the 1960s and continues today. His *Collected Poems, 1947–1980* (Harper & Row), was published in 1984.

from *Meditation and Poetics*

It's an old tradition in the West among great poets that poetry is rarely thought of as "just poetry." Real poetry practitioners are practitioners of mind awareness, or practitioners of reality, expressing their fascination with a phenomenal universe and trying to penetrate to the heart of it. Poetics isn't mere picturesque dilettantism or egotistical expressionism for craven motives grasping for sensation and flattery. Classical poetry is a "process," or experiment—a probe into the nature of reality and the nature of the mind.

That motif comes to a climax in both subject matter and method in our own century. Recent artifacts in many fields of art are examples of "process," or "work in progress," as with the preliminary title of Joyce's last work, *Finnegans Wake*. Real poetry isn't consciously composed as "poetry," as if one only sat down to compose a poem or a novel for publication. Some people do work that way: artists whose motivations are less interesting than those of Shakespeare, Dante, Rimbaud, and Gertrude Stein, or of certain surrealist verbal alchemists—Tristan Tzara, André Breton, Antonin Artaud—or of the elders Pound and William Carlos Williams, or, specifically in our own time, of William Burroughs and Jack Kerouac. For most of "The Moderns," as with the Imagists of the twenties and thirties in our century, the motive has been purification of mind and speech.

You need a certain de-conditioning of attitude—a de-conditioning of rigidity and unyieldingness—so that you can get to the heart of your own thought. That's parallel with traditional Buddhist ideas of renunciation—renunciation of hand-me-down conditioned conceptions of mind. It's the meditative practice of "letting go of thoughts"—neither pushing them away nor inviting them in, but, as you sit meditating, watching the procession of thought forms pass by, rising, flowering, and dissolving, and disowning them, so to speak: you're not responsible any more than you're responsible for the weather, because you can't tell in advance what you're going to think next. Otherwise you'd be able to predict every thought, and that would be sad for you. There are some people whose thoughts are all predictable.

So it requires cultivation of tolerance towards one's own thoughts and impulses and ideas—the tolerance necessary for the perception of one's own mind, the kindness to the self necessary for acceptance of that process of consciousness and for acceptance of the mind's raw contents, as in Walt Whitman's "Song of Myself," so that you can look from the outside into the skull and see what's there in your head.

The specific parallel to be drawn is to Keats's notion of "negative capability," written out in a letter to his brother. He was considering Shakespeare's character and asking what kind of quality went to form a man of achievement, especially in literature. "Negative capability," he wrote, "is when a man is capable of being in uncertainties, mysteries, doubts, without any irritable reaching out after fact and reason." This means the ability to hold contrary or even polar opposite ideas or conceptions in the mind without freaking out—to experience contradiction or conflict or chaos in the mind without any irritable grasping after facts.

The really interesting word here is *irritable,* which in Buddhism we take to be the aggressive insistence on eliminating one concept as against another, so that you have to take a meat-ax to your opponent or yourself to resolve the contradictions—sexual contradictions or political contradictions—as the Marxists took a meat-ax to their own skulls at one point, and as the neoconservatives at this point may take a meat-ax to their own inefficient skulls. A current example might be the maniacal insistence that the Sandinistas are the force of evil and that our C.I.A. terrorists are patriots like George Washington. That's a completely polarized notion of the universe—the notion that everything is black and white.

A basic Buddhist idea from A.D. 150 is that "Form is no different from Emptiness, Emptiness no different from Form." That formulation is one that Keats and all subtle poets might appreciate. The American poets Philip Whalen, Gary Snyder, Kerouac, and Burroughs in their work do appreciate this "highest perfect wisdom," both in their own intuition and from their study of *Prajnaparamita* texts.

As part of "purification" or "de-conditioning" we have the need for clear seeing or direct perception—perception of a young tree without an intervening veil of preconceived ideas; the surprise glimpse, let us say, or insight, or sudden Gestalt, or I suppose you could say satori, occasionally glimpsed as esthetic experience.

In our century Ezra Pound and William Carlos Williams constantly insist on direct perception of the materials of poetry, of the language itself that you're working with. The slogan here—and henceforth I'll use a series of slogans derived from various poets and yogis—is one out of Pound: "Direct treatment of the thing." How do you interpret that phrase? Don't treat the object indirectly or symbolically, but look directly at it and choose spontaneously that aspect of it which is most immediately striking—the striking flash in consciousness or awareness, the most vivid, what sticks out in your mind—and notate that.

"Direct treatment of the 'thing' whether subjective or objective," is a famous axiom or principle that Pound pronounced around 1912. He derived that American application of twentieth-century insight from his study of Chinese Confucian, Taoist, and Japanese Buddhist poetry. There was a Buddhist infusion into Western culture at the end of the nineteenth century, both in painting and in poetry. Pound put in order the papers of "the late professor Ernest Fenellosa," the celebrated essay on "The Chinese Written Character as a Medium for Poetry." Fenellosa/Pound pointed out that in Chinese you were able to have a "direct treatment" of the object because the object was pictorially there via hieroglyph. Pound recommended the adaptation of the same idea: the Chinese poetic method as a corrective to the conceptual vagueness and sentimental abstraction of Western poetry. In a way he was asking for the intercession of the bodhisattvas of Buddhist poetry into Western poetics because he was calling for direct perception, direct contact without intervening conceptualization, a clear seeing attentiveness, which, echoing in your brain, is supposed to be one of the marks of Zen masters, as in their practice of gardening, tea ceremony, flower arranging, or archery.

Another slogan that evolved around the same time as Pound's and with the same motif was William Carlos Williams's famous "No ideas but in things." He repeats it in his epic *Paterson,* a little more clearly for those who haven't understood: "No ideas but in facts." Just the facts, ma'am. Don't give us your editorial; no general ideas. Just "give me a for instance"—correlate the conception with a real process or a particular action or a concrete thing, localized, immediate, palpable, practicable, involving direct sense contact.

Another Pound phrase that leads the mind toward direct treatment of the thing, or clear seeing is: "The natural object is always the adequate symbol." You don't have to go chasing after far-fetched symbols because direct perception will propose efficient language to you. And that relates to another very interesting statement, by the Tibetan lama-poet Chögyam Trungpa: "Things are symbols of themselves." Pound means that the natural object is identical with what it is you're trying to symbolize in any case. Trungpa is saying that if you directly perceive a thing it's completely there, completely itself, completely revelatory of the eternal universe that it's in, or of your mind as it is.

A classic example of William Carlos Williams in America seeing minute particulars clearly, precisely, thoroughly, is in the most famous and most obvious of Imagist poems, "The Red Wheelbarrow." Because the thing was seen so completely the poem seems to have penetrated throughout the culture, so that people who are not interested in poetry—high school kids or thickheaded businessmen—know this as the totem modern poem.

so much depends
upon

a red wheel
barrow

glazed with rain
water

beside the white
chickens.

Why did he focus on that one image in his garden? Well, he probably didn't focus on it—it was just there and he saw it. And he remembered it. Vividness is self-selecting. In other words, he didn't prepare to see it, except that he had had a life's preparation in practicing awareness "close to the nose," trying to stay in his body and observe the space around him. That kind of spontaneous awareness has a Buddhist term for it: "the Unborn." For where does a thought come from? You can't trace it back to a womb, a thought is "unborn." Perception is unborn, in the sense that it spontaneously arises. Because even if you tried to trace your perceptions back to the source, you couldn't.

To catch the red wheelbarrow, however, you have to be practiced in poetics as well as practiced in ordinary mind. Flaubert was the prose initiator of that narrowing down of perception and the concretization of it with his phrase "The ordinary is the extraordinary." There's a very interesting formulation of that attitude of mind in writing poetry by the late Charles Olson, in his essay "Projective Verse." This is kind of caviar, but William Carlos Williams reprinted this famous essay for the transmission of his own ideas to another generation. It contains several slogans commonly used by most modern poets that relate to the idea of direct seeing or direct awareness of open mind and open form in poetry. Here's what Olson says:

> This is the problem which any poet who departs from closed form is especially confronted by. And it evolves a whole series of new recognitions. From the moment he ventures into FIELD COMPOSITION [Olson means the field of the mind] . . . he can go by no track other than the one that the poem under hand declares for itself. Thus he has to behave, and be, instant by instant, aware of some several forces just now beginning to be examined. . . .
>
> The principle, the law which presides conspicuously over such composition and when obeyed is the reason why a projective poem can come into being. It is this: FORM IS NEVER MORE THAN AN EXTENSION OF CONTENT. (Or so it got phrased by one R[obert] Creeley, and it makes absolute sense to me, with this possible corollary, that right form, in any given poem, is the only and exclusively possible extension of the content under hand.) There it is, brothers, sitting there for USE.

By "content" I think Olson means the sequence of perceptions. So the form—the form of a poem, the plot of a poem, the argument of a poem, the narrative of a poem—would correspond to the sequence of perceptions. If that seems opaque to you, the next paragraph from Olson's "Projective Verse" essay might explain more. He says this:

> Now the *process* of the thing, how the principle can be made so to shape the energies that the form is accomplished. And I think it could be boiled down to one statement (first pounded into my head by Edward Dahlberg): ONE PERCEPTION MUST IMMEDIATELY AND DIRECTLY LEAD TO A FURTHER PERCEPTION. It means exactly what it says, is a matter of, at *all* points . . . get on with it, keep moving, keep in, speed the nerves, their speed, the perceptions, theirs, the acts, the split-second acts [the decisions you make while scribbling], the whole business, keep it moving as fast as you can, citizen. And if you set up as a poet, USE, USE, USE the process at all points. In any given poem always, always one perception must, must, must [as with the mind] MOVE INSTANTER ON ANOTHER! . . . So there we are, fast there's the dogma. And its excuse, its usableness, in practice. Which gets us . . . inside the machinery, now, 1950, of how projective verse is made.

I interpret that set of words—"one perception must move instanter on another"—as similar to the dharmic practice of letting go of thoughts and allowing fresh thoughts to arise and be registered, rather than hanging onto one exclusive image and forcing Reason to branch it out and extend it into a hung-up metaphor. That was the difference between the metaphysically inspired poetry of the thirties to the fifties in America after T. S. Eliot and the Open Form, practiced simultaneously by Ezra Pound and William Carlos Williams and later by Charles Olson and Robert Creeley. They let the mind loose. Actually, that's a phrase by one of the founders of our country: "The mind must be loose." That's John Adams, as reported by Robert Duncan in relation to poetics. Try that on the religious right. Leave the mind loose. One perception leads to another. So don't cling to perceptions, or fixate on impressions, or on visions of William Blake. As the young surrealist poet Philip Lamantia said when he was asked in 1958 to define "hip" as distinguishable from "square": Hip is "Don't get hung up."

So we have, as a ground of purification, letting go—the confidence to let your mind loose and observe your own perceptions and their discontinuities. You can't go back and change the sequence of the thoughts you had; you can't revise the process of thinking or deny what was thought, but thought obliterates itself anyway. You don't have to worry about that, you can go on to the next thought.

Robert Duncan once got up and walked across the room and then said, "I can't revise my steps once I've taken them." He was using that as an example to explain why he was interested in Gertrude Stein's writing, which was writing in the present moment, present time, present consciousness: what was going on in the grammar of her head during the time of composition without recourse to past memory or future planning.

Meditators have formulated a slogan that says, "Renunciation is a way to avoid conditioned mind." That means that meditation is practiced by constantly renouncing your mind, or "renouncing" your thoughts, or "letting go" of your thoughts. It doesn't mean letting go of your whole awareness—only that small part of your mind that's dependent on linear, logical thinking. It doesn't mean renouncing intellect, which has its proper place in Buddhism, as it does in Blake. It doesn't mean idiot wildness. It means expanding the area of awareness, so that your awareness surrounds your thoughts, rather than that you enter into thoughts like a dream. Thus the life of meditation and the life of art are both based on a similar conception of spontaneous mind. They both share renunciation as a way of avoiding a conditioned art work, or trite art, or repetition of other people's ideas.

I remember Kerouac falling down drunk on the kitchen floor of 170 East Second Street in 1960, laughing up at me and saying, "Ginsberg, you're a hairy loss." That's something that he made up on the spot, a phrase that just came out of his mouth, and I was offended. A hairy loss! If you allow the active phrase to come to your mind, allow that out, you speak from a ground that can relate your inner perception to external phenomena, and thus join Heaven and Earth.

Thoughts Sitting Breathing

OM—the pride of perfumed money, music food from China, a place to sit quiet.

MA—How jealous! the million Pentagon myrmidons with dollar billions to spend on Rock & Roll, restaurant high thrones in sky filled with Electric Bombers—Ah! how jealous they are of the thin stomached Vietnamese boy.

NI—Lust in heart for the pink tender prick'd school-boy upstairs bedroom naked with his books, high school locker shower, stretching on the bed, the young guitar player's ass

PA—Impercipience, cat meows natural words at the window, dog barks cheerful morn, cockroach feelers touch the wall, the fly buzzes long long on the sunny windowsill lying upside-down in deathly prayer exhausted, man bends over oblivious books, buds stick forth their heart-tips when ice melts New Year's eve, green grass shoots show 'neath melted snow, screams rise out of thousands of mouths in Hanoi—

DMI—alone the misery, the broken legs of carcrash alcohol; gimme another cigarette, I ain't got a dime for coffee, got no rupee for rice ain't got no land I got hunger in my gland my belly's swollen potatoes my knees got cut on the Tanks—

HŪM—the pigs got rocks in their head, C.I.A. got one eye bloody mind tongue, fiends sold my phonograph TV set to the junkman, Hate that dog shat my rug, hate Gook Heaven, hate them hippies in Hell stinking Marijuana smog city.

OM—Give it all away, poetry bliss & ready cash for taxicabs, walk Central Park alone & cook your beans in empty silence watching the Worm crawl thru meat walls—

MA—sit down crosslegged and relax; storm Heaven with your mental guns? Give up let Angels alone to play their guitars in Hollywood and drink their Coke-snuff in mountainside bathroom peace—

NI—Light as ashes, love for Neal sublimed into Poesy, love for Peter gone into the Vegetable garden to grow corn & tomatoes—

PA—Dog bark! call the mind gods! scream happiness in Saigon behind the bar my mother in throes of Police vomit rape! that garbage can I threw in Atlantic Ocean floats over Father Fisheye's sacred grave—

DMI—I forgive thee Cord Meyer secret mind police suborned the Student Congress Cultural Freedom & destroyed Intellect in Academe Columbia Harvard made great murder Indochina War our fantasy-bomb gutted New York's soul—

HŪM—Miserable victims flashing knives, Hell's Angels Manson Nixon Calley-Ma, all the cops in the world and their gangster lovers, car salesmen Wall Street brokers smoking in rage over dwindling oil supplies, O poor sick junkies all here's bliss of Buddha-opium, Sacred Emptiness to fix your angry brains—

OM—the Crown of Emptiness, relax the skullcap wove of formal thought, let light escape to Heaven, floating up from heart thru cranium, free space for Causeless Bliss—

MA—Speech purified, worlds calmed of alcoholic luxury & irritable smoking, jealous fucking rush thru taxicab cities, mental cancer pig war fever machines—Heart through throat, free space for Causeless Bliss!

NI—How vast, how brightly empty and how old, the breath within the breast expands threefold, the sigh of no restraint, sigh love's release, the rest and peacefulness of sweethearts' ease, from Heart to Heart—free space for Causeless Bliss!

PA—Dog bellies crying happy in the snow, worms share mind's heaviest part, elephants carry Angels whose animal trumpets blow from abdomen deep navel up into the heart—free space for Causeless Bliss

DMI—Down in the pecker, the empty piece of wood—Everyone I fucked is dead and gone—everyone I'm gonna fuck is turning to a ghost—All my penis blessedness never'll get lost, but rise from loins & come in my heart—free space for Causeless Bliss

HŪM—I shit out my hate thru my asshole, My sphincter loosens the void, all hell's legions fall thru space, the Pentagon is destroyed

> United States armies march thru the past
> The Chinese legions rage
> Past the Great Wall of Maya

And scream on the central stage
I loose my bowels of Asia
I move the U.S.A.
I crap on Dharmakaya
And wipe the worlds away
White House filled with fuel gas bombs
Slums with rats' faeces & teeth
All Space is fore-given to Emptiness—
From earth to heart, free space

for Causeless Bliss

January 1, 1973

"What would you do if you lost it?"

said Rinpoche Chögyam Trungpa Tulku in the marble glittering
apartment lobby
looking at my black hand-box full of Art, "Better prepare for
Death" . . .
The harmonium that's Peter's
the scarf that's Krishna's the bell and brass lightningbolt Phil Whalen
selected in Japan
a tattered copy of Blake, with chord notations, black books from
City Lights,
Australian Aborigine song sticks, green temple incense, Tibetan
precious-metal finger cymbals—
A broken leg a week later enough reminder, lay in bed and after few
days' pain began to weep
no reason, thinking a little of Rabbi Schacter, a little of father Louis,
a little of everything that must be abandoned,
snow abandoned,
empty dog barks after the dogs have disappeared
meals eaten passed thru the body to nourish tomatoes and corn,
The wooden bowl from Haiti too huge for my salad,
Teachings, Tantras, Haggadahs, Zohar, Revelations, poetries,
Koans
forgotten with the snowy world, forgotten
with generations of icicles crashing to white gullies by roadside,
Dharmakaya forgot, Nirmanakaya shoved in coffin, Sambhogakaya
eclipsed in candle-light snuffed by the playful cat—
Goodbye my own treasures, bodies adored to the nipple,

old souls worshipped flower-eye or imaginary auditory panoramic
skull—

goodbye old socks washed over & over, blue boxer shorts, subzero
longies,

new Ball Boots black hiplength for snowdrifts near the farm mailbox,

goodbye to my room full of books, all wisdoms I never studied, all
the Campion, Creeley, Anacreon Blake I never read through,

blankets farewell, orange diamonded trunked from Mexico Himalayan sheepwool lugged down from Almora days with Lama
Govinda and Peter trying to eat tough stubborn halfcooked
chicken.

Paintings on wall, Maitreya, Sakyamuni & Padmasambhava, Dr.
Samedi with Haitian spats & cane whiskey,

Bhaktivedanta Swami at desk staring sad eye Krishna at my hopeless
selfconsciousness,

Attic full of toys, desk full of old checks, files on NY police &
C.I.A. peddling Heroin,

Files on laughing Leary, files on Police State, files on ecosystems all
faded & brown,

notebooks untranscribed, hundreds of little poems & prose my own
hand,

newspaper interviews, assemblaged archives, useless paper-
works surrounding me imperfectly chronologic, humorous later
in eternity, reflective of Cities' particular streets studios and
boudoirs—

goodbye poetry books, I don't have to take you along anymore on
a chain to Deux Magots like a red lobster

thru Paris, Moscow, Prague, Milan, New York, Calcutta,
Bangkok, holy Benares, yea Rishikesh & Brindaban may yr prana
lift ye over the roof of the world—

my own breath slower now, silent waiting & watching—

Downstairs pump-organs, musics, rags and blues, home made Blake
hymns, mantras to raise the skull of America,

goodbye C chord, F chord, G chord, goodbye all the chords of The
House of the Rising Sun

Goodbye farmhouse, city apartment, garbage subways Empire
State, Museum of Modern Art where I wandered thru puberty
dazzled by Van Gogh's raw-brained star-systems pasted on blue
thick skyey Suchness—

Goodbye again Naomi, goodbye old painful legged poet Louis,
goodbye Paterson the 69 between Joe Bozzo & Harry Haines that
out-lasted childhood & poisoned the air o'er Passaic Valley,

goodbye Broadway, give my regards to the great falls & boys staring marijuana'd in wonder hearing the quiet roar of Godfather
Williams' speech
Goodbye old poets of Century that taught fixed eye & sharp tongue
from Pound with silent Mouni heart to Tom Veitch weeping in
Stinson Beach,
goodbye to my brothers who write poetry & play fiddle, my neph-
ews who blow tuba & stroke bass viol, whistle flute or smile &
sing in blue rhythm,
goodbye shades of dead living loves, bodies weeping bodies broken
bodies aging, bodies turned to wax doll or cinder
Goodbye America you hope you prayer you tenderness, you IBM
135-35 Electronic Automated Battlefield Igloo White Dragon-
tooth Fuel-Air Bomb over Indochina
Goodbye Heaven, farewell Nirvana, sad Paradise adieu, adios all
angels and archangels, devas & devakis, Bodhisattvas, Buddhas,
rings of Seraphim, Constellations of elect souls weeping singing
in the golden Bhumi Rungs, goodbye High Throne, High Central
Place, Alleluiah Light beyond Light, a wave of the hand to Thee
Central Golden Rose,
Om Ah Hum A La La Ho Sophia, Soham Tara Ma, Om Phat Svaha
Padmasambhava Marpa Mila sGam.po.pa Karmapa Trungpaye!
Namastaji Brahma, Ave atque vale Eros, Jupiter, Zeus, Apollo,
Surya, Indra
Bom Bom! Shivaye!   Ram Nam Satyahey! Om Ganipatti, Om Sa-
raswati Hrih Sowha! Ardinarishvara Radha Harekrishna farethee-
well forevermore!
None left standing! No tears left for eyes, no eyes for weeping, no
mouth for singing, no song for the hearer, no more words for any
mind.

Cherry Valley, February 1, 1973

Returning to the Country
for a Brief Visit

Annotations to Amitendranath Tagore's Sung Poetry

"In later days, remembering this I shall certainly go mad."

Reading Sung poems, I think of my poems to Neal
dead few years now, Jack underground
invisible—their faces rise in my mind.

Did I write truthfully of them? In later times
I saw them little, not much difference they're dead.
They live in books and memory, strong as on earth.

"I do not know who is hoarding all this rare work."

Old One the dog stretches stiff legged,
soon he'll be underground. Spring's first fat bee
buzzes yellow over the new grass and dead leaves.

What's this little brown insect walking zigzag
across the sunny white page of Su Tung-p'o's poem?
Fly away, tiny mite, even your life is tender—
I lift the book and blow you into the dazzling void.

"I fear that others may know I am here;
An immortal may appear to welcome me."

Right leg broken, can't walk around
visit the fishpond to touch the cold water,
tramp thru willows to the lonely meadow across the brook—
here comes a metal landrover, brakes creaking hello.

"You live apart on rivers and seas . . ."

You live in apartments by rivers and seas
Spring comes, waters flow murky, the salt wave's covered with oily
   dung
Sun rises, smokestacks cover the roofs with black mist
winds blow, city skies are clear blue all afternoon
but at night the full moon hesitates behind brick.
How will all these millions of people worship the Great Mother?
When all these millions of people die, will they recognize the Great
   Father?

"I always remember the year I made it over the mountain pass."

Robins and sparrows warble in mild spring dusk
sun sets behind green pines in the little valley
High over my roof gray branches sway gently under motionless
   clouds
Hunters guns sounded three times in the hillside aspen
The house sat silent as I looked above my book,
quiet old poems about the Yi & Tsangpo Rivers—
I always remember the spring I climbed Glacier Peak with Gary.

Cherry Valley, April 20, 1973

Why I Meditate

I sit because the Dadaists screamed on Mirror Street
I sit because the Surrealists ate angry pillows
I sit because the Imagists breathed calmly in Rutherford and
  Manhattan
I sit because 2400 years
I sit in America because Buddha saw a Corpse in Lumbini
I sit because the Yippies whooped up Chicago's teargas skies once
I sit because No because
I sit because I was unable to trace the Unborn back to the womb
I sit because it's easy
I sit because I get angry if I don't
I sit because they told me to
I sit because I read about it in the Funny Papers
I sit because I had a vision also dropped LSD
I sit because I don't know what else to do like Peter Orlovsky
I sit because after Lunacharsky got fired & Stalin gave Zhdanov a
  special tennis court I became a rootless cosmopolitan
I sit inside the shell of the old Me
I sit for world revolution

July 19, 1981

Susan Griffin

Susan Griffin is a prominent essayist, poet and playwright, and a student of vipassana and Vietnamese Buddhism. Her collection *Woman and Nature: The Roaring Inside Her* (Harper & Row, 1979), is one of the foremost statements regarding the relationship of feminism and ecology. Her latest book of poetry, *Unremembered Country* (Copper Canyon Press), was published in 1987.

Torture

for Carolyn, Claribel & Michele

Unremembered country

As if taken suddenly
into a strange house
until slowly
you see

you are a part of the tissue
of the lungs
bringing breath
to this body.

What you witness here
is unspeakable

even to speak the words
partakes of the brutality
of these events

which pass between
these couples

the one who inflicts
the one who suffers

with this kind of suffering
the unhealing scar
is visible immediately
you can imagine the white streak
even before the hand moves

that hand
so human
gripping the instrument

does the instrument still
believe in innocence?

All that I know I heard secondhand. Now I am telling you. Michele
came back from Chile with the story of a woman who was tortured. She
spoke to the woman herself. The woman could not speak of her own
torture in any reasonable way. Her mind had given way, which is what
the torturers wanted. They knew of this kind of fragility in her. They
told her that her children were dead. This was not true. Michele told us
the woman had an absent look on her face as she told her the torturers
could not be blamed for saying her children were dead. Michele said she
could not forget the expression of this woman's face that was beaten
down and empty. And in turn, I cannot forget Michele's voice, telling
the story, that edge there of one who has listened, and is not certain what
can be done, except to tell, over and over, to tell.

To this I add another story. I heard it from Claribel. She is a poet. She
has told this story herself in her own language, a very intense Spanish that
breaks perhaps even more harshly over those soft syllables, as she talks
about the woman from Salvador, too ill to torture physically, and how the
guards would rape the other women, and then gathering together the con-
doms used in these rapes, thrust them into her mouth. Only later do I want
to ask her how do we tell this story so that it does not become another facet
of the original assault, a cruelty of words? The question did not arise as she
told it, her face, her hands reaching apologetically for cigarettes, coffee,
those of us who listened, shaking our heads. Phrase by phrase, carefully
each piece of the tale was reconstructed in this way, as if we were seam-
stresses assembling garments for a passage away from or into this life.

The
instruments
the glass cutters

used at Chartres
must have been
sharp
to cut such
clear lines
a range of color
like music.

What, then, shall we do?
Must we have
such lines cut
deeply into
memory
until we know
all the stories of
suffering by heart?
Is this
the only way
the suffering
will stop?

I wake very early
a high wind cleans the trees
which sparkle and shine as I
write and then
fall into sleep again, dream.
I have entered
the room of the stories,
outside a woman stands
holding a stop watch.
As if I have entered
a room full of
radiation, my time
must be limited, but
the clock stops as I
look up. The ceiling
is very high, and
there, at the top
colored windows
let in a choir of light.

Born Into a World Knowing

This will happen
Oh god we say just give
me a few more
breaths
and don't let it be
terrible
let it be soft
perhaps in someone's
arms, perhaps tasting
chocolate
perhaps
laughing or asking
Is it over already?
or saying *not yet. Not
yet* the sky
has at this moment turned
another shade of blue,
and see there a child
still plays
in the fresh snow.

Amnesia

You have deserted yourself, gone
deep into the mind of an
amnesiac, that one you thought
you had something with,
what should you ask of your own
non-existence, testimony? A
portrait? The picture
for example of the goat's head
perpetually eating a wildflower
who stares with an ignorant look
from the surface of your desk.
Things are not always
the way they are supposed to be.
You are trying to search
for endings, to call things
this or that, when you ought
to walk across the room,
open a book, go out even

to the corner, stand for a moment.
We are only impressions
that change
not only daily but
at every moment.
You tell this to someone who calls.
He is feeling what you are feeling.
What we think of as interruption,
you say, is substance.
Try to remember, you speak now to yourself,
who were you before you took flight?
You were the one who would one day
take flight. Laugh, you say,
look at the goat's head, you are
fond of it, you like to think of it
eating paper, eating everything, all
you have ever imagined, yourself,
the one who does not remember,
and there in the goat's stomach
or in the grass, the soil where the
goat stands, you and she will
find yourselves, the ones you abandoned,
the world.

Ocean

for Naomi

Strength comes in waves.
Only some know this.
They don't tell.
They know only in unknowing.
They go back millennia
are small, terrified
within the sea and the cell.
They have let go the line of history.
They no longer know
what they knew.
Like children suffering
they enter uncertainty completely.
And like children they
seem to be weak and trembling
in the shadow
of the largest wave.

Sam Hamill

Sam Hamill was brought to the literature of Buddhism through the writings of Kenneth Rexroth. He is a poet, translator, and editor at Copper Canyon Press and teaches creative writing in schools and prisons. Author of a dozen books, including *Basho's Ghost* (Broken Moon, 1989), his essays on poetry, Zen, feminism, and translation are gathered in *A Poet's Work: The Other Side of Poetry* (Broken Moon Press, 1990). His translation of *Oko no hosomichi*, Basho's famous travel diary, has been published under the title *Narrow Road to the Interior* (Shambhala Publications, 1991). *Only Companion*, an anthology of Japanese *tanka*, is also forthcoming from Shambhala Publications.

Sitting Zen, Working Zen, Feminist Zen

When the Third Patriarch of Zen, Sengtsan, was still a student of the Second Patriarch, Hui-k'o, he went to his Master and said, "I am diseased; please cleanse me of my sin."

Hui-k'o said, "Bring me your sin and I will cleanse you of it."

Sengtsan thought a long time. "I cannot get at it."

"Then I have cleansed you of it."

This story and many others from R. H. Blyth's *Zen and Zen Classics* filled my days aboard a troop ship bound for Yokohama more than a quarter-century ago. Eighteen years old, I had squandered my adolescence in and out of jails until a judge suggested I "seek discipline in the service of the U.S. Marine Corps or spend a like amount of time in the custody of the state." I had read a little about Zen Buddhism, mostly things suggested by Kenneth Rexroth. As I would slowly discover over the following decades, Zen means sitting. But I will always be grateful to R. H. Blyth for his little books of commentary and translation, and I continue to read them for the sheer intelligence of the prose.

While stationed on Okinawa, reading Blyth, Suzuki, and others, I learned to sit zazen. I visited temples and attended lectures. I sat almost daily, my military schedule permitting, but only for very short periods—fifteen or twenty minutes per day. I extended my stay there to pursue my studies. More than a quarter-century has passed since those two years concluded, but my practice remains relatively unchanged. Out of this early practice, I adopted a standard of nonviolence, the position of the conscientious objector, a view I hold to this day.

Hui Neng, the Sixth Patriarch, says we sit zazen not in order to become enlightened, but because we *are* enlightened. In his extraordinary little volume of "Essays in Zen Buddhist Ethics," *The Mind of Clover*, Robert Aitken devotes a brief piece to the term *samu*, a term D. T. Suzuki translates unsatisfactorily as "labor." As Aitken points out, *sa* means "production—tillage or harvest"; *mu* means "to devote attention." Thus, we remember the words of Pai-chang, "A day of no samu is a day of no eating." Pai-chang's words work in two directions at once. "No work, no food," is barely adequate to his insight. He also means that we are nourished by our devotion and attention to labors.

At a time when all emphasis was being placed on zazen, the Rinzai monk Hakuin went around Soto meditation halls and poked the monks, "Get up and go do something useful, the work is part of the koan!"

And that is the story. Whether we call it by its Chinese name, *tso-ch'an,* or whether we know it from the Japanese *zazen,* we cannot know it without *doing* it. Talking about sitting is not sitting. In order to comprehend attentive inaction, one must begin with contemplation. Dialogue won't help. I do not sit in order to "become enlightened." Millions of people have died at the hands of those who professed to seek enlightenment. I sit in order to sit. If Hui Neng believes my sitting is evidence of enlightenment, he may also wish to account for my shortcomings—call them my "endarkenments."

The other side of sitting is *samu*. Not simply working, but investing in devoted labors. There are plenty of monks raking sand in elegant temple gardens in Japan who never really see the sand they rake. There are some who think the sand is only a metaphor, some who think it a legend or a fable, a symbol, a tradition. Perhaps there are even some who believe Zen can enter the heart through the eye.

Raking the sand, there is plenty of sand to be raked, and indeed some of it seems at first to be the sands of one's own life, sands of the hourglass, or sands from a remembered beach. *Samu* suggests a right-mindfulness toward one's work, toward *all* of one's work. Raking the sand, one sifts through illusions and deceits, through guilt and embarrassment and anger, until, eventually, slowly and carefully raking the sand, one gets at last to the sand.

The work is part of the koan.

Action is measured by inaction, inaction informs action—the Tao of zazen. Zen discipline comes down to this—attentiveness; doing and not-doing; being. As with poetry, insights attainable through the practice of zazen arise out of attention to detail, to daily moment-by-moment attention to detail.

Americans often get caught up in the notion of highest perfect enlightenment. We live in a culture that has invested heavily in lies promoting the idea of immediate self-gratification. Caught between our illusion of prosperity and the hard reality of homelessness, poverty, despair, and murderous foreign relations, we often try desperately *not* to see. Sometimes this is accomplished by turning over our own individual responsibility to "faith," to religion. Some even attempt to escape into Zen. But Zen is not an evasion of personal accountability.

Some Zennists believe in sudden complete realization; some believe in gradual clarification. Some follow teaching that emphasizes koan study; some emphasize recitation of the sutras. What are we to say when each claims the one way to nirvana?

I have never been to nirvana and I don't know anyone there. In *this* world, samsara, the cycle of birth and death, I am witness to the innumerable births and deaths of each inevitable day. Nirvana is not my problem in exactly the same way in which Christian heaven is not my problem. Nirvana, heaven, the gods and goddesses—all good. But because I know I will die, because I live my own death as surely as I live my own life, I inhabit the world of samsara. "Born like a dream in a dream world," Muso says in a poem, "I shall pass like the morning dew." Asked whether Amida Buddha's western paradise really exists, Ikkyu responds with *Amida-hadaka-monogatari,* or *Naked Speaking About Amida,* saying it is *minna mi*—"all within the body." Ezra Pound quotes Confucius, "A man's Paradise is his own good nature."

Here is a poem—an incantation or a sutra perhaps. I made several pilgrimages to Hasedera, the temple of Kannon, bodhisattva of compassion, in Kamakura. There, I had been deeply moved by thousands of little figures of Jizo, buddha of children and travelers. They had been placed along the steep hillside steps, one by one, by women who had lost children. Some were for infants who died at birth, some for children who had died, but most were for the souls of aborted pregnancies. Often, the little stone figures wore hats or bright bibs, or carried toys. Some had bright umbrellas resting on their shoulders.

Climbing higher, rinse mouth and hands, light incense, and enter the temple of Kannon. In the temple hush, souls of the children become a silent choir, and the four o'clock bell resonates over hills surrounding the city.

Later, outside on the high verandah overlooking the bay, hawks ride long curls of air up and away, over the hills, a few seagulls call, and a faint strand of cloud or mist settles on the horizon. Erotic love, Rexroth used to say, is one of the highest forms of contemplation. Birth-and-love-and-death, nirvana, Jesus, and the Buddha, even the temple of Kannon itself—all within the body.

Ten Thousand Sutras

after Hakuin's Meditation Sutra

This body is the body of the Buddha.
Like ice and water, the one is always in the other.

In the middle of the lake
we long for a drink of water.

Adrift in Samsara
we dream of blissful Nirvana.

This body is the body of the Buddha,
this moment an eternity.

Saying I love you, the deed is done—
the name and the deed are one.

With you and without you
the line runs straight—

your body is the body of the Buddha,
there is light beyond the gate.

This love I give to you
is the love that comes from Kannon.

Every breath a sutra.
Going or returning, it's the same.

Our bodies are the bodies of the Buddha,
our names are Kannon's name.

No word can adequately say it,
yet every word must praise it—

in silent meditation
destroying evil karma,

in silent meditation
inhabiting the Dharma—

this body is the body of the Buddha,
your body is the body of the Buddha.

Open arms and eyes to Samsara,
embraced by the thousand arms of Kannon!

In the perfect mind of *vivikta-dharma,*
the truth of solitude,

our body is a temple
not a refuge.

Praise our body
even in Samsara,

our bodies are the body of the Buddha,
our bodies are the body of the Buddha.

"Our body is a temple / not a refuge." The line has been with me for many years, but I cannot remember whether I first wrote it or read it. It is Hakuin, of course. The word and the deed become one. Just as there is buddhahood or enlightenment in lovemaking, there is also *mu,* "nothingness." And there is solitude. And eternal joy in the giving. And monumental grief.

Jizo is really more for us, for those who remain in this cycle of birth and death, than for the children. It is we, ourselves, individually within our own deepest moments of solitude, who seek assurance or solace from without. Jizo? We are Jizo.

In *The Blue Cliff Record,* there is a story of Yun-men, who observed that below Dragon Gate, the entrance to nirvana, there were many gills and scales. He means that many a good monk becomes attached to the idea of nonattachment, clinging to an illusion just as foolish as clinging to a Cadillac. I discussed this koan with Keida Yusuke during one of his visits to my home in Tokyo. Keida Sensei later translated my name into Japanese, selecting characters as follows: *Ha*—wave; *miru*—watch or look; *Sa*—sand or beach; *mu*—dream. Playing with this new name while thinking over our talk about Yun-men, a poem began to take shape.

Watching the Waves

to Keida Yusuke

For fifty years I've drifted,
carried on wandering waves
like a single grain of sand
from a beach a world away.

Yun-men raised his dragon staff:
it swallowed earth and heaven.
Gills and scales at Dragon Gate,
all these years chasing waves!

You return to your cottage
nestled in northern mountains.
I remain in the city,
red dust burning in my eyes.

Moonlight troubles the waters;
mountains and rivers remain.
Blinding light every morning;
in the evening, clouds and rain.

The reader should see, in addition to koan 60 in *The Blue Cliff Record,*
Ikkyu Sojun's poem, "Peach Blossom Waves" in *The Crazy Cloud Anthology.* In the third stanza, the "red dust" refers to evidence of the
"pleasures of the world." The first couplet of the fourth stanza refers to
Zen "barriers" that remain between myself and "highest perfect enlightenment." The "blinding light" is zazen or silent self-illumination.
"Clouds and rain" is an ancient euphemism for lovemaking.

Ryokan extolled the virtues of incantation of the *nembutsu,* the Buddha's name. Yung Chia says in his *Song of Enlightenment,* "Our illusory
unreal body is the Cosmic body." Hakuin says our body is the body of
the Buddha.

Making love, sitting zazen, bringing an attitude of devotion to all one's
works—seeing one's own carelessness for what it really is when that time
comes, I could say, "Sitting zazen improves the quality of one's life." I
could say, "If more people sat zazen, the world would be the better for
it." But that doesn't mean anything. Jung called for universal individu-
ation. Zen has no missionary tradition.

If Zen practice is to remain abundant, if we continue to embrace its
ethics, then we must also participate in feminist zen, we must discover
just who are the matriarchs, and we must learn from them as we have
learned from the patriarchs. Kannon, bodhisattva of compassion, comes
from the Chinese Kuan Shih Yin, who in turn comes from the Indian
Avalokitesvara. Sometimes masculine, often feminine, Kannon's compassion lies at the heart of my practice. She-who-sees-the-world's-cries.
Her listening lies at the heart of her vision.

I seek a balance between masculine and feminine, between social activism and solitude, between heaven and earth, between the impossible
perfection of grace and the equally impossible sadness of sin.

I seek not the asceticism of zen, but its social engagement; not the activism of the feminist, but her passionate contemplation. What's in the heart of it? Gratitude.

Gnostology

Each return is a blessing,
a birthing. I come back
again in the last light
of evening and the blue cups
camas raises to catch
the mist are dripping,
blackberries turning
blue from green, and down
the narrow Strait of Juan
de Fuca, foghorns
faintly sound.
     I stand
a long time outside, listening
to the dripping leaves
and nighthawk cries.
Behind me, the dark house
drips from the eaves.
        I slide
the wide door open
and breathe the scents
of stale beer and cigarettes
I smoked last week. The same
books clutter the table.
The same poem dies
in the crude last unfinished
line I couldn't make
to breathe.
      I ease
into my tattered chair in
trembling light as the sunset
slides into a shadow
ghosting the dark Pacific.
Somewhere, the tide is

staggering over stones at
the feet of incoming swells;
the gulls are scavenging,
looping a last time over
brine, searching for edibles
tangled in the wrack.
          The moon
slips between two cedars,
razor thin and curved into
a dazzling sliver of ice
simmering in the fog.
The dark of night settles in
on strong, steady feet.

This silence is not
profound—it's an old
friend, my beautiful dark
daughter I haven't seen
in years, a longing, a soft
exquisite ache. An hour
flies.
    Another.
          This life's
a summer reverie, a dream
flashing past unnoticed
at the edge of sleep, a
simple gesture: a touch
or kiss of a friend.
          Finally,
I rise
and step out of my clothes.
I stand on the porch in the mist,
suddenly naked,
lightly goose-fleshed,
more alive than I have been
in days. My whole body
responds to mist and air,
the moist touch of evening
bristling hairs of belly
and legs, and I feel
my nipples' erection,
my scrotum draw up
against my groin, my toes

count every grain of earth
beneath my feet.

Out in the blank space
of night, thousands
and thousands of systems are
at work—lighting
galaxies, whirling the billions
of years into a ball.
                      Are
the ants asleep inside
their catacombs of fir?
Are the chloroplasts
resting their eyes?
                With no prayer
on my breath, without
hope or fear, without asking
what it is or what the seasons know,
I gather
a long, slow breath,

breathe it,

kneel,

and bow.

Helenic Triptych

Forehead on forearm, eyes unfocused,
he listens to rain pelting wet earth that smells
of dreams and destinations, of departures which
preceded no arrival. Alone with the long afternoon,
he longed for starlight through windows,
for the soft, hollow breath of the sea as it sounds
through the broken conch of the human voice
traveling its distance alone.

There was a time he thought of his body
as a temple for Helen, a time when the twin fires of his tongue
were his daughters, Justice and Mercy, but
that is the way of the young. Helen,

kidnaped by Theseus much as our bodies are taken:
for the moment—before the life escapes into Hades—
and we waken to dawn confused, everything forgotten,
everything but Helen.

And so he sets sail from Troy, forehead
bent to forearm, the afternoon slipping by
with its cargo of dream and remembrance.
So that is how the summer died.

O

At dawn, he'd taken
a solitary step and entered
the nearly perfect syntax of the world.

It would be simple to die for a Helen.
It would be easy to set sail, to turn one's back on the ruins,
to acquire the grammar of wisdom
at the small cost
of some small life:
to perfect a civilization.

Arrival is not destination, nor death
a suitable answer.

Each step the first step; each step the final:
each road a crossroad: each tree
articulates a tree.—It is that which comes closest
but passes, that suggestion of perfection,
that makes the flesh its home.

O

And now, he knows, the evening comes
with its torment and its thugs
demanding taxes. And then the anonymous night
with its quicklime of desire,
its starlight and retribution.

That is how this window came to look out
of grief, on the charred monuments of Troy:
it would be good to give one's life for the beautiful
if the beautiful would last. But the world
casts us out and it is impossible to touch anything
except one another. So we reach out when we can

for the outstretched hand of another
knowing that when it is withdrawn . . .

Head tilted forward
almost as though to pray, he buries
his eyes in his forearm.

And the gesture
is almost perfect.

A Dragon in the Clouds

It is solstice,—
hot, dry,
air too heavy to move,
the mountains hazy blue.

I have been baking in the sun
with Euripedes' fable of Helen.

And now, quietly,
a finch has flown down from the cedar
to perch on the windowsill.

And I realize
she is curious,
she is watching,

and has cautiously stepped closer.

The beauty of the tragic,
the tragedy of the lovely,

she doesn't know or care to remember.

She knows two things:
the world is flat,
and that she lives

on this side
of the only river
she cannot fly across.

She looks at emeralds
in the grass and sees
only common seed.

And now she has come closer
once again,

her head cocked,
surveying my naked body.

Her eyes are large
and wearied by their knowledge,

like Kawabata's eyes,
which knew
only sadness and beauty.

I close my book very slowly,
lay my head on my arms,
and look her in the eye:

she has become my lover
and my Dharma master.

Morris Graves says birds
inhabit a world without karma.

Thirty-one new yellow daffodils
bloom in the little garden.

Alder seed covers everything
with little flakes of rust.

A breeze through evergreens.
Distant bird-trills.

When Hui Neng tore up the Sutras,
his bones were already dust.

Jim Harrison

Jim Harrison is a poet and novelist living in northern Michigan. His most recent books are *The Woman Lit by Fireflies* (Houghton Mifflin, 1990) and *Theory and Practice of Rivers and Other Poems* (Clark City, 1989).

Everyday Life

I often think that because I am quite remote up here in northern Michigan from others who practice, and am intensely stubborn, I learn so slowly that I will be dead before I understand very much.

But "who dies?" is a koan I poised for myself several years ago. To know the self, of course, is hopefully to forget the self. The especially banal wine of illusion is to hold on tightly to all the resonances of what we see in the mirror, inside and out. In our practice the self is not pushed away, it drifts away. When you are a poet there is a residual fear that if you lose the self you will lose your art. Gradually, however (for me it took fifteen years!), you discover that what you thought was the self had little to do with your own true nature. Or your art, for that matter.

When I learned this I began to understand that the period of zazen that lays the foundation of the day is meant to grow until it swallows both the day and night. Time viewed as periods of practice and nonpractice is as fanciful a duality as the notion that Zen is Oriental. The kapok in the zafu beneath your ass is without nationality. The Bodhidharma and Dogen saw each other across an ocean river that is without sex, color, time, or form. What is between Arcturus and Aldebaran?

I was wondering the other day about this body that wakes up to a cold rain from an instructive dream, takes its coffee out to the granary to sit on a red cushion. The body sees the totems of consolation hanging around the room: animal skins, a heron wing, malformed antlers, crow and peregrine feathers, a Sioux painted coyote skull, a grizzly turd, a sea lion's caudal bone, a wild turkey's foot, favored stones, a brass Bureau of Indian Affairs body tag from Wyoming Territory, a bear claw, a prehistoric grizzly tooth. These are familiar, beloved objects of earth, but the day is not familiar because it is a new one. The bird that passes across the window is a reminder of the shortness of life, but it is mostly a bird flying past the window.

"The days are stacked against / what we think we are," I wrote in a poem. The point here, albeit blunt, is that when you forget what you are, you truly "see" the day. The man who howls in anger on the phone an hour later because he has been crossed is a comic-figure dog paddling in a sump of pride. He wasn't conscious enough at the moment to realize that there is evil afloat in the land, within and without. This condition can be called "self-sunken." A little later, when he takes a walk on the shores of a lake, he does himself a favor by becoming nothing. He forgets being "right" or "wrong," which enables him to watch time herself flickering across the water. This is a delightful illusion.

The hardest thing for me to accept was that my life was what it was every day. This seemed to negate notions of grandeur necessary for an interest in survival. The turnaround came when an interviewer asked me about the discipline that I used to be productive. It occurred to me at that moment that discipline was what you are every day, how conscious you are willing to be. In the *Tao-te Ching* (in the splendid new Stephen Mitchell translation) it says, "Act without doing; work without effort." So you write to express your true nature, part of which is an aesthetic sense that reflects the intricacies of life, rather than the short circuits devised by the ego. Assuming the technique of the art has been learned, it can then arrive out of silence rather than by the self-administered cattle prod to the temples that is postmodernism.

After this body eats a tad too much for lunch it returns to the granary, stokes the fire, and takes a nap with its beloved dog, who, at eleven, is in the winter of her life. A distinct lump of sorrow forms, which, on being observed, reminds the body of the Protestant hymn "Fly, Fly Away," and we are returned to the fragility of birds. The sense of transience is then embraced. When the dead sister reappears in dreams she is always a bird.

On waking with a start, because it is the dog's nature to bark on occasion at nothing in particular, the work is resumed. There has been an exhausting effort in recent years through the form of poetry and novels to understand native cultures. The study of native cultures tends to lead one far afield from all you have learned, including much that you have perceived and assumed was reality. At first this is disconcerting, but there are many benefits to letting the world fall apart. I find that I have to spend a great deal of time alone in the natural world to be of use to anyone else. Above my desk there is a wonderfully comic reproduction of Hokusai's blind men leading each other across a stream.

Whatever I have learned I owe largely to others. It was back in 1967 that I met Peter Matthiessen and Deborah Love, then Gary Snyder, though in both cases I had read the work. But in these formative stages of practice the *sangha* is especially important. George Quasha introduced me to the work of Chögyam Trungpa—*Cutting Through Spiritual Materialism* is an improbably vital book. Shortly thereafter I met Bob Watkins, a true Zen man, who had studied with Suzuki Roshi and Kobun Chino Sensei. The work of Lucien Stryk has been critical to me, though I have never met him. Then, through Dan Gerber, I met Kobun himself, who has revived me a number of times. Through all of this I had the steadying companionship of Dan Gerber, who is currently my teacher. Without this succession (or modest lineage!) I'd be dead as a doornail, as I have been a man, at times, of intemperate habits. I'm still amazed how the world, with my cooperation, can knock me off Achala's log back into the fire. There is something here of the child who, upon waking, thinks he can fly, even though he failed badly the day before.

There is an urge to keep everything secret. But this is what protestants call the sin of pride, also greed. They have another notion relevant here, that of the "stumbling block" wherein the mature in the faith behave in such a way as to impede the neophyte. There is sadly a lot of this among Buddhists, the spiritual materialism that infers that I have lived in this town a long time and you are only a newcomer. This is like shouting at a child that he is only three years old. It is also the kind of terrifying bullshit that has permanently enfeebled Christianity. Disregarding an afterlife, he who would be first will be last.

We should sit after the fashion of Dogen or Suzuki Roshi: as a river within its banks, the night sky in the heavens, the earth turning easily with her burden. We must practice like John Muir's bears: "Bears are made of the same dust as we and breathe the same winds and drink the same waters, his life not long, not short, knows no beginning, no ending, to him life unstinted, unplanned, is above the accident of time, and his years, markless, boundless, equal eternity."

This is all peculiar but quite unremarkable. It is night now and the snow is falling. I go outside and my warm slippers melt a track for a few moments. To the east there is a break in the clouds, and I feel attended to by the stars and the blackness above the clouds, the endless blessed night that cushions us.

After Reading Takahashi

for Lucien and Peter

Nothing is the same to anyone.
Moscow is east of Nairobi
but thinks of herself as perpetually west.
The bird sees the top of my head,
an even trade for her feathered belly.
Our eyes staring through the nose bridge
never to see each other.
She is not I, I not her.
So what, you think, having little
notion of my concerns. O that dank
basement of "so what" known by all
though never quite in the same way.
All of us drinking through a cold afternoon,
our eyes are on the mirror behind
the bottles, on the snow out the window
which the wind chases fruitlessly,
each in his separateness drinking,
talk noises coming out of our mouths.
In the corner a pretty girl plays pinball.
I have no language to talk to her.
I have come to the point in life when
I could be her father. This was never true before.
The bear hunter talked about the mountains.
We looked at them together out of the
tavern window in Emigrant, Montana.
He spent fifty years in the Absaroka Mountains
hunting grizzly bears and at one time, wolves.
We will never see the same mountains.
He knows them like his hands, his wife's
breasts and legs, his old dog sitting outside
in the pickup. I only see beautiful mountains
and say "beautiful mountains" to which he nods
graciously but they are a photo of China to me.
And all lessons are fatal: the great snowy owl
that flew in front of me so that
I ducked in the car; it will never happen again.
I've been warned by a snowy night, an owl,
the infinite black above and below me to look

at all creatures and things with a billion eyes,
not struggling with the single heartbeat
that is my life.

Dogen's Dream

What happens when the god of spring
meets spring? He thinks for a moment
of great whales travelling from the bottom
to the top of the earth, the day the voyage
began seven million years ago
when spring last changed its season.
He enters himself, emptiness
desiring emptiness. He sleeps
and his sleep is the dance of all the birds
on earth flying north.

Counting Birds

As a child, fresh out of the hospital
with tape covering the left side
of my face, I began to count birds.
At age fifty the sum total is precise
and astonishing, my only secret.
Some men count women or the cars
they've owned, their shirts—
long sleeved and short sleeved—
or shoes, but I have my birds,
excluding, of course, those extraordinary
days: the twenty-one thousand
snow geese and sandhill cranes at
Bosque del Apache; the sky blinded
by great Frigate birds in the Pacific
off Anconcito, Ecuador; the twenty-one
thousand pink flamingos in Ngorongoro Crater
in Tanzania; the vast flock of sea birds
on the Seri coast of the Sea of Cortez
down in Sonora that left at nightfall,
then reappeared, resuming

their exact positions at dawn:
the one thousand cliff swallows nesting
in the sand cliffs of Pyramid Point,
their small round burrows like eyes,
really the souls of the Anazazi who flew
here a thousand years ago
to wait the coming of the Manitou.
And then there were the usual, almost deadly
birds of the soul—the crow with silver
harness I rode one night as if she
were a black, feathered angel;
the birds I became to escape unfortunate
circumstances—how the skin ached
as the feathers shot out toward light;
the thousand birds the dogs helped
me shoot to become a bird (grouse, woodcock,
duck, dove, snipe, pheasant, prairie chicken, etc.).
On my deathbed I'll write this secret
number on a slip of paper and pass
it to my wife and two daughters.
It will be a hot evening in late June
and they might be glancing out the window
at the thunderstorm's approach from the west.
Looking past their eyes and a dead fly
on the window screen I'll wonder
if there's a bird waiting for me in the onrushing clouds
O birds, I'll sing to myself, you've carried
me along on this bloody voyage,
carry me now into that cloud,
into the marvel of this final night.

Kobun

Hotei didn't need a zafu,
saying that his ass was sufficient.
The head's a cloud anchor
that the feet must follow.
Travel light, he said,
or don't travel at all.

Walking

Walking back on a chill morning past Kilmer's Lake
into the first broad gully, down its trough
and over a ridge of poplar, scrub oak, and into
a larger gully, walking into the slow fresh warmth
of midmorning to Spider Lake where I drank
at a small spring remembered from ten years back;
walking northwest two miles where another gully
opened, seeing a stump on a knoll where my father
stood one deer season, and tiring of sleet and cold
burned a pine stump, the snow gathering fire-orange
on a dull day; walking past charred stumps blackened
by the '81 fire to a great hollow stump near a basswood
swale—I sat within it on a November morning
watching deer browse beyond my young range of shotgun
and slug, chest beating hard for killing—
into the edge of a swale waist high with ferns,
seeing the quick movement of a blue racer,
and thick curl of the snake against a birch log,
a pale blue with nothing of the sky in it,
a fleshy blue, blue of knotted veins in an arm;
walking to Savage's Lake where I ate my bread
and cheese, drank cool lake water, and slept for a while,
dreaming of fire, snake and fish and women in white
linen walking, pinkish warm limbs beneath white linen;
then waking, walking homeward toward Well's Lake,
brain at boil now with heat, afternoon glistening
in yellow heat, dead dun-brown grass, windless,
with all distant things shimmering, grasshoppers, birds
dulled to quietness; walking a log road near a cedar swamp
looking cool with green darkness and whine of mosquitoes,
crow's caw overhead, Cooper's hawk floating singly
in mateless haze; walking dumbly, footsore, cutting
into evening through sumac and blackberry brambles,
onto the lake road, feet sliding in the gravel,
whippoorwills, night birds wakening, stumbling to lake
shore, shedding clothes on sweet moss; walking
into syrupy August moonless dark, water cold, pushing
lily pads aside, walking out into the lake with feet
springing on mucky bottom until the water flows overhead;
sinking again to walk on the bottom then buoyed up,
walking on the surface, moving through beds of reeds,

snakes and frogs moving, to the far edge of the lake
then walking upward over the basswood and alders, the field
of sharp stubble and hay bales, toward the woods,
floating over the bushy crests of hardwoods and tips
of pine, barely touching in miles of rolling heavy dark,
coming to the larger water, there walking along the troughs
of waves folding in upon themselves; walking to an island,
small, narrow, sandy, sparsely wooded, in the middle
of the island in a clump of cedars a small spring
which I enter, sliding far down into a deep cool
dark endless weight of water.

The Idea of Balance Is to Be Found in Herons and Loons

I just heard a loon call on a t.v. ad
and my body gave itself
a quite voluntary shudder,
as in the night in East Africa
I heard the immense barking cough
of a lion, so foreign and indifferent.

But the lion drifts away
and the loon stays close,
calling as she did in my childhood,
in the cold rain a song
that tells the world of men
to keep its distance.

It isn't the signal of another life
or the reminder of anything
except her call: still,
at this quiet point past midnight
the rain is the same rain
that fell so long ago, and the loon
says I'm seven years old again.

At the far ends of the lake
where no one lives or visits—
there are no roads to get there;

you take the watercourse way,
the quiet drip and drizzle
of oars, slight squeak of oarlock,
the bare feet can feel the cold water
move beneath the old wood boat.

At one end the lordly, great blue herons
nest at the top of the white pine;
at the other end the loons,
just after daylight in cream–colored mist,
drifting with wails that begin as querulous,
rising then into the spheres in volume,
with lost or doomed angels imprisoned
within their breasts.

Michael Heller

Michael Heller has published five books of poetry, the most recent being *In the Building Place*. His book of essays on the Objectivist poets, *Conviction's Net of Branches: Essays on the Objectivist Poets and Poetry* (Southern Illinois University Press), was published in 1985. He is currently working on a new book of essays and an autobiographical fragment cast in prose-poetry form. He has been a student of Buddhism since 1976.

From the Notes

> For Wordsworth's reader, the poem (and sometimes the world itself) is a created set of hermetic signs. For Tu Fu's reader, meaning is subtly infused in the particular forms of the world perceived and uncertain, perhaps, even to the poet; the poem raises up portentous forms, and in doing so, tells you about both the world and the inner concerns of the poet.
> —Steven Owen, *Traditional Chinese Poetry and Poetics*

"Understand appearance to be the teacher."—Saraha

This statement by the great Indian poet-philosopher continues to have great attraction for me. It is connected with my own thinking on the Objectivist poets, on Maurice Merleau-Ponty's phenomenology, on forms of thought or art that point to the "outside," that open up the petty envelope of self and self-anguish. Herbert Gunther's book *The Tantric View of Life,* with its curious terms and academic jargon, with its abstraction qualifying abstraction, rings certain chords in my head. Occasionally, I find passages that, word-for-word, could have been lifted from Merleau-Ponty's *The Visible and the Invisible.* I am not after something syncretic, however; no real interest in the resonatings of terminologies, in the re-mirrorings of systems, all the false paths of *this* being like *that*. Rather, I find myself ripe for rubrics and mottoes, for pressures and instructions on how to proceed . . . to break through the seductive constellations of human ordering. The other side of that breakthrough would be outer space, something unpredictable? the scrim off or at least exposed. Ultimately these will lead me to a teacher (as far as I understand what it means to find a teacher).

Saraha's statement becomes for me a kind of germ, a linguistic spore of my everyday life, a thought that clings to me and to which I cling like a barnacle to a rock.

Appearance, whatever else it might be, is not union. The word proclaims space, distance, separation, perspective, a litany of outsider terms that have deep psychic appeal. Saraha's thought is, first of all, about otherness and loneliness, a comment on one's precious interiority and, above all, self-ignorance. It is also a salve, a balm, a thing to be recited against one's demons of fear and depression. Perhaps it is also a form of quietism as well.

Which suggests the need for a teacher. One wants to know the world, to live accurately in it, not for some mystical purpose but to go about one's life, to work with others. The teacher steps in and disabuses you of your version of the world, not to supplant it with his but to enable a clearer sense of what is. This is what I take to be the meaning of Chögyam Trungpa's remark that "the function of the teacher is to insult the student."

Saraha's small wedge of words, in the context of practice, could become a personal mantra of sorts, driving words into open space, into the gap that lies between self and world. It suggests not only "knowledge" but connection, a way out of the self or a flow of the self across the magical bridge of words into the world. It leads one as reader to poetry again, to words. And as writer it leads me, not to make worlds, but to wanting to be touched and wounded by worlds. Poems as the possibility of the world's carnality, the body of the world as a word in one's mouth, its savor.

Desire to write an *inscriptive* language, as though, through words, I were first of all trying to haunt my own body, and then perhaps other bodies. To create a form of invitation, "a willingness" as Trungpa said, "to open oneself to the phenomenal world rather than being involved with a strategy of how to relate to it." To enter the space for poetry unarmed, to not want to control any possibility save the following out of the impulse. Isn't this close to the notion of taking refuge, of being a refugee (essentially homeless) without shelter of manner or technique?

Here the usual notions of craft are turned upside down. Normally, craft is containment, mastery, objectification. But what if one had in mind the opposites, dispersal, vulnerability, objectification still (but in the sense that *it* was the path to the reader and not a distancing device)? George Oppen's "The poet suffers the things of the world and speaks them out." Or the painter Arikha's remark that "style is a way of protecting oneself from that which is untrue." "Suffering the world" and "protecting" from untruth, these could easily allude to why the Buddhist outlook is called protecting the mind.

Minor point: such remarks constitute part of the critique of purely formalist notions of art.

Witold Gombrowicz: "The artist who realizes himself inside art will never be creative."

In art, one wants to "treat" an experience so as to receive it back untreated. One recognizes the truth that everything is constructed, but some constructions, just as they come to completion, may be a total surprise to their makers.

Mimesis transformed (in its forms) into language. Walter Benjamin's concept of the mimetic faculty as nonsensuous similarity. Here an idea in language rings faintly of *mahamudra,* the self-existing symbol. This is the sphere of imagination where the view of the "unconditioned" may be glimpsed. Hence through language, the world, cities, lives can be read as sacred (in the sense that everything can be, actually is, under the aspect of *shunyata*). Trungpa writes that the right attitude is to regard the entire world as the floor of a shrine room. To see this as the function of an art. This, in some sense the "outer" teaching.

Which, for the poet as well, is the practice of vulnerability: Somewhere in every act of perception, one is reduced to a word. This is not a word that stands for oneself, nor does it represent oneself. This word (the poem) *is* oneself. And this word is not one that can be enjoyed or taken for comfort. Whatever else is contained in it, the pain of one's death is also there.

And later, this same verbal artifact, read back to its author, will have a solidity, a sculptural quality. Reading it again, one would no longer find that peculiar confirmatory power that came with the first enunciation. Rather, this solidity would be in the form of an archaic monument or gate, something one went by and looked at with all the fascination of a tourist.

My experience and the act of writing are by no means synonymous. I can't *use* meditation to cook up something; indeed, practice seems continually to lead away from the corruptions of use. True, meditation may occasionally throw off the ghostly shadow of nonbeing, which, like a curious, silver gas, permeates and highlights the world about me. An almost painful brilliance. What is seen or experienced afterward might remind of nondualism, not as a concept but as an instance in one's being, a mere snowflake of the unconditioned, cool and bitter on the tongue.

For the poet as a practitioner, the question of what to write down can never be doctrinaire. Even Allen Ginsberg's "first thought; best thought" formulation is in danger of becoming an ideology, a self-sanctifying gesture.

For literature, one must be exceptionally careful of esoteric terminology, of "borrowings." We delude and endanger ourselves by appropriations and promulgations of lore that is culturally bound, that requires initiates. "If a man learns theology before he learns to be a human being," wrote Ludvig Holberg, "he will never become a human being."

The view from practice and the view from the act of writing poetry: occasional synonymy. Victor Segalen's poem "The Sealless Reign" (in his *Steles* of 1914) reads like a Buddhist *via negativa*. Segalen postulates the "reign of no seal," which turns the world from being a theater for projections, a clustering of conception, history, and authority, into a surface off which all thought runs like rainwater off a stone. Poetry, whether in the zero flick of haiku syntax or in the monstrous alternate worlds of Dante and Milton, works on the edge of theistic/nontheistic relating. Practice as constant awareness of the mind's flip-flop along this boundary. Such awareness is also the birth bed of compassion . . . or as Segalen puts it, "the dawning of the day when [one] becomes Regent and Sage upon the throne of his heart."

Water, Heads, Hamptons

"the unbearableness of idyllic literature"—Canetti

My dear,
it is summer. Time to be out of time.
Let us read together the world's newspapers.

But the wind blows away the pages of the *Times*—
they rise, stretch full-length in the breeze like
any vacationer wanting a day in the sun, an even tan
to return with to a city, to proclaim "I too have been away."

Let us read. We can! Memory is our language. We are two
minds that lie athwart each other, two continental plates
with errant nationalities that articulate via subterranean grit.
In time, we will grind this world to powder, to be upraised
and bleached by processes of the seas.

But the wind blows. The surf ripples and slaps with the sough
of all the living and dead it has dissolved, and, with a great
respiratory suck, deposits on the beach what waves
must leave even as they take back what must be taken back.

Ah, you hear the anti-noise where gusts expose the sheet
of crumpled newsprint buried in the sand. What is written
is written. But we will lean close, intent, where
windblown grains pepper the page with faint pings.

    O

It is one of those days when my will seems no more
than the will to conflate utter laziness with a poem
or with roiling sleepily in some good sex. Sleep,

O langorous sleep where I am forgetful of the misery
of history, my brutal West, a dozing Prince
before which all gives way.
                And summer
lightning at the sea's rim transforms the high
gorgeous blocks of clouds into a dance, a shadow-screen
of our imaginable gods: blue Buddha, Shiva of the knife,
Kali who follows footsteps in trackless sand, aereated Christ!

    O

A weird pang of nameless joy. Look, a swimmer's head
is bobbing in the sea. And I point, my finger
like a sunbeam in a barrel. Here's this head

that moves from horizon to beach, this flesh-dot
that seems to swim away from the end
of an entrapping sentence, re-opening its syntax,

and so, for once, is at work against
premature closure. So I identify
a brother eidolon against the tide's flat reach.

    O

Summer's paradise. Its rhythm. But not
the incessant flights of midges swarming in dark air,

alighting on the body through which hope and pain trickle,
those substantial rivers flowing to the seas.

Will you swat the tic of memory and enter into
ever-present babble of flies? Madness of the words.
Old tropes like brilliance of coral shoals on which
waves break and shipwrecks and glittery cabin lights
are extinguished in the deeps.

    O

To the white sands who will speak a name?
The quiet of dusk comes back. Noiseless flight
of gulls inscribes the air and the world goes down
in a rhythm of deepening colors.

Surely the gods we invent bring out the night's phenomena:
flux into perfection, corollas and auroras, St Elmo's fire
for all those who suffer the agonies of speech.

                      Objects, you
no longer offer up yourselves for ceaseless dictation,
no language anyway, our mouths are on each other.
Some lord of silence rises with stars and planets . . .

Photograph of a Man Holding His Penis

for Michael Martone

World o world of the photograph, granular,
Quantumed for composition in the film's grain,
But here blurred, soft-toned and diffuse
Until the whole resolves into an ache, a
Chimerical, alchemical flower, a pattern
Against pure randomness.

As though the process itself exists to mock
What is discrete, is singular. Dot leans on dot,
On the binary of *only two* can make of one a life.

And the myth is partial,
A dream half of need confused with desire.

I too live out this fear, this shadowed aloneness,
The white hand's delicate hold where the genital hairs
Are curled, the groin become a hermitage, a ghastly

Down of our featherings . . .

And the texture is bitter, bifurcate,
A braille of flesh
From which a ghost is sown.

Today, Somewhat After Dante

The wind is blowing; the wind bends everything
but the human will. Thus war and pillage
have written more on the earth's surface than wind.

The Wars, Vietnam, the Greater and Lesser Holocausts,
these names, like those of the Florentine treacheries,
season whatever paradisical truth to poems.

Yet, today, I fall like a blunt object into respites,
walk forgetful among the windblown shrubs
and brackish estuaries on this day of unplanned sun,

happy to be lost in the world's things,
in all this matter and *dura mater,* to feel
when I speak, in each word, a sweet tensile pull of a string.

Afternoon light is penetrant, a blank, absented
fixity. What birds have flown off I will find
in glossaries; old loves I will find in

the mind's book between a cloud and a branch or
a filament of moon in the intense blue. And perhaps
I will stumble, as in a vision, on all the dead,

mother and father included, lining the shore
of Little Tick Island where they will be busy bowing
to that figure of perfect freedom, their self-same minds.

And in the distance, like a memory
of love's midpoint, I'll see the sun flash white
on the salt-caked weather sides of twisted trees.

Mythos of Logos

First the stars or the patterning of stars in darkness, and then
perhaps someone climbing up a mountain to close the gap. Begins
in dusty foothills, then forest, then high empty tundra and piles
of rock, and at the top to brush at with the hand the spangled
emptiness. But the hand feels nothing, sweeps nothing but the
cold air. The loveliness of blackness for the first time brings
solitude. And then one keeps silence at failure, nurses anger
and shame, swallows the bitter taste.

And so the world becomes another place, and now I must confess to
the many things that I forgot to say, was afraid to say, for
fear, for love, for shame, O ancients and splendid hosts whose
words come before and after,

Who have uttered out, one theory goes, what was written in the
gene codes and in the stars' imprints before our speech. And now,
those lucid structures are gantries to my nights, wheeling and
reassembling.

And yes the whole career is night, is crafted out of silence.
And so the sentences out there were not unsaid, nor did they blow
away with stellar dust and stellar time. They settled down about
my head, resembling a dome the exact shape of my skull hidden
from others by a flap of skin.

William Heyen

William Heyen is a former Senior Fulbright Lecturer in American literature and currently Professor of English at the State University of New York College at Brockport. The author of several volumes of poetry—including the forthcoming book *The Host: Selected Poems, 1965–1990* (Time Being Books, 1992)—he is a dedicated environmentalist. In speaking of mourning doves he notes: "I used to think, after reading that they built flimsy and wholly unsatisfactory nests in precarious places, that they were dumb. Now, they seem to me to be at home in the floating world, and to know everything I would want to say. And they do not mourn."

Pickerel

Usually, beginning to remember one of my dreams, I'll ask: Did this happen or did that happen? Was it this way or was it that way? But I have just had a very simple and clear and convincing dream; at least for now, I remember all I need to know about it.

In this dream I am not at all confused. I am sixteen, but at the same time as old as I am now. I am with Karen, my first love, walking toward a wood, and at the same time she is not with me, but with others, and watching me. After a while—and, at the same time, right away—I punt a soccer ball. The idea, I know, is to punt it alongside the dark wood to my right, to keep it in the open field in front of me, of us. This way, I will win a scholarship. In the dream, simultaneously, I both know this and do not know it.

I boom the ball. It's a high kick, curves toward the wood, into the wood. I both regret and do not regret the kick, which I follow into the wood, neither with the others nor apart from them. Deeper in the trees, I look down into a pond, see myself as I was/as I am, and walk away. The ball I am looking for is now a golf ball. It is not that the soccer ball *became* a golf ball. It is that in the world of this unifying dream, golf ball and soccer ball are the same. My past and my present are the same. My innocence and my experience are the same. There are no *ifs*, *ors*, or *buts* here, as there are in my conscious life (where description by way of opposites, in fact, can be trite and boring), no division as there is in even this resolute sentence.

An old man is sitting at a table in the wood selling antiques and golf balls. I know he will become my teacher, and, at the same time in this dream he has been my teacher for many years. "What do you have today?" I ask him. "Same as yesterday," he says. At this point, the dream disappears, but, of course, doesn't, and is still with me. . . .

When I am "awake," everything is split: two brains, going or not-going, having Karen and not having Karen, the living and the dead, winter and summer, gases and solids, the mental life and the physical life, darkness and light, women and men, criminal and victim, anguish and joy, history and future, confusion and clarity. But I realize that within this stunning dream of mine was a rounded revelation (so many of my dreams are angles and fragments) of the nature of the universe, and that right now, despite everything else on my mind from my paycheck to the apocalyptic two-volume 1988 Environmental Protection Agency draft report to Congress called "The Potential Effects of Global Climate Change on the United States," which I've been reading—all species, men and pickerel, are endangered—I can start smiling. It is obvious to me and beyond merely wishful thinking that my deepest self has always known Oneness, or I could not have dreamt it so convincingly.

But these are just words. I've tried here to recount a dream that was the thing itself. Can a poem, by way of vivid leaps and jolts and/or stream of mind upon silence embody and communicate such an experience? To try to suggest cosmic seamlessness mystics—native American and Christian and Buddhist (if there is such a thing as a Buddhist mystic)—have spoken in oxymorons, square circles and cold fires and dry tears and snow blossoms. The great Zen poets help us realize *wholeness:* a dragonfly's motionless speed, the flow of rock and skylark, a frog's fusion with water, the politics of candles and sparrow-monks. I think of a Lucien Stryk translation of Basho: "Moon-daubed bush-clover— / ssh, in the next room / snoring prostitutes."

Poetry, in its relationship to Being, is something like the relationship between Thoreau's pickerel and their pond. He describes them as "the animalized *nuclei* or crystals of the Walden water." And how miraculous it is that we have them: "It is surprising that they are caught here,—and that in this deep and capacious spring, far beneath the rattling teams and chaises and tinkling sleighs that travel the Walden road, this great gold and emerald fish swims." And how priceless, *hors commerce:* "I never chanced to see its kind in any market; it would be the cynosure of all eyes there." And how, after this embodiment, we are connected with them to the great sea: "Easily, with a few convulsive quirks, they give up their watery ghosts, like a mortal translated before his time to the thin air of heaven."

Milkweed swim in the margins of "my" western New York State acre. One summer day I noticed the first slight tinge of a second color in their buds and wrote this poem, called "Ensoulment":

> Before midsummer,
> only hard green
> in the milkweed buds,
>
> but now, as here,
> the first faint mauve light
> does appear
>
> from under sepals:
> even underground,
> how long had it been there? When were
>
> such petals
> ever dead? How could it
> not always have been there?

As did my dream, this poem, this time by way of rhetorical questions, seems able to conceive of Oneness. There is a mauve light here that does not come into being at any one millisecond during the summer, but always *is,* underground or in that place which is at once nowhere and everywhere. And my general sense of the "process" of poetry is this: I wrote that poem, in moments of meditation and semi-trance, to remind my conscious self of what my deeper self (Walt Whitman's "me myself") knows to be true. Did Walt, by the way, achieve satori before or during the composition of those masterpieces of wholeness "Song of Myself" and "To Think of Time" and "The Sleepers" woven, without titles, into the first edition of the *Leaves?* Yes.

There is an "imperishable quiet at the heart of form," Theodore Roethke says. A poem can achieve this tremulous balance, and can be during its writing an aid for the writer, during its reading an aid for the reader, in reaching this. I emphasize the "during"—we *do* surface and begin to talk/buy/dissect/classify/explain. Still, if we remain faithful to that quiet . . .

One of environmentalist Barry Commoner's four fundamental laws of ecology—these hold true at once within earthly and cosmic spheres, tangibly and spiritually, I believe—is that "everything must go somewhere."

There are transformations, but nothing goes away. No ends, no beginnings. Thoreau says that the pickerel are "watery ghosts" that are "translated."

When I was a boy I fished a pond that fed into Lake Ronkonkoma on Long Island. We could catch catfish, sunnies, perch, an occasional bass, but never the beautiful elusive pickerel that disdained our bait. But one late afternoon I saw two of them suspended in the shadow of my head under lily pads four or five feet from shore. (There is a stillness inside stillness, and they were so elementally and electrically still that they still hover in my mind like words I am not yet quite able to say.) I cast worms in front of them—they did not blink or flinch or show the slightest interest. Then, because I was/am a murderer and a creator, I dropped a hook over one's back and snagged it, pulled it to shore, injured or killed it—I don't remember. But, despite me, that earlier image of the two pickerel abides, imperishable, the place of poetry before and beyond the clever and the lethal, abides within the dimension that moment-by-moment spawns the galaxies, that spawns my dream of wholeness in which there is a pond in which, I now know, the pickerel live, and will.

The Return

I will touch things and things and no more thoughts.—Robinson Jeffers

My boat slowed on the still water,
stopped in a thatch of lilies.
The moon leaned over the white lilies.

I waited for a sign, and stared
at the hooded water. On the far shore
brush broke, a deer broke cover.

I waited for a sign, and waited.
The moon lit the lilies to candles.
Their light reached down the water

to a dark flame, a fish: it hovered
under the pads, the pond held it
in its dim depths as though in amber.

Green, still, balanced in its own life,
breathing small breaths of light, this
was the world's oldest wonder, the arrow

of thought, the branch that all words
break against, the deep fire, the pure poise
of an object, the pond's presence, the pike.

Redwings

Maybe you've noticed that around here
red-winged blackbirds aren't rare,
but aren't seen often, either, and then, at distance,
banking away from roads as we pass.

But one morning, I saw a hundred,
more, feeding on seed I'd scattered
under a line of pines planted
more than a hundred years before.

Almost at rest, their feathers folded close,
only yellow wingbars
break their black bodies. But when, as they did,
all at once, they lifted, that *red* . . .

I've tried for a long time, and maybe should,
to tell you how the disembodied redwings
flared and vanished.
I've lost them in every telling.

So much for me. I could die now, anyway.
Could you? We will close our eyes
and rest, in case the blackbirds, in slow motion,
assume again the flames they are, and rise.

Witness

We'd walked into the small warm shed
where spring lambs lay in straw
in the half-dark still smelling of their birth,
of ammonia, the damp grass, dung,
into this world in the middle of a field
where lambs bleating soft songs lifted
their heavy heads toward their mothers,

gentle presences within their wool clouds.
Later, outside, as I watched,
Wenzel wrapped his left arm around a sheep's neck
and struck her with the sledge in his right hand.
The dying sheep, her forehead crushed, cried out,
past pain, for her mortal life. Blood flowed
from her burst skull, over her eyes, her black nose.
Wenzel dropped her to the grass.
When I ran home, I struck my head
on a blossoming apple bough.
Where was the dead sheep?
What did I hear?
Where is the witness now?

I was nine or ten.
Her cry was terror,
so I lay awake to hear her,
to wonder why she didn't seem to know
her next manger, her golden fields.
Her odors drifted through my screen—
the hay at the roots of her wool,
her urine, the wet graindust under her chin,
her birth fluids hot and flecked with blood.
I could hear her bleat
to her last lamb, hear her heartbeat
in the black air of my room.
Where was the dead sheep?
Why did she cry for her loss?
Where is the witness now?

Not to accept, but to awaken.
Not to understand, to cry terror, but to know
that even a billion years later, now,
we breathe the first circle of light,
and the light curves into us, into the deer's back,
the man's neck, the woman's thigh,
the cat's mouse-mossed tongue, all the ruby
berries ripening in evening air.
The dead elms and chestnuts are of it, and do not
break the curve. The jeweled flies sip it,
and do not break the curve.
Our homes inhabit, and ride the curve.
Our moon, our rivers, the furthest stars blinking blue,

the great named and nameless comets do not break the curve.
The odorous apple-blossom rain does not break the curve.
The struck ewe's broken brainpan does not break the curve.
Wenzel nor this witness breaks the curve.

In the shed's dusk where spring lambs
sang to their mothers, in my dark room
where the dead ewe's odors drifted my sleep,
and now, within these cells where her forehead blood
flows once more into recollection,
the light curves. You and I bear witness, and know this,
and as we do the light curves into this knowledge.
The struck ewe lives in this light,
in this curve of the only unbroken light.

In a Ch'ing Dynasty Painting
by Chu Lien

a mantis dangles above cherry blossoms,
old friend cicada in its arms,

blunt-nosed, triangular-winged cicada,
and pale, gray-green mantis who has gripped her

all these years but not yet bitten the dark life that still
shudders and buzzes in its barbed arms—

these partners hanging, upside down,
among the blossoms' transluminous faces.

   (*for Li-Young Lee*)

If You Know Me at All

I once prayed that this acre be the elm's home,
but my elms are dying, or dead. Today I dragged
almost the last torso to the back line
for mouse- and rabbit-shelter over the long winter.

Babe Ruth, whose decorum on formal occasions I sometimes
for the health of my soul have needed to emulate,
said near his end that termites had gotten into him,
and as I hauled elm bats away across autumn,

my right elbow and left knee ground out their lamentation.
But I am used to them by now, and almost
unafraid. Me and the Babe and the elms got
a season or so to go before we're nothing here

but sawdust. I root for them, as you will,
with me, if you know me at all. In elm bark we see
children on diamonds over which the sun passes,
and all our home runs in the cross-cut growth rings.

Jane Hirshfield

Jane Hirshfield was graduated from Princeton University with a degree in creative writing and literature in translation. From 1974 to 1982 she studied Soto Zen at the San Francisco Zen Center, including three years of monastic practice at Zen-shin-ji (Tassajara) and a year at Green Gulch Farm. She received lay ordination in 1979. She has received a Guggenheim Fellowship, a Columbia University Translation Center Award, and other honors. Her most recent books are *Of Gravity & Angels* (Wesleyan University, 1988) and a co-translation, *The Ink Dark Moon* (Vintage, 1990). She lives in Mill Valley, California.

Poetry, Zazen, and the Net of Connection

Not long ago, a poet friend described her latest Christmas-gift project to me: taking used bricks and covering their surfaces with a bright mosaic of broken tile. They make, she informed me, useful doorstops; also, with a bit of felt on the bottom, fine bookends. "I started out just fooling around, and I liked the effect," she said. "Like a package that can't be opened." And I thought how apt a description that phrase is for works of art—how we tend to think of them as gradually revealing an inner meaning to us, but in fact how utterly inseparable the meaning of a work is from its body of paint or stone or words.

Later, I thought also of one of Suzuki Roshi's teaching stories, that of Baso and the tile: One day, Baso—a large, strong monk nicknamed the Horse-master—was sitting zazen in the monastery garden. His teacher, Nangaku, saw him and asked, "What are you doing?" Baso answered, "I am sitting zazen." "Why are you doing that?" asked Nangaku. "Because I want to be a buddha."

Nangaku went to another corner of the garden, picked up a tile, and began to rub it vigorously with a cloth. Soon Baso was there, asking his teacher, "What are *you* doing?" "I am trying to make a jewelled mirror out of this tile," Nangaku replied. "How is it possible to make a mirror by rubbing a tile?" Baso asked. Nangaku answered, "How is it possible to make a buddha by doing zazen?" Of this story, the thirteenth-century teacher Dogen Zenji later said, "When the Horse-master becomes the Horse-master, Zen becomes Zen."

I was introduced to the ideas underlying Buddhist practice by litera-ture, by poetry and writing that were not necessarily explicitly Buddhist, but that reflected Buddhism everywhere in their feelings and imagery—Heian era Japanese and T'ang dynasty Chinese poetry, *No* drama, haiku. Perhaps it is simply because of this personal history, but from the time I began to learn about practice, it has seemed to me that poetry and zazen are parallel and continuous paths: each is an expression of the self in its most complete nature joined with an exploration of the nature of that self.

Zen meditation is a way of feeling one's way forward (or backward, or inward), into one's own deepest experience. It is a way to discover, to uncover, who you already really are. By assuming the posture and atti-tude of meditation, you become a package that can't be opened, a one-ness of wrapping and contents. And poetry can take the same role, the same directionless motion in a life. We write poetry and sit zazen not to become something other than ourselves, a buddha or a mirror, but to know in these activities the original face of our lives. Each is a practice that is its own realization—no less, no more. The point at which these two paths actually meet for me is in a particular kind of concentration that I find fundamental to both. In this concentration, the mind is open, inclusive, alert, receptive to whatever comes, quietly aware; within it, any particular content or focus exists as the reflection of a cloud exists in a still lake, lightly, luminously, and completely. It is in this attentive and wide awareness that any kind of true making happens—emptiness al-lowing form, form allowing emptiness.

To enter the ground of concentration, one begins with the mind of not-knowing. Bowing to a meditation cushion or encountering the mo-ment just before words begin, there is a moment of dwelling in the turning, of attention palpably greeting emptiness. Zen master Zuigan Shigen, alone in his small temple, would call out at odd times to himself, "Zuigan!" and immediately answer, "Yes!" Sitting down to zazen or addressing the white page, we call ourselves to this question: Are you here? Who is here? What is here? And begin to answer. Listening then, noticing and meeting what arises, allowing each moment's fullness and change—doesn't this description of meditation apply equally well to writing? And when Keats writes in one letter that a poet possesses no identity or self, in another that poetic genius matures "by sensation & watchfulness in itself," and in a third offers his famous formulation that the greatest poets' imaginations function through a "negative capability," the ability to abide in mystery and unknowing, doesn't all this point toward the mind of zazen?

In *shikantaza* zazen ("just sitting"), awareness settles through body and breathing to one of seamless, selfless being; in poetry, awareness is through language, through the verbal mind, but also through the body and breath, by way of the music of words, the rhythm of thought. In both, there must be a following of what is. In zazen, it is following the breath that leads to concentration. Following a poem as it rises into being word by word, image by image, also leads to concentration, to thought that comes from the heart and mind both, an understanding encompassing more than simple discursive thought. In virtually every good poem, you can see this mark of widened awareness: an awakened luminosity dwells in all of its parts, regardless of content.

At the heart of how poetry works is a dynamic connection suspended in emptiness: the connection between words and understanding is always a leap across a void, but in poetry, the nature of this leap is made visible. By working near the limits of speech or imagination, a poem raises both the connective power and the openness of language up to consciousness. Hua-yen Buddhism gives us the image of Indra's net, a vision of being in which all things are joined by a wide mesh in which every knot is a jewel, each jewel a universe, and all of them glimmer in the reflected light of one another's existence. This figure of the net, made of both twine and openings, offers a glimpse of form and emptiness functioning together— not one, not two; the knotted jewel-worlds offer the recognition of richness, of treasure, and of many possible ways of being. This sense of interpenetrating boundlessness, of deep freedom, multiplicity, and generosity, is also palpable within the realm of poetry, in its accumulation of constellated worlds—a single web of images, emotions, and meanings that exist in connection to one another, extending infinitely in all directions, moving between mind and mind.

The pleasure of form in poetry too, of its body of sound and meter and rhyme, is the pleasure of knowing the resilience of the structure's net as it embodies grammar and thought; the pleasure of figurative language and metaphor is the realization of how seemingly disparate parts join one another within the mind. Even the pleasure of narrative is, after all, only our sense that between each action and the next there is something that holds, some link between cause and effect. Each of these kinds of connection in a well-made poem is a manifestation of the poet's concentration.

Out of this concentration comes another shared net as well, the wide, supporting net of *sangha*. Strictly translated, *sangha* means the community of those who practice Buddhism, but also, in my own mind, it points to the community of those who may not have practiced, yet share some understanding of our life that I recognize as being not very different from the understanding I turned to Zen practice to explore. If the teachings of Buddhism arise out of a deep experience of concentration (and one hopes, its fruit, wisdom), surely "Buddhist" realization is everywhere possible. And everywhere I look in poetry, I find this is so.

Turning at random to what is now on my desk: in W. S. Merwin's translation of the Argentinian poet Roberto Juarroz, the first poem begins, "A net of looking holds the world together . . . " In these few words, there is Indra's net, an understanding of the nature of awareness, an oblique acknowledgment of transience. Next I see on an index card one of the most quoted lines from the poetry of Czeslaw Milosz, the Nobel laureate: "What is poetry if it cannot save nations or people?" Here is the bodhisattva vow, not to enter the realm of enlightenment until all other beings (down to the last blade of grass, the bodhisattva would say) are saved from delusion as well. And here is a small poem by Rainer Maria Rilke I have been translating, an inscription he put into the copy of the Duino Elegies he gave to his Polish translator:

Happy are those who know:
behind all words, the Unsayable stands;
and from that source, the Infinite
crosses over to gladness, and us.

Free of those bridges we raise
with constructed distinctions;
so that always, in each separate joy,
we gaze at the single, wholly mutual core.

What is this, if not a statement of the experience of the world and its relationship to words that is felt in meditation? Rilke spent years learning to observe closely; his work in *New Poems* is a direct result of this deliberate and reponsive practice of looking. "When the Horse-master becomes the Horse-master, Zen becomes Zen," Dogen wrote; and, "To follow the way is to study the self; to study the self is to forget the self; to forget the self is to be enlightened by the ten thousand things." When Rilke becomes Rilke, forgets Rilke, and turns to the myriad things for his poems, is he not practicing the *sangha*'s understanding?

If poets have a task for which they are responsible to the culture as a whole, to those who share their time and those who follow, I feel that task is to create language that can enable and convey just such deep experience, or subtle experience, or wide experience, and help that knowledge pass from life to life. The job of poetry is to create and enlarge a true understanding, to help the poet and everyone awaken together to the nature of our lives through the clarifying possibilities of words. *Alaya,* the title I chose for my first collection, is a Sanskrit word that means "home" and also, in Buddhist terminology, "the conscious-ness that is the storehouse of experience"—or, put simply, memory. The large storehouse of poetry is the place where seed grain is kept, the way that experience can travel forward, between people and in time. It is a capacious granary, built for the long run. We each bring to it what contribution we can, the harvest of our own fields, filling the grain bins with the many names of home.

Each of our poems names and holds our connected life in this time, in this place, as each spring of water is the storehouse of a particular flavor of earth, each ear of corn the storehouse of weather, of soil, of a thousand years of agricultural choices. As poets, as Buddhists, we are members of many different *sanghas,* storehouses of knowledge, of language, of forms, and of emptiness. Our chosen responsibility is to cultivate the soil of poetry and of our lives; our joy is to carry this responsibility with the same continuous awareness and effortless effort as the earth carries her own cultivation of mountains, swamplands, and rivers.

Recalling a Sung Dynasty Landscape

Palest wash of stone-rubbed ink
leaves open the moon: unpainted circle,
how does it raise so much light?
Below, the mountains
lose themselves in dreaming
a single, thatch-roofed hut.
Not that the hut lends meaning
to the mountains or the moon—
it is a place to rest the eye after much traveling,
is all.
And the heart, unscrolled,
is comforted by such small things:
a cup of green tea rescues us, grows deep and large,
a lake.

In That World, the Angels Wear Fins

In that world, the angels wear fins.
Red hulls pass over like clouds, their shadows
angling down between ropes of sun.
When women who have dived there return,
they do not speak of oysters or pearls.
Shaking their heads they say, "There is nothing."
They say, "We must look somewhere else,"
and twist their black hair in the world of men,
and wade heavily through the grass-scented air.
From this they know loss like salt:
how without it, the tongue grows stubborn and dull,
tastes nothing.
But the wild flavor, the sea, how it moves in them,
hip and thigh—a soundless current, kicking
downward the rest of their lives.

The Stone of Heaven

Here, where the rivers dredge up
the very stone of Heaven, we name its colors—
muttonfat jade, kingfisher jade, jade of appleskin green.

And here, in the glittering
hues of the Flemish Masters, we sample their wine;
rest in their windows' sun-warmth,
cross with pleasure their scrubbed tile floors.
Everywhere the details leap like fish—bright shards
of water out of water, facet-cut, swift-moving
on the myriad bones.

Any woodthrush shows it—he sings,
not to fill the world, but because he is filled.

But the world does not fill with us,
it spills and spills, whirs with owl-wings,
rises, sets, stuns us with planet-rings, stars.
A carnival tent, a fluttering of banners.

O baker of yeast-scented loaves,
sword dancer,
seamstress, weaver of shattering glass,

O whirler of winds, boat-swallower,
germinant seed,
O seasons that sing in our ears in the shape of O—
we name your colors muttonfat, kingfisher, jade,
we name your colors anthracite, orca, growth-tip of pine,
we name them arpeggio, pond,
we name them flickering helix within the cell, burning coal tunnel,
    blossom of salt,
we name them roof flashing copper, frost-scent at morning,
    smoke-singe of pearl,
from black-flowering to light-flowering we name them,
from barest conception, the almost not thought of, to heaviest
    matter, we name them,
from glacier-lit blue to the gold of iguana we name them,
and naming, begin to see,
and seeing, begin to assemble the plain stones of earth.

November, Remembering Voltaire

In the evenings
I scrape my fingernails clean,
hunt through old catalogues for new seed,
oil workboots and shears.
This garden is no metaphor—
more a task that swallows you into itself,
earth using, as always, everything it can.
I lend myself to unpromising winter dirt
with leaf-mold and bulb,
plant into the oncoming cold.
Not that I ever thought
the philosopher meant to be taken literally,
but with no invented God overhead,
I conjure a stubborn faith in rotting
that ripens into soil,
in an old corm that rises steadily each spring:
not symbols, but reassurances,
like a mother's voice at bedtime reading a long-familiar book,
the known words barely listened to,
but joining, for all the nights of a life,
each world to the next.

Inspiration

Think of those Chinese monks' tales:
years of struggling
in the zendo, then the clink,
while sweeping up, of stone on stone . . .
It's Emily's wisdom: Truth in Circuit lies.
Or see Grant's *Common Birds and How To Know Them*
(New York: Scribner's, 1901):
"The approach must be by detour,
advantage taken of rock, tree, mound, and brush,
but if without success this way, use artifice,
throw off all stealth's appearance, watchfulness,
look guileless, a loiterer, purposeless,
stroll on (not too directly toward the bird),
avoiding any gaze too steadfast;
or failing still in this, give voice to sundry whistles,
chirp: your quarry may stay on to answer."
More briefly, try; but stymied, give it up, do something else.
Leave the untrappable thought, go walking,
ideas buzz the air like flies; return to work,
a fox trots by—not Hughes's sharp-stinking thought-fox
but quite real, outside the window,
with cream-dipped tail and red-fire legs doused watery brown;
emerges from the wood's dark margin, stopping all thinking,
and briefly squats (not fox, but vixen), then moves along
and out of sight. "Enlightenment," wrote one master,
"is an accident, though certain efforts make you accident-prone."
The rest slants fox-like, in and out of stones.

Mary Kean

Mary Kean published her first book, *Critical Minutes,* with Rocky Ledge Cottage Editions in 1985. She has worked with choreographers in blending poetry and dance performances and has taught at the University of Colorado and Naropa Institute in Boulder, Colorado, where she was the director of Project Outreach, a program of writing workshops with "at-risk" populations. Ms. Kean lives in White Rock, British Columbia, where she works as a family therapist.

Crisp Blue Shirt

Here she is alone
     his crisp blue shirt so beautifully laundered
     open at the throat and adorned with perfectly ordinary buttons
Is far away like a satellite
Good.
         Good. Good. Good.
Alone is just as she should be
     in her natural habitat:
     moving alone, breathing alone, phoning alone, drawing
     alone,
     paying bills alone.

Alone is an animal
     a tree
     a bear
     nation entire unto itself
She walks around in it like a man in the streets
     like Walt Whitman

or like anyone.

Alone is cool, still mountain lake
   and she, Divorcee, comes hot little deer,
   pursued by rough-haired dogs of Mara
   and drinks,
   and wades into her own solitude.
Oh, beautiful breathless ice-cold solitude
   so claustrophobic, staunches the heart
   brings her to her senses
Good old tree.
Good old bear.
    Good crisp blue shirt.

Poetry

Dawn divides itself:
the definite grey & the definite
combustion into day.
The porch fills up with poems.
It might rain.
Where I live, people hang their laundry on the line.
Tables, chairs and even lamps are tallow.
Tomorrow Cindy will have a name for the magazine.
A swan flies through the dining room.
The yard fills up with poems.
I play tapes, clean the oven & call my lawyer.
The dial on the phone is white hot;
my hand, a fan of flames.
I know so many people. Each one owns a little tile.
Let's invite them over,
place the tiles and see the child of illusion.

Reality

Torn with deception, men in bed
wait for their children.
Women at their computers meet & smack
like crickets.
At dusk the house is quiet as a painting.
Moon calls her children resting like bulbs.

A man appears from the eye of a dancer.
The house scatters like shrapnel.
Hordes of phantoms blossom & faint.
In the morning borders ravel & despair
so who knows where what is said at lunch
comes from: the coffee or the cream?

Parachute Sestina

Who would ring in on such incredible sense?
Who would drop by at such a time, indeed,
who *could* drop by without an aid, a parachute
or with feigned indifference pretend not to grasp
what event is taking place, has taken place as routine
a sort of discipline, almost a resistance, like the French.

In World Wars in Europe completely isolated, the French
had to be very alert, n'est-ce pas? Had to have the sense
to appear ordinary, to appear only normal, routine,
passing the days of occupation preparing meals, indeed
hardly interested in the enemy much less able to grasp
the significance of maneuvers, matériel, troops arriving by
    parachute

and that is where we are now. Only an entrance, say, by parachute
of a little silk goddess. I think in theater the French
copied Greeks and brought in to save the day, literally to grasp
out of the jaws of fate, the heroine who didn't have the sense
to get herself out of a jam or else as in our own situation, indeed,
the jam has gotten the better of everyone and become the routine.

Wouldn't you think one of us could see it as a routine,
could coax the others to leap, parachute
out of the B-29 of continuous patterns. Yes, indeed. Yes, indeed,
now we understand what we are discussing. It is the French.
It is their logic. Their open-hearted, intelligent sense
and sensibility. They understand passion and what it is to grasp
on to concept. To grasp on to a thought; to grasp
and to hold to one's idea of the world, which makes the world
    routine
makes it dry up, become grey, lose its fresh sense
of itself. So a desperate action is again called for. A parachute
action. The ripcord, fail-safe packaging. In the French

culture a situation should never deteriorate so. Indeed

that *is* culture. *Is* civilization: *being* in action, in deed
as well as in word or thought, free from the deathly grasp
of passion and at the same time passionate. The French
describe these expressions of passion as faux pas. Routine
gestures of discursive mind. We cannot parachute
to some Switzerland without some sense

of that routine. Without some grasp of what motivates, the
    parachute
is just another thought and becomes captured like the French
who, at one time, for all their culture & good sense were *not* free.
    Indeed.

Sphinx

There is a wind, dry as an old Pharaoh.
Your smile, smooth as a sphinx,
and I am crayfish, curled around your arm.
A bird twitters like Nefertiti;
the cat's first clean yawn says Ra.

There is a wind, dry as an old Pharaoh.
bird twitters
        at Nefertiti
        old Pharaoh cold in the window
            Nefertiti at the window
                Nefertiti   a bird
        bird at the window
                    Nefertiti   bird
                                        bird
                bird at the window.

Our friends in the cattails are mummies;
We are painted as a boating party,
Anubis at the prow. His dark presence
says Death but we know
he means Once.

Magpie

mocks black and white cat.
Every day I wear a sweater.
The little mountain behind me wears
a rainbow like tropical fish. Land
is the piñata with all its surprises.
Sounds of animals. Flashlights.
Our lives back to back.
Tears really mean, "Taste this fire."

Robert Kelly

Robert Kelly has published numerous works, including *Under Words* (Black Sparrow, 1983), *Not This Island Music* (Black Sparrow, 1987), *The Flowers of Unceasing Coincidence* (Station Hill Press, 1988), and *Doctor of Silence* (McPherson & Co., 1988). He came to Buddhism in 1982 "as a way of compassionate participation in the world." He studied with Kalu Rinpoche and studies with Lama Norlha, to whom the poems here are dedicated. He teaches at Bard College in Annandale-on-Hudson, New York.

Going With the Poem

Language is the intersection of consciousness with society.

This is where our work must be done.

What work?

The unexpected. The dog that did nothing in the nighttime. The sentence that opened, between one word and another, like the bronze door of a cathedral, to show the sea. The moon, her hair, his hand—anything you please. In other words: in other words.

For a long time I thought it was a political necessity to de-reference language from its customary occasions—there might be some benefit from crisscrossing the wiring at the base. Deep in the planet of our incarnation the uncountably many relays switch on and off. Language, that gauge, gives our best local mapping of those (strictly) endless modifications motivated by everything else. Our syntax is our habit. What we take ourselves to be—wanters, haters, indifferentists—is the sum of what is said about us, and what we say about ourselves, not just out loud, but in the ceaseless discourse of the head (if that's where you hear it), the never-stopping paean to our own self-nature, the sacred and terrible jabber of all-day-long and in the dark it turns into dream.

The poem we have learned to make is an experiential one, whose value arises from the *deed* we do in the act of reading it. Buddhism's own name for itself is the Dharma—that is, Reality, everything that is the case. Buddhism is not a religion, it is reality. What we call religion is *one* of the means Buddhism uses to change reality.

And it must be changed. That is the Rilkean, Lorcan, Mallarméan momentum, the shared thing, the alchemical Tongue Work that makes the poetry of this century different in many ways from the recent centuries of its antecedents, and joins it with its beginnings in Homer and Veda.

The poem is not an artifact, not a picture of reality; it is a weapon or at least a tool in the ceaseless and necessary battle for simple vigilance, *pour éveiller,* wake up—the basic meaning of the verbal root *budh-* of which the past participle is *Buddha,* the One Who Woke Up.

How to make sense of ruin. The torso perfected by its absences. *You* must change your life—that's the word to stress when you read that amazing line aloud at the end of Rilke's poem. And this changing is a process, a continuity (*tantra*) within the huger faith in which our faith in poetry as a sort of revelation functions. Our work is to inscribe the consequences of reverence, to register the strange and particular knowings that arise from even an occasional devotion to the happiness of all beings. Poetry is only one of the infinite ways in which the *buddhavacana* can speak, the voice of the Awakened One waking us. But it is a way. The Buddha they say can manifest as a man, a woman, a picture, a bowl of rice, a word.

For all the smallness and meanness of most writers, they propose a compassionate intent: to say a word everyone can hear,

a word that comforts and heals.

In our day, in our life, poetry has a work.

This is how I tried to define it in the back pages of my most recent collection of poems, my first since going to Buddhism:

> Trying to understand and examine how
> through the composition of poems
> the organs of enlightenment
> can begin to open
> and begin to work
> for the benefit of all.

For the benefit of all, not just the talker, the poem shapes itself in sylla-bles, which are breath-patterns, deep metabolic rhythms it borrows from the body of the writer, the ground swell. This is a signal of what is personal (body) transcending itself into what is sharing, shared: Speech.

Speech is the deep sound of language, the blood of society, the archaic system of phonemes always focused currently, precisely. Speech is lan-guage, the urgent semantics of everyday "meanings" ensnared in all the magical guesswork of the mother tongue that reveals the mind.

Not particularly the mind of the given writer, that's hardly the point; though that mind lies bare in the poem, its nudity is not the aim of the process, but a means of it.

The poet is someone with nothing to say.

Poets are people who have momentarily stilled or silenced what-they-want-to-say, so that they can speak. What is revealed in the poem is the mind of all beings who use language.

The mind of life speaks us in detail, and language is responsible to it. Into the condensing text, a poem works all the ordinary and extraordinary skills that comes its way from our searches among the materials: medi-tation, what is called thinking, what is called dreaming, from conversa-tion, libraries, annals, archives, ritual, introspection, argument, analysis, lovemaking, daydream, remembering, looking, looking out the win-dow. Then the musical powers of syntax, all our listening, all our artful structurings of the line, sound, all the elaborate posturings of metrics, all begin to act: the poem.

A poem is activity, a nest of sounded deeds. The deeds are shared by reader and writer equally, transpersonally, unpossessed.

And what they share is one focused, coherent dance of all that's going on. The activity of poetry is to reconnect the reader and the reader's society with the underlying ever-present glory we take as behavior. There is an internal politics of the poem: the spontaneously arising text is responsible to all the constituencies the poet contains and momentarily represents. My needs are my permissions. What I hear is sacred: in one ear and out the mouth.

Silence is the life of poetry. Not the silence of the uncommitted, but Vimalakirti's silence, that shook the world like a lion's shout,

the silence that hears us at the end of every line of poetry.

Maitreya

Snow lies blue under the trees' shadows and strong where the sun
    strikes everywhere else.
Across this snow Maitreya comes walking.
He is walking towards us.
He is clear red in color like ruby or garnet and seems to our eyes
    about seventy-five or eighty feet high.
He is taller than the highest trees and his features although distinct
    are hard to see because they are as bright as the sky.
The sky is very bright.
These are new woods.
I have been in places where the trees are old.
The house down by the river is very old and the ruins away to the
    south even older.
What stands there is the front wall of an old brick house with two
    corners intact.
Above where the front door had been the empty arch still stands.
The bricks are very red against the very blue sky.
These are experiences about which it seems necessary to use a share
    of *verys*.
How long the arch will go on standing is neither clear nor a matter
    of much hope.
Already one brick is certainly coming loose.
We are walking north over the empty fields.
People have passed before us on foot and on skis.
There are the tracks of one sled.
Perhaps a father pulled his son deep into the woods along this trail.

The way fathers wait for their sons and then keep the sons waiting
all the rest of their lives takes some of the keenness away from the
vivid blue-skied red-knitted woollen capped joy in a simple image
of a father and his son we saw a little while ago.
A father was pulling his little son on a sled down through the
woods.
Maitreya comes toward us moving south to our north.
He is red and clear and taller even than the quick-growing pines
where last autumn we saw the fox couple out strolling.
No one for a minute or two is afraid of anything.
But we are waiting too.
What he means or what it means to see him is that we accept the
necessity of loving everything that is alive.
We accept that as an obligation and the blue sky of clearest winter
noon turns red and walks towards us.
Now that he is closer we see he is really taller than we had thought
before.
Now that he is close it seems we can see nothing higher than he is.
Anything that is really coming towards us is about necessity.
Necessity means obligation.
The obligation is to be red and walk towards everyone with love.
He walks towards us because we are looking towards him.
The obligation is ours.
That doesn't mean love is easy or not easy.
Sometimes it is sometimes it isn't.
He walks because it is his nature to be coming towards.
Without going from where he is not staying he is always coming
towards.

Melencolia

after Albrecht Dürer

Be near me then, it is only a design.
Only a door painted on the wall of your room.
Go in and out. It shows a man almost naked
whose folds and shadows are prussian blue
but whose flesh where the sun strikes it
is the color of raspberries in milk
an hour after immersion. Sugar. This
is the Theologian. He is falling from heaven.
For over a week his skin has endured

the facility of his descent. The soft
bronze hairs on his forearms are burnt off.
This earth his landing place is still a sunset off.

2.

What have I sacrificed. What is the arrow
that took my eyesight, shot
from inside my cranium out, yearning
for a world it pierced me to behold.
Listen. What was the tambourine
Sally clattered as she took off her skirt
in one wide unwrapping gesture meaning me
in? At the fifteenth degree of the sign
Saturn is exalted in Libra. Buildings
are understood, measurements are known,
people understand the frustrum of a cone
by formula. The music of an immense order
peoples our love. One by one
the numbers follow him down from heaven.

3.

All that matters is this meaning?
No. He falls
and what sustains us is the detail,
pores of the skin, the map
of all our difference.
I want to tell you simply that
his body Language is who falls.
When his body touches earth we leave the room
by the spontaneously self-enchanted door.

4.

Midafternoon the heat came back.
It was a farmer with his mate,
his son with a mattock ope'd the earth
and we were two, all of us two
and never one, no one.
Midafternoon the farmer
forgot to hear his Bruckner 8th.
All those opalescent spaces
were actual spaces; he moved
within them and the earth closed.

5.

This is then what Saturn sent:
the golden age, the afternoon
between the beech tree and the lilac
in the place called Europe.
The endless books of the philosophers,
the bridges of Koenigsberg.
But most a sense that our palaver
feeds and is fed by a secret stream,
a simple current underneath the mind
that is the mind.

Objections to the Unsatisfactoriness of Cyclic Existence

Then it if rain we again become another instancing the same
Myth takes to her breasts simply cornfield moonlight
Varnish or resin embedded weather from home The Blue Powder
There root sews seams kettle spits fire hiss so many universes
Planning a trip to the nursery arch as April pond by gloaming
Little lures space deep Lucreville trolley's smart mnemonic clang
Not Marx not not Marx peach peach and bowl milk and
    circumstance read as if it said what he said
Pythagoras and Mary coming between the gates and Russell Square
    other argument to the museum
For long we however want or never glaze on tea ware
To define the world: *Nothing remembering something*
Won't eat try doctoring—a simpler gathering her herbs
Goes grass now this is cubic go away a gong a gong still dark
Codiaeum something named pond beside town I admit my whole
    life study has been Kabbalah
Organize remote a part a ball her white clothes isle of it
Join national cod banks a nation is salt it under differences his
    mistress body unalarmed
Sky in the island willow Sally's discontinuous affections
Sandbox the nothing you can say is not the nothing I mean
Listen it was me in the blue envelope Antarctic passenger
Hook of an apple cloud edge of an edge.

Horse

Waiting at the stable for the horse to be born
the Imperial Stables
with Lipizzaners toe-dancing up the parvis
delicate hooves make
small clods to rise and fall,
                              the earth
                      is a manner of dancing,
when will the last horse come?

The horse with the orange light in its eye,
the horse on fire, the calico horse,
the horse with the polished mirror bright aluminum rump mane of
    milkweed and dame's rocket tangled,
the horse with Latin teeth and Chinese heart,
the horse with his hoof in your lap
his wet muzzle annoying the nape of your neck wisely,
the horse with a grumbling belly the horse
with a crow on its head and a cat on its back
and the cat has blue fur, the horse of judgment,
a horse full of politics a horse full of new quarried stones shining
    white in the sun, a horse
is waiting for you, his yard-long pole is looking for you,
when will you arrive at the human destination,
when will the prefigured certainties dissolve into one spontaneous
    touch,
when will you let the last horse find you,

the horse with Roman nails stabbed into its withers,
the horse dripping with sun,
the horse whose shadow covers a dozen acres and whose cry
wakes you between midnight and dawn,
the horse with crazy eyes like a doting papa,
with eyes not like Stalin not like John Dillinger's eyes,
the horse with honey stuck in his throat
clearing his throat forever whence pure vowels are born among
    men,
the horse upside down, the horse stuffed with silk and linen and
    books printed in Pali,
the horse at the barricades, the green horse who stumbles on the
    wind,
the big horse who remembers your mother, the horse

who makes you love your mother, the horse
with a telephone cord garlanded round his neck,
the horse who talks to the world suddenly and in a quiet voice
braying the truth of the matter, the horse in orange leaves,
the horse with horns on its head, on grass halms grazing,
the horse on sale in New Orleans, the old horse at the mill, the horse
dragging the barge on the Erie canal,
the horse a slave rides all night for weeks to the North,
the horse ramping a mare in Putnam County, a horse
who will never go back, a horse with three
holy men on his back escaping into the dark,

when will you remember your liberty,
when will you let the green horse come,
last of a thousand horses, the horse that's here even now, right now,
the horse in your cellar, the horse on your roof,
the horse in your kitchen huger than sunlight,
the horse who sleeps standing up, whose eye
stares out of your navel, the horse in your bone,
the horse with the head and hooves of a horse,
the horse running towards you on the avenue of light,
the horse that was the first thing I saw when I died?

David McKain

David McKain won the 1987 Associated Writing Programs Award for
Creative Nonfiction with *Spellbound: Growing Up in God's Country* (University of Georgia Press, 1988). He has published three books of poetry,
including *Spirit Bodies,* which won the Ithaca House Poetry Prize in 1990.
He teaches at the University of Connecticut, where he coordinates the
creative writing program and directs the Connecticut Poetry Circuit.

The Birdcarver

Wanting us to see more than decoys
he talks with a knife about his dream:
to free the birds that nest inside the mind,
carve them out of words until they soar.

The white cedar's nearly gone, he says,
sold for posts and fences—
that's the wood for the long-beaked shore birds,
for their hull, nothing else will do.
For fan-tail, ring-neck or mallard,
the soft white pine from Utah.

But the neck of the shore bird curves,
turns to head, then swerves
into a beak
from an everyday branch of blueberry—

that's the thing of it,
find the right day, be ready to see,
come up on it eye-level,

the exact right stem, one
you've passed a hundred times
now curlew, Hudsonian, heron.

The native white cedar,
cut it winter from the swamp,
drag it on a sled across the ice
to season a year up on stickers—
that's a big part, getting out.

Then know calls, migrations, the moon—
like anybody with wood and time,
making something out of nothing.

Coppers

Swatting spots she called flies
my grandmother rocked in her bathrobe:
at war, she flattened tin cans with her heel.
All winter long we huddled in the kitchen:
"The world makes sense," she said.
"Just clean your plate. It won't rain."

She knew how to hang green peppers,
wallpaper, and an axe to its handle,
swelling the hickory in a bucket overnight.
She grew potatoes under straw without a Book
of Glossy Giant Peas. We all saved string
and stuffed rags around the windows.

Floodtime I hung out in the woods all day
waiting for a sign the Lord had made
the river swell, combed the grasses down
and drowned the rows where buckwheat
sprouted with the corn. The yellow water
chased the copperheads uphill to town.

The poisonous snakes were everywhere.
They hid beneath loose cellar stone
and curled inside a broken bucket by the well.
But when we found one in a grocery bag
the men strapped on calf-high leather boots
and shouldered long-forked poles and guns.

My fingers in my ears, I ducked
across backyards to hear the shot
and watch the thin blood trickle down
the scales of the writhing belly.
One copper, one shot. From the men
I learned not to torture, not to waste.

Witching

The man who witched brought three sticks:
one like a breastbone from a giant crow,
one a cherry slingshot, forked and polished.

The third was wired, broken at the union
by a pull beneath the earth against
both hands. He showed me callouses.

We hiked in where I'd seen the buck
standing on the quarry ledge, up ahead
the rise of cedars where we built the house.

Stumbling over roots and branches, he
pitched behind what seemed a walking plow.
He held the handles of his stick mid-air

without a steel cutting edge or horse,
then cursing, flung the rod aside to rub
his blistered palms. People here say

by now he's fooled himself. He grabbed
my hand, cupped it over his to feel
the quiver, the heat of the broken stick.

But when he asked if I believed in dowsing,
I couldn't say I did. I said I believed
he had a map inside, hidden lakes and rivers.

I said enough to make him laugh and get me
off the question. Even now, drinking water
from the well, I think he knew his craft

and how to shuffle through the leaves, arms
straight out like a sleepwalker. In stutter
step, shake and stagger, walk high on water.

Opening Day

Gusts of wind cruise like fish
through bare branches of oak and dogwood
by the river. I've come here to read
a letter from a friend locked up in prison,
trying to understand how he has found the heart
to write about cowbirds singing at his shoulder,
about seagulls flying upriver.

The damp air smells like a bucket
half-buried in leafmold—rusted out,
filled with bullet holes and earthworms.
He writes they have a garden where
they grow their own corn and tomatoes,
leaving plenty for the deer and woodchuck.

One Sunday morning he skipped Mass
to dig worms and cut a fishing pole
while the cook smuggled in a jug of wine—
the guard, a few sticks of dry kindling.
Then the three of them squatted in a circle
behind the tool shed, coaxing a spark
from the wet leaves, feasting in the drizzle.

Months earlier, in court, a reporter asked
why he had sprayed "Auschwitz" on a US Trident,
hammering in its nose-cone. At first he shrugged,
as though everyone knew the answer, but then,
in the same quiet voice of the letter, bemused,
he smiled and said, To make a dent in history.

I carry the crumpled letter in my wallet
to remember what it's like to be angry—
angry enough to smuggle paint and a hammer
into an airshow; plant corn and tomatoes;
drink wine; walk in the mist before anyone
else gets up, the seagulls yammering upriver.

for Vincent Kay

Brushfire

After supper, the moon full of smoke,
Jim and I walked down Eleven Mile Road
toward Chrystal, the wind rustling
through the seedpods, sounding like birds
scratching for grain in the ditch
beside us. In the moonlight, a burst
of starlings flew up like black leaves
to the only tree in the cornfield.
I could see the tips of their feathers,
white and silvered for winter.

"I fart like a horse when I walk,"
Jim said, and he kept on walking,
blowing on his hands to keep warm.
He struck a match for a smoke,
then bent down and lit the husks
of dock and chicory. Brighter
than moonlight, the flames jumped up
over our shoulders, crackling
toward his son's trailer. Lights
went out, heads shot up at the window.

"Why'd you set the weeds on fire?"
Jim's wife asked when we got back,
but Jim just hiked up his trousers
and laughed. "Who wants to know?"
he asked, "Donny?" Mrs. Dailey nodded.
From the porch, we could see a man
and a woman beating sparks into the sky
with a rug and a shovel. In an hour,
Don barged in trembling, his hands
and face black, his trousers singed.

"How come you set my yard on fire?"
he challenged his father. "Them weeds,
you mean? I see you and Millie
whackin at 'em over there," Jim laughed.
Mrs. Dailey kept her head down, ironing.
Don ran a finger through his eyebrows,
flinging sweat on the floor like a curse.
Shaking, he looked at his father hard
before he finally smiled, then stormed out
into the cold simplicity of winter.

Jackson Mac Low

Jackson Mac Low is a writer, composer, and visual and performance artist. Of his twenty published books, *Representative Works: 1938–1985* (Roof Books, 1986) is a sampler of his various kinds of work. His most recent publications include *Pieces o' Six* (Sun & Moon, 1991), *Words nd Ends from Ez* (Avenue B, 1989), and a second edition of *French Sonnets* (Membrane, 1989). He has received over a dozen professional awards, including a Fellowship in Creative Writing from the National Endowment for the Arts, a Guggenheim Fellowship for Poetry, and a Fulbright Grant. He has been a visiting professor of creative writing at the State University of New York at Binghamton.

Buddhism, Art, Practice, Polity

Buddhism has exerted an important influence on my life and work since the early 1950s, when I first encountered Zen in the writings of Dr. Daisetz Teitaro Suzuki (and soon after in his classes at Columbia University) and in the music and conversation of John Cage. (From about 1945 to 1953 I considered myself a Taoist.) It continues to do so, even though I have strong reservations about the "church polity" of most of the Buddhist groups I have encountered.

Unlike many of my contemporaries, however, I have seldom consistently practiced either meditation or other Buddhist disciplines, while at the same time I have not, like some artists, notably Mr. Cage, completely eschewed practice outside of work in the arts (which both of us have regarded as a religious discipline in itself). I have during certain periods of my life meditated and/or repeated mantras daily, but at other times I've done so only intermittently or not at all. At times I have regarded my work in the arts as a religious or quasi-religious discipline, but at other times I have thought of art as a strictly "secular" activity.

To some this attests to no very strong commitment to Buddhism on my part. I do not think this view is correct. I am committed to the basic truths of Buddhism, but in this short essay I want to deal directly with those aspects of Buddhism that have most influenced my artistic work, as well as with the polities of the groups within which Buddhism is taught and practiced.

From Zen I gathered the conviction that giving one's complete attention to any dharma (perception, form, feeling, etc.) may lead to a direct insight into reality, and that such insight can free us from suffering, which, as Buddhism teaches, pervades all sentient existence. (Briefly, through this insight the world of suffering, or *samsara,* is revealed to be basically the world of blissful awareness, or *nirvana.*) This way of perceiving is often characterized in Buddhist literature as "choiceless awareness" or "bare attention."

Being "choicelessly aware" is perceiving phenomena—as far as possible—without attachment and without bias. Artworks may facilitate this kind of perception by *presenting* phenomena that are not chosen according to the tastes and predilections of the artists who make them. One way of doing this—though not the only way—is to bring phenomena (including language) to the perceivers of the artworks by means of chance operations or other relatively "nonegoic" methods in which the artist's tastes, passions, and predilections intervene much less than when artworks are made in other, more traditional, ways.

One cannot claim that the artist's "ego" is altogether "evaded" by using chance operations or similar methods. Making artworks always involves skills that even the most untraditional artists draw upon. To use a key Buddhist term, chance operations themselves are "skillful means" through which the latent seeds of enlightenment may be awakened and matured. The most modest claim is that chance operations and related methods make it possible for artists to "let things happen" with somewhat less intervention from the artist's ego than when the more usual "expressive" methods are followed. Both the artists and the perceivers of the artworks may then experience dharmas relatively unencumbered by the artists' passions, opinions, tastes, and predilections.

However, no matter how many decisions, structural and/or material, are made through chance operations or related methods, some must be made by the artist. The use of such methods itself results from a decision. The devising of systematic-chance and similar methods of making and presenting artworks (e.g., of composing and/or performing or delivering poems, musical works, or verbal or verbal-musical performance pieces) always requires some decisions, for instance, concerning the sources of materials and kinds of structure or absence of structure. Besides, even when works are composed, and their delivery or performance regulated, by means of chance operations, the performers must always *interpret* the results of the latter; that is, they have to make decisions.

Therefore, around the end of 1960 I moved the center of decision making in performances of "Simultaneities" out *to the performers themselves*. ("Simultaneities" are various types of performance works that usually, though not always, include verbal elements and often others, such as sounds produced by musical instruments or noisemakers, projected images, and/or physical actions.) Since then I have been composing the scores and general rules for their realization (including certain limitations and exclusions), but the performers' own rule-guided choices, made, *during the performances,* in relation to whatever they are concentratedly hearing, seeing, and so forth—including ambient sounds, sights, and other perceptibles—determine how they make use of the materials provided in the scores. What both performers and audiences come to perceive is a joint production of the composer (who may or may not use chance operations) and the performers—as well as, in a real sense, the ambience. (The realization that the ambience is an inescapable element of every performance undoubtedly comes from Buddhism, notably Zen, as well as Taoism.)

Before the end of 1960, I had specified in-performance chance operations *to regulate delivery* during simultaneous performances of *Stanzas for Iris Lezak* (written May–October 1960; published Barton, Vt.: Something Else Press, 1972; see pp. 412–22)—the first group of works made by acrostic "reading-through" methods I devised in April 1960—and *to determine a performance method* for each of the numbered "Asymmetries" (nonstanzaic poems made by similar methods) realized in any particular performance. (See *Asymmetries 1–260* [written October–December 1960; New York: Printed Editions, 1980], pp. xiii–xxv and 252–55.)

In most subsequent performance works, however, including such open-ended series of Simultaneities as the "Gathas" (begun 1961—the name indicates that they are specifically Buddhist poems, and a large number of them are based on Buddhist mantras), the "Word Events" (begun 1961), and the "Vocabularies" (begun 1968), the performers decide, at once communally and individually, most of the performance parameters that had been regulated by chance operations in earlier works, though chance operations or related methods were used in composing most of these scores and plans. (See examples in *Representative Works: 1938–1985* [New York: Roof Books, 1986].)

Most of the above works are "indeterminate" in that the materials may be used in an infinite number of different orders. However, when performing *The Pronouns—A Collection of 40 Dances—For the Dancers* (New York: Mac Low, 1964; 2d ed. London: Tetrad, 1972; 3d ed. Barrytown,

N.Y.: Station Hill Press, 1979), a series of dance-instruction poems composed by a "diastic" reading-through method devised in 1963, each dancer or other performer decides on actions that interpret in turn *each successive line* of one or more of the poems in whatever way she deems appropriate. The succession of lines is fixed, but the variety of interpretations is infinite. (Each poem may be read alone, or before, during, or after its realization as dance or any other kind of performance—another area of decision making.)

Allowing performers to make significant decisions may seem at odds with the original endeavor to diminish the role of the ego in art. However, it both diminishes the role of the author-composer's ego and helps make the performers more conscious of both ego and nonego, just as participation in such works (whether as author-composer, performer, or audience) encourages the attitudes of choiceless awareness and bare attention that are basic to Buddhist practice.

Another Buddhist consideration that influenced the move to expand performers' decision making during performances comes from Tantric (e.g., Tibetan) Buddhism: the teaching that highly conscious work *with and through* the ego (as against the ego's uncritical "expression") can lead to enlightenment. Attentively making choices in a communal performance situation is, I believe, such a conscious working with and through the ego, embodying the Buddhist paradox that one may be choicelessly aware even when making choices. (I have experienced this often when writing poems—verse and prose—and when making other artworks not by using chance operations but by giving close attention to successive "intuitive" choices, a practice I've frequently followed, both before 1954 and in recent years, as well as intermittently in the intervening years.)

One of the realizations that may come to the author-composer, performers, and audience is that "the ego" is by no means unitary—that what each person calls "herself" comprises many often mutually contradictory strands and is pervaded by elements derived from—even imposed by—other people and both the language one speaks and the society one lives in, as well as "presocietal nature."

I cannot pretend that the motivation for this sharing of decision making is solely Buddhist. It was also inspired by political convictions: those associated with nonviolent communal anarchism, a politics that seems to me consonant with Buddhism and that I've espoused since 1945. (Unlike many other nonviolent communal anarchists, however, I have taken part in electoral politics during the last twenty-five years, since both compassion and wisdom demand attention to the short-term consequences of electoral choices—often crucial to the lives of untold numbers of sentient beings—as well as to long-term societal and personal changes.)

My political attitudes have strongly influenced my discomfort with the various Buddhist groups (Zen and Tibetan) with which I've had contact since the middle 1950s. (I'm *not* referring to Dr. Suzuki's classes—he never claimed to be a Zen master, "merely a university professor.") The authoritarian, indeed absolutely monarchical, relation of the teachers to the students (this is what I intend by "church polity" in the first paragraph of this essay) has always driven me away, even from groups led by teachers from whom I've learned a great deal and by whom I've been inspired.

I understand that knowledge confers authority in the context of teaching, but its extension to the political constitution of the groups within which it is exercised seems entirely uncalled for. I cannot believe that it is impossible to give basic teaching and instruction for practice without acting like an absolute monarch. I'm convinced that this is an unnecessary remnant of the historical situations within which Buddhism has developed.

Of course, religious authoritarianism is by no means confined to Buddhism—it is all but ubiquitous. It occurs within every religion and has been a major point of contention throughout history. But it is especially painful to experience it within the religion of compassion and wisdom. I continue to search for a Buddhist group within which the authoritative moment of teaching occurs within a libertarian or democratic polity.

May–July 1989, April 1990
New York

from Rinzai on the Self, or "The One who is, at this moment, right in front of us, solitarily, illuminatingly, in full awareness, listening to this talk on the Dharma."

Recognize I neither sure, All I
O neither
These, he emptiness
Sure, emptiness liver front,
O recognize
"These, he emptiness
  O neither emptiness

Who he O
I sure,
All these
Must O must emptiness neither these,
Recognize I quite he these,
These, he I sure,
I neither
Front recognize O neither these,
O front
Understands sure,
Sure, O liver I these, All recognize I liver You,
I liver liver understands must I neither All these, I neither quite
   liver You,
I neither
Front understands liver liver
All who All recognize emptiness neither emptiness sure, sure,
Liver I sure, these emptiness neither I neither quite
These O
These he I sure,
These All liver kidney,
O neither
These he emptiness
Dharma he All recognize must All."

                    *   *   *

Revolved is nirvāna. Subject all is
Ordinary nirvāna.
The holy, enter
Subject enter land find,
Ordinary revolved
"The holy, enter
 Ordinary nirvāna. Enter
 What holy, ordinary
 Is subject,
 All the
 The holy, is subject
 Maitreya's ordinary Maitreya's enter nirvāna. The,
 Revolved is great holy, the
 Is nirvāna
 Find revolved ordinary nirvāna. The
 Ordinary find
 Understanding? Subject,
 Subject ordinary land is the all revolved is land you,

Is land land understanding? Maitreya's is nirvāna. All the is
  nirvāna. Great land you,
Is nirvāna.
Find understanding? Land land
All What all revolved enter nirvāna. Enter subject subject,
Land is subject the enter nirvāna. Is nirvāna. Great
The ordinary
The holy, is subject
The all land knowing
Ordinary nirvāna.
The holy, enter
Defiled holy, all Maitreya's all."

Right, is not saunters all is
Only, not
There he even
Saunters even listening front,
Only, front
"There he even
  Only, not even
  Who he Only,
  Is saunters,
  All there
There he is saunters
Moment, Only, moment, even not there,
Right is garden, he there
Is not
Front right Only, not there
Only, front
Of saunters,
Saunters Only, listening is there all right is listening you,
Is listening listening of moment, is not all there is not garden,
  listening you,
Is not
Front of listening listening
All who all right even not even saunters saunters,
Listening is saunters there even is not garden,
There Only
There he is saunters
There all listening karmic
Only, not
There he even
Dharma—he all right moment, all."

Reject. In not see at in
O not
The who elements.
See elements. Listening Followers,
O reject.
"The who elements.
 O not elements.
 Way! Who O
 In see,
 At the
 The who in see
 Moment O moment elements. Not the see,
 Reject. In coming-and-going. Who the
 In not
 Followers reject. O not the
 O Followers
 Use see,
 See O listening in the at reject. In listening You,
 In listening listening use moment in not at the in not
    coming-and-going. Listening You,
 In not
 Followers use listening listening
 At Way! At reject. Elements. Not elements. See see,
 Listening in see the elements. Not in not coming-and-going.
 The O
 The who in see
 The at listening coming-and-going.
 O not
 The who elements.
 Dharma who at reject. Moment at."

Requisite is not seek are is
Of not
The have externalities
Seek externalities learners faith,
Of requisite
"The have externalities
 Of not externalities
 What have of
 Is seek,
 Are the
 The have is seek
 May of may externalities not the,

Requisite is great have the
Is not
Faith requisite of not the
Of faith
Unessential seek,
Seek of learners is the are requisite is learners you,
Is learners learners unessential may is not are the is not great
    learners you,
Is not
Faith unessential learners learners
Are What are requisite externalities not externalities seek seek,
Learners is seek the externalities not is not great
The of
The have is seek
The are learners knowing
Of not
The have externalities
Do have are requisite may are."

Remaining it needed [Zen]. All it
O needed
The he extraordinary
Should extraordinary life. Followers,
O remaining
"The he extraordinary
 O needed extraordinary
 Way, he O
 It should,
 All the
 The he it should
May O may extraordinary needed the,
Remaining it goes he the
It needed
Followers remaining O needed the
O Followers
Urgently should,
Should O life. It the all remaining it life. You,
It life. Life. Urgently may it needed all the it needed goes you,
It needed
Followers urgently life. Life.
All Way, all remaining extraordinary needed extraordinary should
    should,
Life it should the extraordinary needed it needed goes

The O
The he it should
The all life. Can
O needed
The he extraordinary
Dharma. He all remaining may all."

*   *   *

Really indeed not Zen-man all indeed
O not
The how easy
Spend easy learners Followers,
O really
"The how easy
O not easy
Way, how O
Indeed spend,
All the
The how indeed spend
Many O many easy not the,
Really indeed glued how the
Indeed not
Followers really O not the
O Followers
Unfathomable, spend,
Spend O learners indeed the all really indeed learners yet,
Indeed learners learners unfathomable, many indeed not all the
    indeed not glued learners yet,
Indeed not
Followers unfathomable, learners learners
All Way, All really easy not easy spend spend,
Learners indeed spend the easy not indeed not glued
The O
The how indeed spend
The all learners know
O not
The how easy
Difficult how all really many all."

Mahakala

Mahakala is the wrathful manifestation of Avalokiteshvara
Avalokiteshvara is the Bodhisattva of compassion
Mahakala manifests wrathful compassion

Bewilderment signs of deities awake shakes powdery trellises
Patience ingratiates
Is noninterference **not** always the best policy?

Mahakala's is manifestly not noninterference
Or wrathful compassion's manifestation is noninterference
Toward whom or what is Mahakala wrathful?

Why are most religions one way or another angry?
If they're not angry why do they seem so angry?
Why do even Buddhisms seem angry?

Ask a silly question you'll get a silly answer
Wrathful compassion is active protection
What kind of entity is Mahakala?

Many-deities daunts my Quakerish Protestantism
One is at the edge of the thinkable
Why **any** deities if Buddha said no-deity no-self?

Why call energies or kinds of energy deities?
Aren't things confusing enough without charismatic terms?
Whoever thinks Spirit is better ain't Buddha

1 March—2 August 1988
New York

6 Gitanjali for Iris

I

My you
Gain is rainy life
See
The Here end
Gain rainy end again the end see the
Feet. Utter. Cry know
Is Now,
The outside when Now,

(18 seconds of silence)

Is
Life outside void end
The outside
Feet. Utter. Cry know
My you
Gain is rainy life.

II

Midnight, your
Gifts is river, light,
Sing
Thy humble every
Gifts river, every and thy every sing thy
Flute unbreakable captive keep
Is not
Thy of whom not

(10 seconds of silence)

Is
Light, of voice every
Thy of
Flute unbreakable captive keep
Midnight, your
Gifts is river, light,

III

Me You
God is renew life
Sleep
The heart even
God renew even again, the even sleep the
Fear undisturbed. Come keep
Is noontide
The on with noontide

(13 seconds of silence)

Is
Life on venture even
The on
Fear undisturbed. Come keep
Me You
God is renew life

IV

My Your
Ground is resting languidly
Sack
To He earth,
Ground resting earth, and to earth, sack to
Frayed unbreakable, court knew
Is not
To only weeping not

(5 seconds of silence)

Is
Languidly only voyage earth,
To only
Frayed unbreakable, court knew
My your
Ground is resting languidly

V

Master, your
Garment is renew linger
Strength
Trust hard entrance
Garment renew entrance a trust entrance strength trust
Finery, unholy colour knew
Is not
Trust on wall not

(3 seconds of silence)

Is
Linger on vaguest entrance
Trust on
Finery, unholy colour knew
Master, your
Garment is renew linger

VI

Morning You
Gleam in resonant life
Shame

Thee. He eyes
Gleam resonant eyes and thee. Eyes shame thee.
From up come Kindle
In not
Thee. Of wall not

   (15 seconds of silence)

In
Life of vain eyes
Thee. Of
From up come Kindle
Morning You
Gleam in resonant life

Printout from "The"

   THE WIND BLOWS.
THE RAIN FALLS.
 THE SNOW FALLS.
  THE STREAMS FLOW.
  THE RIVERS FLOW.
   THE OCEANS RISE.
    THE OCEANS FALL.

  THE BUSHES GROW.
THE MOSSES GROW.
  THE FERNS GROW.
THE LICHENS GROW.

   THE TREES SWAY IN THE WIND.
THE FLOWERS SWAY IN THE WIND.

  THE INSECTS ARE HATCHED.
   THE REPTILES ARE HATCHED.
THE MAMMALS ARE BORN.
THE BIRDS ARE HATCHED.
 THE FISHES ARE HATCHED.

THE PEOPLE SAIL ON RAFTS.

THE LICHENS GROW.
THE FLOWERS GROW.
THE MOSSES GROW.
THE TREES GROW.

THE INSECTS GROW.
THE REPTILES GROW.

THE BUSHES GROW.

THE INSECTS GATHER FOOD.
THE BIRDS GATHER FOOD.

THE PLANETS SHINE.
THE MOON SHINES.
THE SUN SHINES.

THE TREES DRINK.   THE FUNGUSES DRINK.

THE MOSSES TURN TOWARD THE LIGHT.
THE FLOWERS TURN TOWARD THE LIGHT.
THE TREES TURN TOWARD THE LIGHT.

S. J. Marks

S. J. Marks's book of poems *Something Grazes Our Hair* was published in the spring of 1991 by the University of Illinois Press. His poem "Zen Sequence" was published in 1990 as a limited edition chapbook by The Wooden Spoon Press. An earlier book, *Lines,* was published by the Cummington Press in 1972. He has published poetry in the *American Poetry Review,* the *Iowa Review,* the *New Yorker,* and other periodicals. S. J. Marks is the Clinical Coordinator of the ADAPT Program (which treats substance-abusing pregnant and postpartum women and their children) at Albert Einstein Medical Center / Philadelphia Psychiatric Center and is a psychotherapist in private practice in St. Davids, Pennsylvania.

Cold Places

The sound of the wind is hard—
it pummels the large pines and cedars
and brings the sound of approaching winter,

it comes through a rift left by a sudden emptiness in my heart.

The heaviness of aging presses on us,
a loneliness tinged with sadness;
you're sleeping—you know nothing of what's happening.

The whole of evening light
is sucked into the silver maple,
so the inside of the tree is warm with it.

That distant sound is the thunder of winter.

I see your nipples,
large, swollen, and dark,

I hear the first drops of night rain
spatter the window.

What flows behind my eyelids
from your arm is the deep current of life,
it's what we have
to help us remember that no matter where we are
we are together.

I remember Kawabata's
impotent old men
sleeping with young girls,
pursuing the vanished happiness
of being alive.

Your sleeping face soft in the gentle light—
nothing's more beautiful than your young face
in dreamless sleep.
Straining my ears, I think I hear
faint late-autumn wind blowing down across the hill
behind the house. Warm breath
from your parted lips comes to my face,
the dim light from the lavender bedroom walls flows down
inside your mouth. Your breasts are round and high
and fit in the palm of my hand. I lean over
and take them in my mouth.

Regrets, sadnesses flow in and out of me—
your glowing skin and scent are the forgiveness for sad old men.

The sound goes on and on—informing me of the cold,
inside and out, withered leaves still cling to the branches.

The gray of winter morning
is
by evening
a cold drizzle.
Then the drizzle turns to sleet.
The stones are wet, the fallen maple leaves have not
been raked away.

Losing Myself

I sit drinking wine, and, for a long time, don't notice the dusk.
The delicate sweetness of pink emperor lilies fills my nostrils.
I get up and walk and see again the faces of old friends
as if they were here.
The birds are silent,
you're asleep. No one else is around.
The way through the trees seems never to end.
On the rocks along Gulph Creek
the moss is slippery, rain or no rain.

To Go Through Life Is to Walk
Across a Field

How delicious to walk into the stillness—
the mist surrounds us, we sink into the tall wild grasses,
the meadows blur in the heat,
the edge of the sky's purple.

You're dozing—you're not asleep, but dreaming
you long for sleep.

Gulph Creek cuts through the valley.
I'd like to know
what will happen in the rest of my life.

I remember the people in Chekhov's plays saying good-bye,
"We shall never see each other again," or
"I'll never see you again."

The wind's everywhere—
in the trees, in the rain, in the house, in this poem,
in death, everywhere.

In the evening light
the maple tree glows red.
I feel the warmth of your hands.

The birches, the street, our faces lit
by a car's headlights.

Home now,
raining, the sound of
water running down the drainpipe
heard
in this room.

I came to you because I know
suffering warms the coldness of life.

November Woods

for Masao Abe

Gray sky, mist, the trees black and wet,
branches dripping rain,
soggy ground and oak leaves squish under my feet.

A day of unknowing, of knowing I do not know,
a day of uncertainty,
the day of my life.

Somehow,
I breathe easier here—
in the cool damp air.

I move through the woods,
moving slowly through the drizzle,
stepping carefully on the spongy wet leaf mold on the forest floor,
rain spattering the trees and fallen leaves
deadens the sound of my footsteps.

We change what yesterday did to us.
After watching my mother being operated on for adrenal cancer,
and, sitting with and talking to my just-born daughter
who I know will die in four hours,
I can hear what is. All of what is. Whatever it is.

I walk to where you're staying,
to your class,
to hear you say these kind thoughtful words,
"You do not know what water is. You might visit the Zen master
and ask him. He may pour the jar of water into a glass and say
by word or gesture, 'Please drink it,' " and, later in another context,
"He may say, 'When you have none, I will take it away from
  you.' "

Two things more—
after class, you tell me how you fell on the snow and ice
in New Haven and bruised your shoulder and side; I take leave of
    you,
and, a few hours later, my shoulder and chest ache so much,
I have to take to bed and sleep. Then, in Washington
on the weekend at the Freer Gallery,
Zou Fulei's plum branch—
spring's like breath,
it goes but must return,
the smoky mist dies out,
the empty room's cold,
this ink branch keeps its shadow on my mind—

Barbara Meier

Barbara Meier is a painter, teacher, writer, and poet. She began studying Zen meditation with Suzuki Roshi in 1967 and moved to Boulder in 1974 to practice Tibetan Buddhism with Chögyam Trungpa Rinpoche. She is a past member of the Board of Directors of the Buddhist Peace Fellowship, with whom she spent time in Nicaragua. She has had several one-woman shows of her paintings and is the author of *The Life You Ordered Has Arrived* (Parallax, 1989) and the forthcoming *Sonnets From the War Zones*.

Allow

The sound of Tibetan horns. The sky opens.
All manner of domesticated mammals are
waiting to be let in. The feeling is benign.
Fluid and liquid boomerang.
The pleasure is waiting.
We allow the language of bonds
to shape itself:
gaunt, porous, umbilical.

Vertebral Mountains

The funnel from Big Ideas to
my little life gets wider.
Driving away; the desert's roar
navigates me home. Returning to
B vitamins like insulin, a dozen
magazine subscriptions

waiting at my door.
Fruit trees in the back yard:
nicest thing anyone's ever said.
We're talking now of transmutation;
power and magic are words
that come up a lot.
I write my name in vast dust,
revise, even erase.

Nuns

What's most fun
about Sonny Rollins' set
is watching Ethie
across the club
having a good time.
She is high as a kite . . .
INTO it, bopping, nodding
in rhythm. The rest
are dead to the beat
except Sidney
who remembers our talk
a decade ago:
Vietnam nuns who failed
to self-immolate, so
hurled themselves, top-speed,
against the barbed wire.
"I *saw* you then . . ."
he recalls, just as Sonny swings into
"Oleo," one of my all-time
favorite tunes.

from Sonnets From the War Zones: Nicaragua

I.

Rosa Angel Blanco is born with dark hair and dark glasses
her clothes soaked to the skin. She
gets in an old Buick, drives to the border
Snipers. Mortars. Militia arrives

She hides motionless behind the barricades
Suddenly a problem: no more kissing in the kitchen
Is this obvious or not?
Shrapnel. Abductions. A ritual
to witness. "Real life with dignity."
She can't bear to be there in the dead
of night caught in the crossfire
with those lifeless bodies
Her wounds primarily mental
her memory fills up with blood

3.

Adobe nights. Warm. Rosa Angel
poses in an 18th-century crown
of twigs, gnarled and martyred
A reunion. A meeting on the isthmus, the jetty
A rowboat. She's never navigated these waters
before in the cold green night. She wonders
if she really can swim
She'd rather stay on the bridge for now
There's nothing on the menu just clouds
Diabolical shadows threaten
Shhh—the hostess weeps, carries her children
She's grabbed by the open gash below her jaw
dragged to a more hidden location
The blue Rosa talks about is black.

10.

Fraternal blood shed like an ocean
A drawing of three fingers, the three years
Rosa dissolved in her prison of heroism
This current treaty, rare and precious
Beyond dualism, like irreconcilable space
Headless bodies once floated downstream
In the states: ceremonial pomp; the sacrifice has been
to cut the pockets from cashmere coats
Handfuls of bullets are put on the President's shrine
Rosa Angel is graced with naive and simple truths
Reconciliation was always her big ticket
Her tribulation: to convert the wrap-up
of an honorable revolt to the resurrection
of a tree from which flowers all flowers

II.

Plastered brick walls, some painted, some not
Gaudy, yes, like the atrocities. Never again
Crowded. No space. No water
Rosa Angel is solicitous, gushing in halting
rapid Spanish, how a gun was held to her heart
Villa-Lobos guitars are heard in the streets
Agog with grief there's
a cul-de-sac of options
An internal reservoir of strength
allows seeing: an aerial photograph
Those lieutenants were frothing pure barbarism
no magic, no mercy. Rosa Angel survives the war
the same kind of artist in the moonlight as by day
History has fallen in her lap

Dale Pendell

Dale Pendell works as a software engineer with laser printing systems. From 1973 to 1983, he lived on San Juan Ridge in Nevada County, California, where he founded *Kukso: Journal of Backcountry Writing,* practiced zazen in what later became the Ring of Bone Zendo, and cofounded the Primitive Arts Institute, a nonprofit educational organization teaching primitive and traditional arts and crafts. He now lives in Santa Cruz with his extended family and publishes occasional chapbooks under the imprint Exiled-in-America Press, the most recent being Ana Rossetti's *Tulips,* translated by Susan Suntree and Nancy Nieman.

Some Reveries on Poetry as a Spiritual Discipline

O

Another attempt to cut corners: archery, motorcycles, photography, poetry. Why not
spiritual discipline as spiritual discipline?

And poetry as

> "continue to have fun"
> —Thich Thien-An.

Advice I try to take to heart.

O

Poems are physicks: medicines for soul and planet and culture, and likewise, formulae: equations of power instantiating the subtle dynamics of the spirit.
"We may laugh a lot but we're not kidding."

Never trust any religion without clowns. I sd that.

    ○

The poetry connection came through Basho via Blyth. Blyth says that, not that it ever would, but if it did, come down to a choice between Zen and poetry, Basho would've chosen poetry.

At one time this statement seemed full of portent, an essential point to get straight, now, what . . .
    ??

"Not that it ever would."

    ○

    We need only consult the elders. Orpingalik, the Netsilik poet, and his peers—what we should call traditional poetry, but is instead called "ethnopoetics," to find that poetry has been performing spiritual functions from earliest times:

    *healing: not only charming songs, but further, the song itself. What Orpingalik called his comrades in solitude: "All my being is song, and I sing as I draw breath." Connecting, in the magical sense, through sympathetic evocation, "becoming one with," then shifting the frame of reference, dissolving the frame of reference, and thus, by extension,

    *subverting: breaking the grip of habit, perspective— iconoclasm: cracking eggs, breaking images: that all of them advance and flow through. Is somebody pointing? The clowns get to work here, the Buddhists called it Dharma.

    *community: shared experience, song sharing with friends, mocking enemies, word exchange with other life forms.
    charming songs sung to the weather.

Three treasures.

    ○

If there be a discipline to it, poetry teaches listening.

The short haiku-like poem may be unexcelled here. Listening for the poem, listening and waiting, so that, in the midst of everyday activities, there it is: sudden, sad, poignant, or funny (sabi, wabi, shibui, etc. . . .)

Poetry, like Zen, is an experimental science.

    ○

physicks/physics: words & ideas colliding at the speed of light—
sifting through the debris for a high energy resonance.
Low energy resonance.
An echo.

O

Start with yourself.
Not to slight SELF-comforting, self-exploration, redefine private,
begin with the self. That is to say,

with things. In my own poetry, I have noticed a shift away from
spiritual themes, or from linking Buddhist ideas/teachings with
shamanistic metaphor. Now much more involved with the
particular—assault on the entrenched idea that inanimate objects
don't have "souls."

O

The first thing to do is to kick spirituality in the rear—hard enough
to send it through the window.

The first thing.
The last thing.
Start from where you are.

O

First/last/kick/sitting in the sun,
drinking poison:

don't be private,
don't be negative,
don't use words,
"don't steal, don't lift"
don't obey rules.

O

Basho's admonition: "nothing that stinks of Zen."

well . . .

bliss-bestowing hands, why should they care. In fact, what's with
this "bliss" thing. It's a dark age, do what you can. Some illumi-
nate. Some just rattle the cages.

O

Cherry blossoms falling—
I'm unemployed
for one week.

Woodcutting

Speak from the heart.
She speaks from the heart and lies.
Doesn't matter. Be quiet.

You told me to speak.
You are stupid.
Yes? I don't think so. Anyway,
I know who you are.
You   are a pine tree.
You are rounds of a pine tree,
Sixteen inches long, two feet across.
You are rotten. You have mushrooms
Instead of blood. You are a fly
On my back. You are that big long fly
Caressing together its back legs. I
Could eat you.

You are sawdust in my socks.
You are two weeks of this heat wave.
Don't get smart with me, woodcutting work.

You are too heavy to lift.
You are filling my truck.
You are who started talking first.
No. I am who started talking first.
You let go of my splitting maul, please.

You are gasoline mixed 16:1 with oil.
You are too god damn loud.
Someday you are going to cut my foot,
    you son of a bitch.
You are my hard hat that keeps slipping in the sweat.
Time to drink. Where is the water?
Sharpen the chain. Watch your step.
Yellowjackets, watch out!
Don't lift with your back.
Don't worry, Mother, your words are imprinted in my mind!

Time to pee on the ground.
Where?
There, on those gooseberries.

Who *said* that?
Who's *talking?*
Who *started* this?
Look. A whole truckload
Of wood.

Mountains and Rivers,

"wine-hearted solitude," as Jeffers called it,
we stretch out, or bunch up, dharma friends:
Will to the front, Jill anchoring, or shifting,
places changing.

"California chapter of the National Joke Society"

on the trail.

Secret Lake algae blown/green bloom, soap or something:
biggest crayfish I've seen,
scuttling about beneath on the rocks.
I pump water through a filter.

We gradually move above the Jeffrey pines, into the lodgepoles.
At Fremont Lake
I caught the scent
of bitter cherry,

so elegant and sweet.
Tangles surround the camp.

dearest daughter:

We are up now at 9,200 feet. The air is thin, and it is
cold. We had a very hard hike today—lots of uphill—we climbed
1200 feet in about two miles: steep!
I heart that it was snowing here yesterday afternoon. I am
VERY glad I brought my long underwear. Tomorrow we try the
ascent of Mt. Forsythe.

Sunday AM: again at Lake Harriet.
Our schedule:

5:30	conch
6:00	zazen
7:30	breakfast, "unless delayed by coffee"
9:15–9:30	trail meeting and Dogen reading
10:00–10:30	head out
6:00	dinner
7:30	zazen
9:00–9:30	retire

Surprising how little loafing time there is: pumping water, cooking, cleaning pots, packing up camp. Here's who was along:
Reed, Ginny, Jill, Will, Sheelo, Vonna, Masa, Jim, Dale, Nelson, DeOnne.

Dogen:
Blue mountains continuously walk; a stone woman gives birth to a child.

If it's level or downhill, or your pack is light, call it walking or backpacking, but when you hit the uphill, it's backslogging.

Back-slogging,
             cd be some rock n roll song,
             "back-sloggin' "

up and up,
backsloggin', breath and step,
  blue mountains continuously walk.

  You should study blue mountains.

Backsloggin'.

There is a samadhi called the exhaustion samadhi.
It requires most vigorous hiking.

Things to bring next time:
  an insulated plastic cup like Masa has;
  a bigger towel, the better to be a water dog like Sheelo.

After the layover we are native. Juniper, white pine.

Finding a camp means finding two camps: one for the kitchen and
another for the zendo. And then another, away, threading
through boulders, around stunted pines, up the hillside, around a
bend. Look well and there's a perfect hojo at each camp. This
is where the members of the Joke Society trade their bits.

Walking down the life zones: white pine/juniper, lodgepole pine,
walking into the pit, finally back down to the Jeffreys.

Long ago there was a buddha called the Shrugging Buddha. Bodhisattvas, monks, nuns, and laypersons would ask questions of great
earnestness and profundity, and the Shrugging Buddha would
just laugh and shrug his shoulders. One day they set a trap for
him. He got caught.
What did he do then?

Backsloggin. Blue Mountains continuously walk.
        Not just sometimes.

Blue Mountains said: "There is a teaching beyond koan practice,
what is that?"

The work of mountains is to investigate mountains thoroughly.
Walking and breathing, sitting and breathing.

There are mountains hidden in sky. There are mountains hidden
in mountains. There are mountains hidden in hiddenness. This
is complete understanding.

   Frost, mountains rippling in the lake, swallows diving
and flitting. Mist rises from the lake as we wait for the sun.

Anthony Piccione

Anthony Piccione was born in Sheffield, Alabama. He graduated from East Texas State University, the University of Texas–El Paso, where he studied poetry with Robert Burlingame, and Ohio University. He has taught at Ohio University, Northern Illinois University, and the State University of New York at Brockport, as well as in Turkey and the People's Republic of China. His most recent book of poetry is *Seeing It Was So* (BOA Editions, 1986).

Outside

After the first sleet snow the talking goes silent.
Inside my long walk, testing the cold in clumsy stiffness,
field and woods drifting over, away into the bone length of it,
the weather we can't, alive, reach, I measure, measure, lose.

Autumn lingers like a room, a face we glimpsed as we locked
our greenhouse against winter. And for the deermouse, trapped
or lodged by choice, we stumble back again and again
to set out cracked corn and a tent of shirts.

Still, an awkward distance presses tight
behind my walking, windows iced and growing faint,
head leaning into the shearing wind, time and
place a small light around my feet.

Visit From a Friend

Spring flood again. Went out to not write the poem,
to not find my name under the uprooted poplar,
to see my white feet as just mine, two small
lazy things to be loved one at a time.

His car pulls in. Too fast. Still, I dream with animals.
So hard to know what century this is. Sitting here,
like this, cities lean in around the brickmaker.
Legs numb for years. Shift. Move.

While my tall friend points rightly to books and men,
we watch a hummingbird surround the slow mind of the sky.
Soon the only thing moving, we know, is what we think.
Now the whole history of libraries blazes like a match.

If this is not the world, why are we here?
Well, we will call this silence the universe
where our children find their play in all directions,
and this time forgive them us, if it goes that way.

Opening the Cabin at Mid-Winter

Now, this is really splendid, a gift!
The mad scrawl of mouse dung over my desk,
dark tunneling through the ruins of mattress,
dumb scrabbling feet gone still in the walls,
all of this where nothing was! Joy balanced
on a hair, bright sky unfolding, and rage.

TWO POEMS AFTER WINTER

A Small Prayer to Everything

Is there somewhere we shouldn't look? What wins with a trick?
To the dark Mothers, and the Fathers of outrage,
and anything powerful that calls for my heart, take it.
It happens that I am finished with fear. I don't know why
I got here, nor what it means to dive all night towards God,
but I'm awake now, beside this slow buffalo who chews
even the sunlight as it falls on the grass.

Well, I am going to lie down here, for nothing.
Love to you, to the brain we share: it holds only where we go.

This Day of Spring, We All Go Outside

Kneeling in the high grass, patching a fence, at last
I climb down from that spindly mind that held the skies
of winter off, losing, losing. Now the whole world
is busy. Our dog plunges everywhere with no name.
The two little ones play and play. My wife lies
down naked in the back fields of sun, it's our land.
Her breasts are so white, so utterly soft, so free
of meaning I go over just to be near. I love this laziness.
Today, I know, I will worry no more weeds from the word-brain,
today. I tell her, I give myself to the buffalo.
We laugh and shove each other. Totally happy,
our teenage daughter rides past on the small yellow tractor.

Ice Fishing

I stand two days staring
into the black hole.
The slowness fills
with seawater. Ice mountains
blaze all around.
Every thing's mind sweeps over me.
We meet our own eyes.

Atoms

How we fall all night towards each other,
the speed of longing gathered in our far-flung hearts.

Trying to Read in My Study

Buddha, St. Theresa, Lao Tsu, the dancing
bears in the window backed with storm.
A blackbird crosses left to right.
The empty window brighter.

George Quasha

George Quasha is the author of several books of poetry, including *So-mapoetics* (Sumac Press, 1973), *Giving the Lily Back Her Hands* (Station Hill Press, 1980), and *In No Time* (Station Hill Press, 1991), and the editor of *America a Prophecy: A New Reading of American Poetry from Pre-Columbian Times to the Present* (Random House, 1973) and *Open Poetry* (Simon & Schuster, 1973). He is also the publisher of Station Hill Press, an artist, and a bodyworker. He lives in Barrytown, New York, and practices Tibetan Dzogchen, under Namkhai Norbu Rinpoche, as well as Lama Tharchin Rinpoche. He also practices t'ai chi and ch'i-kung under Master T. K. Shih.

A Virtual Account

In the tall tale of my life as poet I am aware of three broad stages or personal epochs: First, a sense of "vocation" *in* poetry. Second, the awareness that the vocation has extended to the domain of language—all communicative relationships, all interchange with others, and all participation in any medium that has the potential to communicate—and that the distinction "poetry" is, by its history and by its nature, always in question. Third, an emerging view that the value or more accurately the *virtue* of the poetic act lies in the integrity of its process, the authenticity of its inquiry, and the power of its opening in the domain of language.

I suppose the first of these stages constitutes some sort of apprenticeship. The second comes with the discovery of having a work, a work that's inseparable from the full range of one's concerns. And the third arises in the broader field of refocusing the sense of self. This involves a kind of shift in noetic ecology where the intensification of presence and responsiveness paradoxically extends the periphery of identity beyond the field of sentience. I would say that it is here that one begins to assume responsibility for what lies outside the range of (ordinary) direct experience but is somehow still within one's field of resonance. The ability to consciously and articulately work within one's resonant (yet ultimately transentient) field is primarily a function of practice. And where the medium of practice is in the broadest sense linguistic the vehicle of study and teaching is poetics—or parapoetics, the working principles of what lies outside poetic consensus yet declares itself to be poetry.

Somewhere along the way, nearly two decades ago, I began to see that the poetic and the noetic could not be held apart, that the issues of one must bear upon the other, and that a shift in one domain must eventually show up in the other domain. I embraced this bond between language and mind as fundamental to the practices appropriate to each, and I studied each through the lens of the other. What I suppose to be a natural anarchistic perspective has always made me uncomfortable with nominalizing, categorizing, institutionalizing, or otherwise reifying my practices and affiliations (poetic or noetic), but as a fundamental of poetic practice I have openly raided every available esoteric tradition and none more consistently than Vajrayana Buddhism.

That my personal practices have since the early 1970s derived mainly from Buddhist and Taoist traditions in no way compromises my stand that poetic inquiry must happen in unnameable free space, because I see those traditions as essentially and in the truest sense anarchistic. William Blake is for me the Western master of this stance.

I would also say that Blake was for me the first teacher—a source of guidance rooted in a poetics of self-transformation and at the same time somehow "outside" culture, literature, personality, life in all its relative manifestations. From him I got the view of work as a path beyond limitation—of the poem as "infernal method" by which one breaks the spell of consensus and follows the "golden string" to the open space of choice.

Where Blake's subversive vision meets Buddhism is in Vajrayana, particularly Dzogchen (the "Great Perfection" teaching), and the view of *shunyata* or "emptiness" as openness, spaciousness, intrinsic completion, or primordial perfection and of compassion as energy, not only in the psychological sense, which is relative, but in the absolute and ontological sense. Cleansing the doors of perception means seeing *what is* with naked awareness. The poem that comes from this view is not a claim to enlightenment but an act of commitment to open space. Its aspiration is to perform its work with integrity and in such a way that reading becomes aware of itself—or, better, *in* itself—so that, through its own process, reading subverts attachment and generates yet finer, freer awareness.* I speak here of the poet's own reading, no less than another's.

The poet who has this stand is not simply "taking a position"—which implies a certain fixity, requiring defense and perhaps aggressiveness in advancing the position—but making a declaration, whose force is ontological by virtue of the source of that act in personal realization. I see now, in a way I did not some years back when my poetic stance, while not fundamentally different, was perhaps unintentionally assertive, that authentic poetic declaration is arrived at spontaneously—that in a sense one discovers the stance, not before the fact or even after the fact, but *in* the fact. The mode of ideological transaction out of such a stance tends to be dialogical rather than polemical, because dialogue is at the heart of how the poet is knowing reality and of the kind of speaking and listening that happens. Moreover, one comes to an awareness of the limitations of polemic—that often it does not create a new listening, that in fact it may do the very opposite, closing down the very space in which the new poetics could take root. Polemic attempts to gain ground by displacing another position, and in this way it can perpetuate the illusion that there is something "outside" to gain. Dialogue, on the other hand, seeks further engagement and realization and can remain consistent with a principle of nonduality.

Another gift to poetics from William Blake: that the "prophetic" poem—one that *acts ahead of itself* rather than by reference to what has significance already—is a space in which meaning happens. It is a skillful means, a "technology" or *tekne* of saying, that creates possibility. It engineers or guides a journey. And it is alive, almost a living being, a Dante's Virgil whose hand grips the prehensile mind and engages it in a process of knowing its further reality. Reading as an act of *unconditioning* Blake saw as subversive to a culture that lives by consensus. His visionary poet, as technician of the possible, is willing to frustrate and perplex the mind in order to stand outside its drivenness and attachment, its mechanism. At the same time he creates a context in which the mind can come upon itself, extend its capacity to know itself as source, face its responsibility as author of experience, embrace a certain tropism toward

---

*I am tempted to say "reading self-liberates," where "self-liberates" is reflexive, translating a Tibetan Dzogchen term (*rang grol*) that is notoriously difficult to represent in English. In one sense I take it to mean "become mind-degradable" (as in "biodegradable"), wherein the products of mind, such as concepts and other reified projections, quickly melt down and return to the active field of mind energy. Another way of saying it is: when a mind-event self-liberates, it realizes an intrinsic state of possibility in which the energy that performed the mind-event becomes free in and of itself. To this all-important task of practice I am saying there is a poetic equivalent.

essential delight in being while denying nothing that seems true—and all this within a field of sometimes terrifying intimacy.

Where text is viewed as an opportunity for practice, for noetic shift, the Dharma offers unexpected instruction, not as precepts for behavior but as indicating energies within the processes of language. One may be directed beyond automatic fascination with what happens within the foreground of attention. The mind may learn to follow subtle impulses that seem unanchored; or it may identify with the periphery—the context (or perhaps circumtext)—of a moment or event. "Composition by field" (Olson, Duncan) and "systematic chance operations" (Cage, Mac Low) are tactical theories addressing aspects of this potential shift of focus, displacing the radical of composition. Paradoxically, this reorientation involves an extraordinary degree of active presence, a willingness to follow freely according to the integrity of the moment and within the self-direction of the field. The issues of style, of form, of shape, of appearance are matters of discrimination in practice, intrinsically open, as free (and not free) as language. I see the root issue as integrity in *writing into the space outside the poem, outside the known.*

Practice is like "placing a jar in Tennessee." It causes the slovenly wilderness of ordinary consciousness to rise up around it. Wallace Stevens's "Anecdote of the Jar" is a paradigm of the poetic act as artifact placed in the "natural" world. Transformation is a name for the poet's self-realignment within the poetic act, a somewhat mysterious event that takes place at the level of context, and this happens less by direct effort to change or manipulate the context than by a radical alteration of focus. The point of practice is to find the new focus (or what Cage calls "unfocus"). The power of a gesture shows itself in the waves sent to the perimeter of the field, the recipient who registers the charge. For me the "social role" of poetry has to do with a certain self-discipline arising in awareness of how any act alters all acts. Responsibility as "keeping the ability to respond" (Duncan) is an issue of wakefulness, like being awake to others in the performance field. (In this domain Jackson Mac Low has been for me the preeminent teacher.) If I had to define poetry in a phrase I would call it *speaking with listening.*

This view leaves open the whole issue of the "source" of the poem, whether or to what degree it is "given" (in Blake's or Spicer's sense) or otherwise displaces the agency of composition. Removing mental obstacles, cleaning out cultural debris, cleansing personal obscurations, even "giving a purer sense to the words of the tribe"—these are among the activities shared by radical poetics and Buddhist practice, which surrender expectation to listening and aesthetic prejudice to an open state of attention. Poetry's most challenging ontological claim is to be the space that preserves the very possibility of authentic language. In the teachings of Dzogchen there is mention of *lhug-pa,* a term, like the Taoist t'ai chi *nonresistance* that implies a state of relaxed alertness, an alive clearing that is at once empty of conditioning and full of potency, flexible yet uncompromisable, a state of presence that is outside the passive/active duality. What happens there can seem to be a gift from the Wisdom *Dakinis.*

Recently while formulating these speculations I had a dream that seemed urgent enough to write down, yet I couldn't really do it. Once I had given up I recognized that the "message" of the dream was not its content but its special state of awareness. My mind sort of rotated around a realization: that "we" (those, I suppose, who share the awareness) carry a special energy, as though something were on fire inside. A controlled burn, it becomes alchemical; otherwise it consumes everything to the point of burnout. The foretaste of realization is connection—being plugged in, the powerful current running in the channels. Practice is what manages the heat—cultivates the energy, draws it out, teaches us how to behave to its laws. Whether the practice is poetic or meditative, the discipline is intrinsic to the activity; and any expression carries the charge of the realization, a virtual resource open to others who know how to get it.

Thomas's Secret Sayings

How do I hold her in me as I speak
She is a real woman every time she is
No man hath spoken more the more there is to speak
Find what it is in here and it will never go away
Don't stop and there is a turn the other side of the tongue
Look up the birds the sky it is the sea not out there but in there
Out here as you know her so will you be her
Her out or her in you grow older to make her a child again Ask
Hiding in plain sight she comes always into her being
She is a real woman every time there is
And everything in free fall means everything engraves
And nothing covered will remain without being uncovered
And the lion becomes man consumed by man
How do I hold her in me even if I speak
I perform operations upon the traces of her sentence
Do not tell lies and do not do what you hate since all is plain
If you have ears take this large fish
Psyche sews seeds and reads
Fell on rock failed to root and no ears

On the other hand there are the fruitions
I hold you and wait for you to blaze
Away and away to have passed to have been beginning
First one and then two and then what
The more there is to speak than which none hath spoken more, thus
Go to the one who goes to the one who goes to the one who goes
   to the one
Do what you lie and tell what you hate since all is plain
You are like a righteous angel you are like a wise philosopher
You are the more there is to say for whose sake
Who goes to none
I am your master because I am not the one you think
Every one thing I have ever said is two
For whose sake heaven and earth came together
Nor your master because you get high on the measure
Every time she is a woman she is as real as she is
Tell me who am I like
Throw stones and let the fire burn you up
To say these things is her every wish
If it's there eat it

A Nod to the Numen

He spooks us to speak him.
A spike around the neck
hangs him, speechless.
This speech is his necklace.
I dig in his side with my spurs,
a thankless task
for the power of the foot.
He rules the toes and the tongue.
Duende, the bull dies
for the pleasure of the act
of death-making. The poetics
of exit, when and where
to yield
to the cut-off.
       How it goes
off its own deep end.
That is the spook of the speaking.

A knot in the prose has *duende.*
He punches La Catalina with a boar's hoof
and Don Juan chuckles.

We cannot preserve the feel of this talk,
we can only notice the *frisson*
and let it go. The old man's wisdom
is only across the room
in relation to your sense of loss.
And: The pleasure of the side that greets the spur
is a given line. It's all given,
the pleasure and the pain, and given up.
The catch is in the angle of its
disappearance. I disappear with it.
No poem, no talk, no nothing
is preserved. Nourish this
absence, as a knot in the brain
moves forward
as the knot in the tongue.

The catch is what keeps me here.
That's the catch
in this *duende* affair.
The biggest catch in the game
is the game. It goes on
at the scheduled time.
As a bonus, Buddhism
helps you write dialogue. That
is a given line, from across the room.
Listen, says the Dialogue
to itself, don't screw up
the reception. Attention
   is
is the catch, I'm caught
before I know it. No loss
no win, but the ball in the air
—and now we're in Tibet.
Bullfighting in Tibet.
Everybody dies.

If it says itself until it takes you
apart
it's *duende*.
"My vocabulary did this to me,"
he said on his deathbed.
How do we deal with that?
It deals with us.
Were the given words received in spirit

of forgiveness? Blake, Blake,
Blake calls us back from the doubt of words,
doubt in words, death in word,—
if it's so given
so it is given.
It is the catch of itself, and we
are its game.
    Look, we have
come through, a ways.
Becoming what we make.
Serious business.
Everybody dies. Words die
for us, in us, as we are apart
on the Earth.

      1975

Further Fingers for the Further Hand

To want to be happy.

What is the word I was looking for?

Undoing.

The dark

crowding itself out

in full view.

Morphic Resonance

Form
sounds
name
like
sound
forms
shape
things

Jed Rasula

Jed Rasula has lived in Finland, Germany, Alaska, Colorado, Indiana, California, and up and down the eastern seaboard of the United States. He is the author of a book of poems and calligraphics, *Tabula Rasula: being a book of audible visual matters* (Station Hill, 1986), editor of the poetry magazine *Wch Way*, and is on the editorial staff of *Sulfur*. He currently teaches at Queen's University in Kingston, Ontario.

Sound and Savor

> *the body is a great bell*
> *that sits like a hull*
> *over a voice*
> *summoning sound*

I recently came across this fragment from a notebook, dated September 1980. It arose during (and was probably copied down in the midst of) a conversation with Charles Stein. It encapsulates much of my sense of writing, of practice, of where and how writing and practice come together.

There are two integral relations with writing: as practice, and as production, or materialization. The practice returns the act of writing to its inner modality, aligning it with the postural sum of body-image, proprioceptive faculty, pneuma or breath, the axiomatic uprightness of the spinal column. Such practice is the ecological interface between the imaginal body and the material residuum of the encompassing field. It is primarily practice, and only incidentally *writing*.* (It is often, for me, as readily drawing or painting, gardening or walking.) It's a pure gift, then,

---

*My sense of such practice is informed by yoga and by t'ai chi, and not, strictly, by sitting meditation.

when a discernably shareable text comes into existence as a result of this practice.

The appropriate word for these texts is *blessings*. The functional parameters of such writing I have designated as *The Memory Theatre* since 1975. The rooms and templates, groves and caves of initiatory reverie into the charms of life constitute the scenes, incidents, compressed palpitations of organic devotion that end up coating the surfaces of the memory theatre. I suspect that, taken together, all the instances throughout my life in which I have felt summoned by the resonating hull of that bell have constituted the primal theatre (the inaugural sense of incident being, at age seven, a spooky but reverent ascent up a mountain in the Susquehanna River valley to visit some Indian burial mounds.) *The Memory Theatre* is a title that only partially applies to writing: I've come to recognize aspects of my life as pertaining to the Memory Theatre as irrevocably as any text I'm likely to produce.

But there have been texts, episodes of writing, concentrated and unremittingly *sent* from beyond my local and partial resolve or will. "The Field & Garden of Circe" is one that has sporadically stung me, and in stinging sweetened my sense of purpose in writing as practice, as nothing else has. "Circe" and the other *Memory Theatre* writings, in the plenum of my own existence, are enduring evidence of a Buddhist precept; I quote from Shunryu Suzuki's *Zen Mind, Beginner's Mind:* "Waves are the practice of water." Writing is the practice of language. *Writing* is a practice in ways that speaking is not. Talk, conversation, dialogue—these are inexorably socialized, made public and expedient, as the ground of social exchange. I don't mean to suggest that writing as such is immune from the pressures of expectation and demand that are the burden of socialization; but it can act as a sort of shrine, to shelter detachment, and to nourish a sentience not socially bound. The pivot of praxis is somatic, individual (which doesn't mean "private" or even personal). But any practice involving language can only remain interiorized for a limited time. Inevitably the moment arrives when the share of words encompasses others in its passionate expenditure.

To be an actively publishing writer is to intervene in the practice with a purposiveness not necessarily part of the practice as such. "Just write," like the precept "just sit," should be enough. But publication alters the medium: it organizes and intensifies the writing, shaping, and nurturing it. Performative and gestural possibilities are gleaned. My own commitment has been as far as possible to connect production or materialization of the writing with the sense of its value for me as practice—to make of these different engagements a compound, a union, a praxis.

Most significantly this has meant developing a perspective on the text as circumstantially variable. My book *Tabula Rasula,* for instance, was initially prepared in a xerographic edition running to some four hundred pages. To prepare it for a manageable publication it had to be reduced to one hundred pages. This meant not "selecting" a quarter of the manuscript (as if it were a torso of meat to be carved up) but recomposing (*composting* is my preferred term) a new book from the old, using all the typographic and calligraphic skills at my disposal that were specific to a different medium. I have worked extensively as a typesetter and designer, and could approach my own writing, when it came to a final publication, only from a perspective fully responsible to what I knew of the medium of print. This was no longer design but a furtherance of composition.

Another aspect of my writing has arisen directly out of the manifest sense of *public* in publication. In practical terms this sort of writing is "constructivist," oriented to possibilities of assemblage that address the occasion of hearing or reading, rather than the moment of composition. (For these texts, in fact, there's no such "moment.") At its extreme this writing is thoroughly lapidary: *Accidental Research* is the title of a manuscript incorporating much writing I did in the midst of other engagements (child rearing, carpentry: circumstances forbidding more than the briefest attention to the asides of writing something down). Where the creative concentration comes is in the final stage of piecing out chunks for further deliberation. Compositionally it's a matter of arranging mosaic clusters.

In the title pieces for *Accidental Research* there's no attempt to provide overall continuity of a speaking voice. Instead, the sentence or phrasal units swarm like antibodies into the Language Homunculus, the "what is said of what is said" that hibernates inside the text. *Accidental Research* is public—of the polis—in the conviction that an antibiosis is at hand in the human world. As "an association between two or more organisms that is injurious to one of them," the humanization of the planet has instituted governance as such—including any and all political regimes whether left or right—as injurious to the organisms of earth with which we're bound, no longer in symbiosis, but in antibiosis. These writings conscientiously handle a hyperbolic and presumptuous apparatus: the withered and stunted public language in our time. This cosmetic gadgetry—the artificial life-support system that constitutes common parlance today—sustains a smothering fiction of history as a developmental/evolutionary maturation of the species. In other parts of *Accidental Research,* like "New Rev. on Cell. Path. Porn" (in *Temblor* 7) the writerly surface is flushed with a rhetoric that makes the language bristle with all its accumulated alien parasites, its abrasions and contusions, as it is pressed into service for the prevailing emotional greed of the century's twilight. This kind of writing, in its own very different way, attempts a reclamation of our right to language, which I would affirm, in all my work, as the most inalienable of all rights.

My poems included in the present anthology derive from the first sense of practice outlined above. They are measured somatic topoi, imagos of calm, gratitude, sedimented *rasa*. Rasa: the sap or soup of earthly delight, cultivated out of savored (flavored) incarnation. They practice a rapport with the curious factor of *faith* that circumscribes such practice, making the glance (Orpheus looking back over his shoulder, or Cobra—*bhujangasana*—in yoga) suffice. Making the glance suffice.

from The Field & Garden of Circe

"The roar of the sea, largeness of the tide, the blue horizon, the sun burning, excite it."—Richard Jeffries, *Sun Life*

Even though you are heavier now
you will float on water & be like ice.
Everywhere you look you will be a parent
swelling & drifting, layer by layer,
pressed to the black stone known as coal
for millions of years on a piece of shale
the explorer's dogs were absorbed
for a liquid to turn to gas
for the chaffinch grateful for help
for the elegant delicate beak
for the glucose flurry "building with light"
naked & crouched in a nook of rubble
a dog a horse a self-willed wolf
like guarding a house with a bumpy tongue
& it doesn't take much just a
few young buds is usually enough,
a succulent slit while the taller the door
her hazardous egg their mouth agape
to skeleton, organs, affection & food
to making noises' spiky case
stippled with heat off a gulf of leaves
so small revolving honey pelt

so hottest point a flaunted sap
the fossil record *most* assent
so equinox decay remains
a good & solid boiler does,
in freshwater snail, in corms of crocus,
in pollen compulsion these flailing salts
this many shines, active a petal
& mineral mysteries list them plough,
a slow alive,
a solemn earth,
a miracle parent, a carrot,
amazing butters that hundreds of out,
that hollowed ocean algae worm by several noun,
sargasso elms not gills but lunge,
such coat of moisture bigger but danger,
nature around the year on over
a crop of sap, a possible rock-hard pear,
cocoon or dormant facet house,
produces branching bees as well,
anatomy rapidly animal lakes,
anatomy rapidly animal lakes,
grumble thorax splashed with yellow
flexible trump & soon may fly
browned on wingtip pumice
immortal maya soaring pillow
each beech attach a history of Venus
—pingala blush in obelisk—
anatomy rapidly animal lakes
the fossil record most assent
to soar on murmur swells the
patter numerical obstinate
loam of the pressure of years
of the story is very invited
and longs for names or
skullborne glues her
syrup a sun life shore to bone
shortwave for years to become
excited the story as light
is food we animal
membrane's karezza narcosis
to *fend*
these cool veins blue past throng

a thaw that soared on cells
by way of manifold pranks
in debts of protein end on end

    O

". . . there is a massive convergence of mobile minds
flying upward on a gradient of surprise . . ."
just waiting waiting & sweet untold "you know
biology branch in memory alive
biology branch entire hill in memory saliva
said to the fly
there probably *is*"
the spider to being alive
the purge desire to fatten its secret
indulge desire to memor erupt

origi
origin
in ast
astrophe
vertig
amor
ashing a for
a passion forest
a metal blur on sunblind sea shone clouded roar
nor even the need to *attain*
a mooth smapping of surf
lits into folds & cusplike rrific absor

Vowels

She dreamt I was talking to myself.
I pressed my beak to a crack in the shell.
I talked to a bowl full of water.
They dreamt it was weather.

I meant to point to the keys
rattling inside the tree.
I meant to pertain, meant to incise, meant to specify,
meant to mean.

I meant to mean a pun would say
whatever another might.

Whatever another might.

Doing good is a species enough,
a species itself.

Each broken twig and upturned pebble concurs.
Salamanders brighten *through the stone.*
Directly visible below.
As I am under the cloud.
The mound of my head.
The pond of my god.
For the moment a jonquil.
A tulip, a crown, a clue of wind.
For the moment the moment.

These are my gods I give them speech.

To bubble
To bother
To bring to bear
To brace, to ring, to flare up hot nest oracle door.
A gate the autumn pours from trees.
Shaking with wrath, reading the eggs, shining the keen,
I learn and sort. It leaks and fits.

These are my gods I give them speech.

These odds and ends.

Each by each.

The Hollow

    The garden blackens in the rain
this afternoon mist where solitude gathers a body,
        casts a shadow, travels & knocks at house & head

the day is all & *only* beauty's opening duct
  to let my being hollow sound the earth persists desiring so

greetings from January

the cold flowers of stony Pluto are up & about

The Table

the organic tableau
—the billions of years of flowering cells
that have fed me the world—
snatched from the scum of the pond
a ball of gell to shape the lure

written by water in leaves are a book

the deodars tall as a ridge

the slippers of thought in the bush are finches

each cloud is a pond in the air

the earth is a star in the heart

the tree's a straw to squeeze up sap

to "believe" and "leave seed"
    return to a common root

    the black and red lines on the wall were friends
like the parchment stained with a snake
                whose blood had dried by noon
            on the Barrytown graveyard post-office road
        (the sonar of underworld icemelt rubbing his hide)

            and what did I see in the gravel of stars
but the ribs of a cow were clear in the western sky

Alexis Rotella

Alexis Rotella is the author of fifteen books of haiku and poetry, as well as *How Words and Thoughts Effect Your Body* and *The Essence of Flowers (Wisdom for the Aquarian Age)*. An interfaith minister with a doctorate in hypnotherapy, she is a practicing certified Ericksonian hypnotherapist and counselor. Her study of Zen has enhanced her appreciation of the Kabbalah, of which she has been a student for over fifteen years.

Winter chill:
the moon moves away
from the geese.

through the bird skull whistle of wind

soaking up the moon   the snail

This heat:
a pilgrimage of black ants
along the pine snag.

Blackbirds
spring
from a bolt of silk

Lightning:
in the crack of a boulder,
violets.

pause in his sentence   distant crows

Blackberry pickers—
a child's laugh escapes
from an old woman's body.

A head comes out
of the turtle's shell—
the roshi's flute.

At the pool hall
spouting zen
the young stud.

In the marsh
a heron alights
on an old sofa.

After the first snow
rabbit tracks
connecting graves.

A wet spot
on the rock
where the frog sat.

Steve Sanfield

Steve Sanfield was raised and educated in New England. Following a stint in Hollywood's entertainment industry, he lived and traveled abroad, mainly around the Mediterranean, North Africa, and the Greek Islands, where experiments with psychedelics led to the study of Tibetan Buddhism and eventually to a relationship with Joshu Sasaki Roshi, which has continued for the past twenty-five years. He has written seven books of poetry, including *Wandering* (Shaman Drum Press, 1977), *A New Way* (Tooth of Time, 1983), and *He Smiled To Himself* (Shakti Press, 1990). He has also written three books of folklore, the latest being *The Feather Merchants and Other Tales of the Fools of Chelm* (Orchard Books, 1991). The associate editor of *Kuksu: A Journal of Backcountry Writing* and a founding and later contributing editor of *Zero: A Journal of Contemporary Buddhist Life & Thought,* he became the first full-time Storyteller-in-Residence in the United States in 1977, under the sponsorship of the California Arts Council.

A Cycle of Hoops* for the First Snow

Waking this morning
to find the world
covered in white.

> The brown grasses
> seen afresh
> after a night of snow.

---

*I call them hoops rather than haiku, because *haiku* is a Japanese word for a poem usually written according to very specific guidelines. I wanted to step beyond those lines and also add another season—the season of the heart. And further, as Black Elk says, "that is because the Power of the world always worked in circles and everything tries to be round. In the old days when we were a strong and happy people, all our power came to us from the sacred hoop of the nation, and as long as the hoop was unbroken, the people flourished."

Even that junkpile
I meant to put in order
is perfect.

On moonlit snow
even my shadow
is cold.

The power of snow
to make all things
new.

Snapped in two:
that tree I never
should have planted.

Tracks in the snow:
what happened
while we slept.

*   *   *

Empty woodshed.
Bad back.
Trouble ahead.

Not quite cold enough
to build a fire.
Regretting it all morning.

Gutting the deer
steam rising
in lantern light.

Another season
and no one to talk with
about the last.

Holed up for winter
wondering if anyone
will come.

The steaming kettle
my only companion
this winter night.

Fifteen kinds of mosquitoes
but they all
sound the same.

—Everglades

The loudest sound:
the quail
at dawn.

So cold
even the words
freeze.

More and more
sure of
less and less.

True eloquence:
the rattlesnake's
warning.

The first narcissus
and his nose
all stuffed up.

Emptying the piss pot
he notices the moon
pours it on himself.

Sleep on the couch she says
cutting his fantasies
in two.

Remembers
beginning to masturbate.
Can't recall if he finished.

Cleaning house.
Poems scattered
everywhere.

Love poems
scribbled for one
now sent to another.

That cricket he rescued
from the dishwater
kept him awake all night.

Sends himself
a welcome home card.
It never arrives.

Rain on the roof.
A cricket in the house.
As it is.

Leslie Scalapino

Leslie Scalapino grew up in Berkeley, California, and has traveled in Asia since childhood. She is the publisher of O Books and the author of a number of collections of poetry and prose, including *The Return of Painting, The Pearl & Orion/A Trilogy* (North Point Press, 1991), and *way* (North Point Press, 1988). She lives in Oakland, California, where she practices Zen.

from The Pearl

Woman wading on long yellow grass.
There's the blue sky. She's wading turmoil and some buzzards are on the grass—that is before her.

Slow low gutting on the long yellow grass.
and the buzzards are on the corpse that is amidst the grass.
hams forward and then back wading—and ahead and behind that in the grass.
In the blue sky. On the slope, hams extended forward. wading.
on it.
rolled down the grass—and the buzzards on one. Cluster flapping.
that is in the blue sky. Cluster flapping on a corpse.
wading on
indentation in the wave of slopes and buzzards start are on a corpse flapping. up.
hams wading up.
in it.
The buzzards in it had been on the corpses, here and there.
Flapping cluster in it on one.

the whirr in that the mixing amidst it in the indentation.

pushed into going into the ocean which is at the edge of this.
On the rise, with the others, who're churning. The water is heavy,
the rise of it. The living have struggled into it. A shot cracks into
it. And a corpse boils. The living churning around it. The lighted
sea.

The other feels a crack in her side the hip that is soaking hanging in the heavy water.

blood that comes into the sea from the humans.

And wading in who're shooting they keep on going cracks of
shots in it.

churning.

heavy mass.

swimming. the rolls. in the waves.

Having the hip that had hung in the water. In the long grass.
Weeds entwined dragging the hip leg lying. Slept deeply before.
The men on the mounted pickup truck emerges through grass. A
shot in the heavy grass. The leg lying twined in the weed and
rolling into the indentation.

Buzzards fly up.

from a corpse in the indentation flapping on it.

which is turned over on its trunk.

trunk of woman low wading now.

her on the long grass.

Rolling into indentation of reddish cattle with gentle white
faces who're kneeling in it. The kneeling gentle cattle beginning
to stand frightened.

The leg is soaked. The kneeling cattle standing, settling, the
twined grass. in among them.

Slept in a matted indentation with them.

the men out of the mounted pickup truck overseeing muffled.

Lying by the steer it is not double.

There's a puff. Crack of shots muffled.

Morning comes. it does not come, how can it? the thick slurred
cattle kneeling eating in the light air.

the lightened white air. Wheeling oneself forward on a cart, a
sled—of the leg. On the sidewalk asking money of the passerby—
in it—on the sled.

it is free

for the one they think. for that other who's asking for the
money.

on the sled—it is.

a soldier affected by the unburied dead covered with the buzzards in the valleys and not turn that inward.
and then he's in the light air
and not figure out how it unfolds
Wheeling on the sled—having slept in the indentation—deer
simply have ticks which become huge until they drop off.
a huge tick in the side of having waded.
they begin singing—soldiers she meets on the road are a choir
and they began singing.
into the area of just pulp—only that
One realizing I have to do this myself.
the leg is soaked. She goes on the sled. There's a sandbar out
along stretching on which are corpses the buzzards had encrusting
flapping. the light air is coming up. no planet. or orb. an orb
floating.
Now it's gone.
And out tangled in the yellow grass, on it. The woman wading.
There's a corpse in the grass the buzzards sapping it whirling. It's
far gone. in the light air.
it can't be that in the long yellow grass
the hams stretch out and running down the slope in the yellow
grass. arms twirling flapping being in the grass.
There are weeds. It's dawn. Encounters sensitive man. as in
trunk of seal lying on her, rearing—their coming. the light air is
coming up. entwined thrashing around. He puts it into her again.
Him rearing, on the trunk
He withdraws it, takes it out
the weeds are still
He puts it back in—on the trunk
Him having gotten an erection
the trunk, the bulb of it in her. after
the dawn

There was this crescent moon hanging with a bright planet in
this blue night sky. They were low
in it
the sack of corpse wavered bulb that was created by some
behavior
they the orbs weren't held
birds come glancing sucked and then released
by the one or the people in their behavior
it's completely irrelevant
just the figure of the plant or the plant

drew a figure of a plant, whereas some other traced it and was given the figure to trace and was praised for it—conceived before. Not ability. There is no such. No community exists, and that is not the matter.

Flatness was construed as (was made to be) a barrier put up against the viewer's normal wish to enter a picture and dream, to have it be a space apart from life in which the mind would be free to make its own connections.

> have it be life

It isn't. The illness was rampant and took two-thirds of the population and that among the country so there were few laborers. They could ask a high price for their labor, being so few. And so cautioned not to. to do as modesty, is their real circumstance which they should see.

> as convention yet
> real—as literal

that modesty means something. not struggling. and being free.

Yet the countryside was unworked—who have mind. having been wiped out there by the illness. And those remaining asked cautioned to work at the same low wages as before—when the buds came out on the trees and it was spring.

The budding trees stood out—heartbreaking, to see people starving lying out. how could one be fool enough to have fallen for those who are cruel as being the heart's companion?

> love

They fan out as a spray, running—yet there is a huge crowd. The cops are among them, and are before them in a phalanx wearing battle-gear. They lob canisters of teargas into them, which fall. There's the sound of them being thrown. A cloud billows out.

> inside in the night the
> teargas wafts to people
> in a gathering

They break the plate glass windows, the glass coming down in waves, of the banks and the shops. In the day—afterward—the trucks carrying the plate glass come. The only work.

Yet decimated. The crowds break the plate windows again and again.

> the laborers come—a few
> working, bringing the plate glass
> which is roped carried on trucks.

Children are playing in the quiet empty yards streets—they come running angry from being chased by a helicopter.

The helicopters patrol, hovering constantly. Chased the children up their own street. Who're made furious.

The people lying starving are the secret—of reality—like the layers of the bud. used to think that and see that is not so.

The (other) is at an Orange Julius stand, having a juice. sitting. She feels ill and is weak, not able to move rapidly or continue on. A cop car stops, and a small crowd gathers around it.

They do something there. Crowded so that she can't see, on the car.

A girl approaches her from there who is thin and dressed raggedly.

She is about fourteen. She wants to hire the (other) to take a package to a house.

She holds it out. It is a small package tied with string. The people around the cop car disperse running, and then before the (other) knows it the girl runs leaving her with it.

so they get to joy

Andrew Schelling

Andrew Schelling was born in Washington, D.C., and raised outside Boston. Early years were spent tramping Thoreau's countryside, following the Taoist adage "avoid the authorities." He traveled to India, then settled in California, wrote poetry, scoured history, studied Buddhism, and worked as a baker, truckdriver, bookseller, and teacher. Two years of Sanskrit studies at Berkeley resulted in ongoing poetry translations. He and Benjamin Friedlander edit *Dark Ages Clasp the Daisy Root,* a journal of experimental poetics. In 1986 he crossed India again, as recorded in his book *Claw Moraine.* His recent books are *Dropping the Bow: Poems from Ancient India* (Broken Moon Press, 1991) and *Ktaadn's Lamp* (Rocky Ledge Editions, 1991).

Mounting the Poetry Vehicle

Buddhism as I understand it doesn't mean true or false. It just means waking up. It's funny, but the parallel is that poetry seems the only place words are not true or false. The question is, do these words wake you up.

It hit me with terrific force when I first encountered the small press and began to read a living poetry. Here I found poets who took to writing as to "the hall of practice." These thought-shapers, following a string of unruly predecessors, were not using words simply to talk about something—they were producing states of consciousness, configurations of language into some *wakened* thing. Poems seemed ideograms of alertness on the page. You could carry them around in your hip pocket, a literal state of Mind.

The texts and personages of Buddhist history have about them a similar vigilance. Gautama Buddha, discussing with friends what he'd found out about Mind under the Bodhi tree, seems not so distant from my own generation. For in India, up till Gautama's day, poetry and philosophy had centered around the ingestion of a troubling psychedelic—*soma*. Yet tripping gave way, somehow, to other disciplines, other techniques of insight. Perhaps *soma* got too unpredictable—useful, like mushrooms or acid for a while, but ultimately lacking in grace. Wherever in this country, during a period of comparable disaffection, psychedelics got applied with intelligence, their use also dropped away over the years. Friends turned to the disciplined training of art, a handicraft, meditation, or to word-powered vehicles, by which I don't just mean mantra, the chanting of formulas. These have their use—but poets demand the precision, the subtlety, acquired by playing the full range of language. Language? A thousand string'd lute—the ear hasn't been born that's heard all its strings.

At some point I met on the field of Poetry the poets of classical Sanskrit. An eloquent if nearly anonymous crew. These writers had drawn careful distinctions between the emotional conditions that flicker across the human heart. And they had developed a poetry to account for each of these states. Sometimes I run into people who will see as "Buddhist" only that poetry which displays a certain *cool*. But the Sanskrit poets, insisting on the heart's self-born intelligence, would find luminous poetry in the heat of any emotion. It's this, Mind alert to its own transformations, that bind for me the twin disciplines—meditation and poetry.

I've seen parallels drawn between Buddhist metaphysics and poetic practice, some of which are clearly useful. But the planet being wide as it is, and Mind such surprising terrain, I'd resist any comprehensive statement of procedure such as "spontaneous prose" or "first thought best thought" as getting to the pith of writing. With some people it might take several dozen years of hard work to loosen up to a point of easy alertness. Buddhist lore's packed with accounts of tough labor carried out for years, gritty patience and gentle humor. I can best describe my own writing practice by a phrase Mel Weissman applies to zazen—"continual refinement."

In other words, you *make* poems. That doesn't just mean technique. It's the same as making love—unfettered urge is there from the start—it's part of our makeup. With some people the raw impulse takes a frightfully demonic form. But the task of refinement—as poet, lover, or contemplative—has no limit. How long do you sit in meditation before posture and breathing are correct? How long is too long for a poem to take shape? Sometimes it occurs on the instant. Other times it is the effort of years.

Not that writing and meditation substitute for one another. They just clarify certain issues in similar ways. One clear correspondence: both demand hard work, but work that accepts *uselessness* as the ground of endeavor. Sure you can write a polemical poem, just as you can "sit" outside the gates of Livermore weapons lab—make it useful by locating it in some special context. But that's different. The eerie word *magic* that haunts poetry, the quiet sorcery that smolders in meditation—not much credence given them by our contemporary world. (India to some degree, parts of Africa probably.) But in the West? Well, poets and yogins are not quite so intimidating as we used to be. So what? Maybe we've gained something, now that contemplatives don't get hired as "doctors of political medicine"—magic poisoners, that is—or poets to wreck crops with spells and curses. This lends a delightful autonomy—call it "breathing room"—to those who want to sit down and write. Or who just want to sit down.

One curious note I'd like to end on. Hardly anyone pays attention, but give or take a hundred years Gautama Buddha was contemporary with Panini, the world's first, probably the world's greatest, linguist. Coincidence? Who's kidding whom? Something big was going on, these simultaneous inquiries into Mind and Language, twenty-five hundred years ago. And it was happening across the planet—Greece, China, Palestine. This I think is where our so-called modernism begins. Practicing Mind and practicing Language. They've been pretty inextricable ever since.

So inextricable in fact that some hold Mind to be nothing *but* the play of language. That contradicts my own experience. Yet words and the way we put them together are at this historical juncture the primary vehicle we've got. Almost everything we know about human life on this planet is locked up inside this mystery. I'd look alongside the established Buddhist lineages for another tradition, a subterranean movement that trades with the world at large. Some elusive, night-wandering caravan loaded with strange goods, picking its way up the treacherous trade routes of History. Call it by a Sanskrit term, *kavyayana*—the Poetry Vehicle. "You don't need no ticket, you just get on board."

Storm Furrows

1

no longer
we this
evening
the cold
returns the
inconstancy
lasts

2

of tea
how a fox
under
jagged rocks
this shirt
but not an
empty sack

3

eyebrows
like bamboo
linger
the last
drinking to
the white
dregs

4

books
highest moon
on the
red-walled
musk of her
vagina

5

over
rises quiet
even insects
to sleep
are ancient
dry

6

are not my
poems my poems
or not or
now—
flickers
dream returns
the cold of
some imagined
was

7

branches
water
but how to
read it
thirty
four years
a sign or
two

8

rain
squaring the
roof at a
slant
notes in the
night of
shadows where
the cat
would
walk

9

    black
wings of
fastflying birds
     in the
       window
     clock lamp
      magic
       wand

10

knowing
if even that
the more
or nothing more
some few
objects
define the
light & shadow
along one's
desk

11

homage sarasvati
     girl with a lute
  the book the night

writing
past
midnight
the beak of
flame the
hiss hiss
of presence
unseen in
the lamp or
is it rain
renewed
in the coastal
redwoods
she lives among

a slip of a
goddess
teeth like beads
of rice—
that white they say—
elusive
but nonetheless
in a hut
word has it
down by some river
or other
    (you
can if you
find her

Armand Schwerner

Armand Schwerner began his meditation practice in 1971, at the Kagyu community at Tail of the Tiger in Vermont, and with Chögyam Trungpa Rinpoche. He subsequently joined the New York chapter of Dharmadhatu, leaving in 1975. In 1981 he began Zen practice with Sensei Glassman at the Zen Community of New York, receiving lay ordination in 1983. He has published fifteen books and continues work on his ongoing—and best-known—collection of poems, *The Tablets*. He published *The Tablets I–XXVI* in 1989.

Notes on a Life in Buddhism

I'd been reading D. T. Suzuki and Paul Reps, among others, for years before the summer of 1971, when I got in touch with the Kagyu community at Tail of the Tiger in northern Vermont, where I would experience my first practice context. Chögyam Trungpa Rinpoche gave a teaching on Naropa that summer. I was distraught, whirled within the maelstrom of a disintegrating marriage, worried about the potentially withering effects of its climate on the development of my two sons. Having no faith in the usefulness of a return to psychotherapy, I was searching for a psychology that—as I then formulated it—existed within a significant metaphysic. The study of Buddhism and the discovery of the subtle insights of *abhidharma* attracted me as if I'd discovered my veritable archaic home. Someone at Naropa—was it Trungpa, or a member of the community, or a voice in a book?—said, "No need to repress; no need to express; every need to recognize." In the course of my return to a home that I intensely feared would turn my new learning into thinnest air, I was happily pursued by that utterance as if by a talisman. The letter from Vermont that gave the New York City address and telephone number of the group still hangs on my study wall.

George Quasha had recommended Trungpa Rinpoche's *Meditation in*

Action a few months before I visited Tail of the Tiger for the first time, a visit that in fact was impelled by my reading of that book and an almost immediate surging sense of indebtedness. I subsequently joined the New York chapter of Dharmadhatu and on January 8, 1973, took refuge in Barnet, Vermont, where I received from Rinpoche the dharma name Chö-kyi Nying-po, "flute of the dharma." After 1975 I continued to study and to practice, but decided it was no longer possible to continue as a member of Dharmadhatu. Some aspects of both the personal and collective climates within which my resignation occurred will become evident from speculations a bit further on. In 1981 I began Zen practice with Sensei Glassman at the Zen Community of New York. I received *jukai* (lay ordination) in 1983 and the dharma name Ho-ka, "song of the dharma." I left in 1985. From 1976 to the present I have been attending *dzogchen* teachings given by Namkhai Norbu Rinpoche, Sogyal Rinpoche, and the Khenpos Palden Sherab Rinpoche and Tsewang Dongyal Rinpoche, in New York City, upstate New York, and Massachusetts.

The first of my fifteen books appeared in 1962, nine years before entering on Buddhist practice. Many of the main lines of Buddhist thought, which I later recognized as much as learned, had been evident in my work before the actualizations of practice. The inescapable wakes following upon such actualizations were manifestations of the great teachers Confusion and Process.

My first attempt at meditation at Tail of the Tiger in 1971 was preceded by weeks and weeks of anxiety. I was sure that yielding to the process would once and for all ruin me for poetry—or would ruin the poetry within me. I could express my concern with a less dualistic formulation only if I had some certainty about the eternal problems of inner and outer, this and that, container and contained. But in the *Sandokai*, a part of every Zen service, inheres an assurance of the imponderable, necessary puzzle of the dualism of absolute and relative:

> The relative fits the absolute as a box and its lid.
> The absolute meets the relative like two arrow points that touch
>   high in the air.
> Hearing this, simply perceive the Source!

The anxiety about meditation soon dropped away, but it remained in its ore awaiting resurrection in a context that would appear later.

Before I trek further into that mine, let me present a few examples of the beneficent radiations of Buddhism in my life and work. It's an impossible conceit to think we can distinguish between the end of one wake-segment and the beginning of the next. Just as one can't seize the particular moment the air's no longer impregnated by the smell of lilac, or as the caressing hand is unable to identify the precise picosecond during which it grazes away from the skin of the beloved, so too I can't stop the riverish shiftings of my life since 1971—can't stop the world, not to get off, but to find The Most Influential Concepts or The Major Spiritual Events. But I have sometimes experienced repeated, unexpected and irrigating droplets of past memories.

One morning in 1972 at Tail of the Tiger I experienced a leap into body-filling thankfulness for the teaching that the buddha-nature is indwelling, revealable, and discoverable, that there is never any need to seek it out in some unreachable place out *there,* a profoundly lightening teaching. Perhaps if during my childhood or adolescence I had experienced mystical Judaism, the teaching about buddha-nature might not have exploded with quite that elemental power. But my experience of the sacred texts in my loosely traditional Jewish upbringing had pointed without respite to the unreachable Otherness of deity, a teaching buttressed by the equally convinced monotheism of environing Christianity.

Another time, one evening in 1983 at the Zen Community in Riverdale, New York, I remember a conversation with my good friend poet Lou Nordstrom, Rinzai and Soto priest; in the course of saying something about my grateful sense of the power of the bodhisattva idea in Mahayana—in the midst of the very utterance—an opening transformed statement into realization. A *life* is made of such moments, whose inflows a simple prose statement can only point to. My poetry seems to me inconceivable outside of the penetrations of the force field of such psychic events.

Some experiences in the course of a *sesshin* at the Zen Community of New York, Riverdale, in 1983, gave rise to the following Tablet:

TABLET XXV

clearly I'm the swimming animal, the light
song or the dark song + + + + + + + + + simple . . . . . .
when it's hot I'm wet, I don't need to celebrate, to
strike two stones together, alone in this small getting older house
humbled by distractable eyes, quiet realm . . . . animal
what happened yesterday? the lettuce drains on the sill
colored liquids going up and down inside me . . . . . . tracks . . . .
. . . . without any time + + + + + + + + + + +
+ +. . . . .
river . . . . . . reaching around behind my left shoulder. never mind.

. . . . reaching around into the hollow
behind my left shoulder, anything, there might be
water, a wasp, clangor lately, the thickness
of the vagina smell of another room, the great matters of my pic-
    tures
whose songs in my dreams look like my story, look like + + + + +
nothing, there's nothing after I cut down the frenzied objects
in the dance, nothing
to celebrate or hide from . . . . iron cinctures
in my shoulders, unnecessary to turn around, back
is back . . . . a phalanx of my teachers'
                                                    changing voices
on the clay road and I lift my head up to the perennial sun, hot
red stone in a blue containing it, or back of it,
so it is there
I in my air here . . . . these small
getting older thighs matted like the floor of the woods
with webs and fists of branches keeping their story
+ letting drop away
their story . . . . ah the ground yesterday
a vast invitation of voices, wet through by flooding,
alive with drone and crawl, track and shimmer of beings in love
with the hazy dusk of water. . . . .
    . . . .
    . . . .
    . . . .
    . . . .
    . . . .
    . . . . hazy . . . .

The scholar/translator's notations:
. . . . *missing section* + + + + + + + *untranslatable*

(I'd been working with my teacher Sensei Glassman's *The Hazy Moon of
Enlightenment,* for which the following lines served as epigraph:

Though clear waters range to the vast blue autumn sky
How can they compare with the hazy moon on a spring night!
Most people want to have pure clarity,
But sweep as you will, you cannot empty the mind.

—Keizan Zenji)

Experiences in the context of five years of Zen practice some ten years after I'd ended my membership in Dharmadhatu drove me to a different level within the resurrectable ore. The early 1980s were a productive period for me; nevertheless, I couldn't understand why I was so bothered by the differences between my sense of the nature of my convictions and my sense of the nature of my teacher's convictions—not just *my* teacher's, but those of many teachers. If I consider these differences as differences between teachers and students, I realize that an aspect of the connection between the two involves dialogue of an idiosyncratic sort. The learners, through the implicit mandates of the teaching situation, willingly suspend critical operations within the relationship. And the teachers in the space provided by the suspension do their work. However, if I, a poet, focus on the difference between the teacher and myself, I can't avoid the recognition that his clay, his plasticine, his rock, his marble, his acrylic and his collage fragments, his flesh, his sound, his soul-texture—his material, in short—is other human beings; mine is me.

What is the attainment of a significant condition? Let's say this condition's recognizable by a qualified other. Qualified? Or it's certifiable by one's own experientially validated practice. Certifiable? Validated? Pervasive as such questions are in the context of spiritual practice, they are equally central in their implicit application to poetry, to kinds of poetry, to levels of poetic arrival. What is the nature of a Hinayana poetry, a Mahayana poetry, a Vajrayana poetry, a *dzogchen* poetry? Are these reasonable questions?

The space of that poetry which is indebted to the active presence of Buddhism in America contains "infinite riches in a little room." For instance, the work of John Giorno, a profoundly committed Vajrayana practitioner, takes on incandescent power in performance. But it keeps its secret. I've never understood the nature of the relationship between his practice and the language and form of his poetry. How does the one inform the others? How can it help doing so? The thematic carryover, yes, but in which way(s) does a particular work—one's own work too—embody or mime or incarnate in its procedures, its being, the textures, sensations, modalities of mandala or of visualization practices, of *shikantaza* ("just sitting")? Such speculations, both rational and intuitive, manifest continuously, enrich and are fed by the loose, real community of poets in the locus of ongoing reciprocal recognitions that constitutes in my life both some of its deepest friendships and the impersonal fount of its productiveness.

Another question rises up: how much can you do in language, language separated from performance, music, rite? Take Tibetan sacred, regularly metered, didactically purposive poetry. For some two years I studied Tibetan and translated *nyingma* texts. For me the essential Tibetan poetry exists not in many of those medieval seven- or eight-syllable verses but in the chants of the Gyuto monks, say, or the lived transformations of visualization practice. But now of course we're dealing with the complex acculturative issues raised by the varying functions of different genres of poetry in either traditionalist or industrial societies. Chuck Stein's work, for instance, seems to me deeply useful in its ongoing attempts to embody aspects of Buddhist practice in image and rhythm and poetically assimilated depths of philosophical speculation. A vast terrain, these poetic practices are informed by varied individual experiences of Buddhism in the last two decades.

It seems to me that as a poet, I had in my choice of a path—my act, my generating, my practice—created a basic, necessary condition that had me feeding on myself in a way that the choice of a teacherly life task essentially obviates. Looking around, I found few paradigmatic instances of useful and significant priest-poets that invalidate these assumptions, and I found a good number of instances in which transformation into priest diluted and enervated the poet. These are instances bound by place and time, instances for which I don't claim universal validity. Personality needs differ; modes of integration vary. But the enervation of the poet, as I perceive the contemporary situation, has also to do with the complex, ambiguous qualities of the idea and reality of a religious community and the texture of his adherence to such a community. Besides, it was more and more apparent that the relatively open nature of American society and the fluidity of role assumptions within it required a lot of hard questioning on the part of any autonomous, responsible person.

I knew the terms of my inner conflict were not trivial. I'd seen monks with artistic and intellectual gifts driven, at the direction of their teachers, into months and years of work in computerized data banks, in long acts of accountancy, and in questionable subjection to manufacturing operations. I'd been involved in many intense conversations relating to the question of the proper role of practitioners, who, I observed, had through the power and need of their spiritual inclinations made choices based more on their acceptance of what the teacher defined as socioreligious necessity than on the essential directions of their capabilities.

My readings in Krishnamurti strengthened my understanding that I was not involved merely in a meretricious struggle instigated by the machinations of ego. Speculations about what becoming a monk would involve were subject to my increasing awareness of considerations about the nature and needs of my calling as poet, most particularly as that choice related to institutional involvements. I left the Zen Community not very long after my ordination. I knew, of course, that Trungpa (among other teacher-practitioners of various arts) was a poet and a calligrapher. And I respect Philip Whalen's work. I believed and still believe, however, that the weight of the evidence and the idiosyncratic dictates of my experience validate my conviction and my sense of the necessity of my choice.

My concerns include matters having to do with the particulars of what Jackson Mac Low, in a letter to Michael Heller about socioreligious matters in American Buddhism, has termed "church polity." Many of us students, in our need to estimate what point we had reached on the spiritual path, were encouraged in that effort by teachings about *bhumis,* stages on the path. We exercised our measuring rods, although most of us, I'm sure, also knew that any mensuration was at best merely one more "skillful means." If we were lucky, we would ripen into a continuous availability to panic—which Trungpa Rinpoche called "the source of open heart and open ground, and which creates an enormous sense of fresh air. That ongoing panic points to the seriousness of the tantric path, which is so overwhelmingly powerful and demanding that it is better not to commit ourselves to it. But if we must get into it, we should take it absolutely seriously."

Adages for life, and for the making of poetry. But in this age of pandemic reification fathers and daughters are daily transformed into wares, and the monetization of the ghettoized Other infects attitudes toward interpersonal love and toward socialization. That reification slows the journey toward the achievement of the stage akin to that which Thinley Norbu calls "play-mind" in the "magic dance," a stage whose energy is the energy of symbolic forms, a special few of which have attained the exemplary power that I will refer to in this context as the *uncanny*—the power conflating both the rational and the prereflective, both the transcendent and the immanent, which we concede to and celebrate in the work of Friedrich Hölderlin and Paul Celan, for example. And thus the monetization of the Other also affects what Wallace Stevens called "the momentous world of poetry."

Consequently the soteriological bonds between the guru and the student take on an idiosyncratic power within the family of the numinous. Considering the proposition Student:Teacher = Poet:Poem, we get an idea of another aspect of the reach of that power when we compare it with ordinary anxieties about the possibility of betrayal in our most intimate relationships. Such anxieties are almost inescapable within the partial reciprocities of relational self-surrender. But we can usually deal with the voltage of these mundane, quotidian concerns; there is a more painful apprehension, the fear that we might become the recipients of the venom of teacherly mishandling. There's much to elicit our acute concern in the momentous world of spiritual practice, a concern that constant reevaluation of authority patterns in spiritual communities would do a lot to allay.

Time after time, and turn following upon turn, we stagger through psychological and spiritual modalities, not too clear about which aspects of which relationships are subsumed in which modality. No issue remains so vexing as the shifting understandings of the functions of psychotherapy or psychoanalysis on the one hand and, on the other, of the quiddities of spiritual work. The teacher is a "spiritual friend"; many hours of deep perturbation attest to the ambiguous nature of our sense of such a function. Such hours attest to our willing suspension of withdrawal from pain in the service of our growing sense of wonder at the embodyings of our unsuspected possibilities.

We're often taught—and we often come to believe that we understand—that the achievement of the state of true studenthood depends upon the capacity to transcend the unenlightened fear of pain, the capacity to experience the workings of faith, grace, and seminal confusion. We think of Milarepa, who was able in his cave to dispel the demons of the mind, seeing that they were merely the demons of the mind. Thus we know that skeptical questioning may help to protect against some disease.

Item—Sometimes what we had finally come to accept as our own projection upon the teacher yields to the realization that our dark mind-edgers had some merit.

Item—The dark hints are the projections of the subject.

Item—The student considers himself "thingified" by his teacher.

Item—It's frightening to be a student.

Item—To be a student requires courage.

Item—It's crucial to find the right teacher.

Item—It's extraordinarily difficult to find the right teacher, more difficult than finding the true lover.

Item—Finding the right teacher, though absolutely crucial, may be impossible.

Item—The teacher, like the unrealized but latent state of the poem, attracts the devotion to the *uncanny*.

Item—Freedom is a necessary condition of studenthood.

Item—The teacher is transparent.

Item—The student experiences the teacher as opaque until he no longer needs to do so.

Item—Thus the teacher is the object of all the student's projections.

Item—But the teacher, being transparent, is not responsible for the student's projections.

Item—The teacher might be contributing to the process eventuating in some of the student's projections.

Item—The teacher is not a psychoanalyst.

Item—The student should not conflate spiritual and psychoanalytic functions.

Item—The student must come to recognize the teacher's idiosyncracies.

Item—A spiritual community rarely furnishes the means for differen-
tiating between the teacher's idiosyncracies and his spiritual
function.

Item—The teacher identifies the student's realization and authenticates
the student's realization.

Zen, like poetry, stresses that ultimately all conceptions are misconceptions—which is not to say there is something "wrong" with conceiv-
ing, but that a hammerlock on an idea serves neither process nor the
growing perception of the boundedness of ideas. Misconceptions contrast with embodiments, incarnations, findings. The faith that moves
mountains is implicated in the appearance of poems and also invents the
teacher; we live among others, and our lives are a compound of ever-new
appreciations relating to the blessings of confusion, to trust, to aloneness,
and to the nature of the "real," the naming of which undoes presence.
One of the powers of Buddhism, like that of Blake and Marx, is its
insistent signaling of the human tropism toward reification and of the
suffering this tendency generates.

TABLET XVII

*'Ahanarshi's trip': this tablet seems to belong to the familiar anecdotal
homiletic genre, though the personal presence, in combination with an almost surreal texture, makes me suspect the intrusion of a relatively recent
hand. An archetype of spiritual friendship does pervade the text, some of
whose quality arrives at later refinements in Judeo-Christianity.*

Ahanarshi . . . . in the Teacher's room . . . . Ahanarshi
+ + + + + + + + for the Teacher . . . . interview
Ahanarshi +
and the vibrations of Ahanarshi's water body were tempest
Ahanarshi did a headstand to [homogenize] his fluids, he used
the [meditation-pillow] to prop himself up on, he sat
in the lotus flower,* Ahanarshi, at the feet of the Teacher

*etymology unclear: may signify a growth, perhaps
a position*

for the space of a meal,* the straggles of his hair [set ablaze]

commonly taken as ½ hour

Ahanarshi, by the Teacher, gently by the Teacher.

Buzz of a fly, buzz of a fly, random visits to the wine cask
Ahanarshi wanted to talk, wanted . . . .
wanted + + + + + + + + + + + + + + + + + but settled; he slid
into [himself], turquoise vase,
dust pieces strike him, Ahanarshi, his crystal body
gong . . . . sea-wind of the double flutes
Ahanarshi sees his heart is a frost-cake, he sees his heart, the smell
of low-tide decay invades his rust nostrils, he inhales
aroma of singed hair he shudders with pleasure in his throat
. . . . + + + + + + + + he, stiff as a penis, prone on the river belly
sees inside to the shoal of sea-robins and flounders and porgies
which never bump, Ahanarshi sees them never touch,
cold under the chocolate river; his head turns warm, he tells
well among the [species] he tells well a while and telling
bewilders . . . . . rage . . . . blows of phlegm into his fat throat
. . . . rest + + + + + + + + + + + + + + + + + + +
is it clear is it clear are you enveloping, Ahanarshi, are you,
or riding at the quiet of an envelopment?
the arced right foot cramps. drive of ice-pins
in the cave behind the left knee. He says, 'pain, pain'
Ahanarshi says 'pain, pain' he reenters his activity
he is present Ahanarshi no longer concentrating now he hears
air circulating in and out of the Teacher he splinters into a mine
of blue-green flints it is clear thousands of painful wisps
ride him, tiny throats, the Teacher says:
                    'we will work together'
The Teacher says 'we will work together'
the single mind . . . . to discover* the Teacher

                    * *invent?*

        [   ] *suggested by the scholar/translator*

    I think I've been playing out the great games of self-definition and
identifying-the-task not only between myself and the teacher but also
between myself and the poem-as-teacher. After the first few years, as the
circle within which Trungpa Rinpoche carried on his salutary work ex-
panded, his students saw him less and less as his activities required increasing travel; Glassman Sensei, on the other hand, lived within the Zen
Community; he was readily available to his students. I understand the
universality of and the need for plurilogue, but it's clearer to me now
why my decisions did not crucially involve either the physical availability

or nonavailability of my two primary teachers. (Of course, the teacher need not appear in a physical manifestation. Gershom Sholem says of the great Jewish mystic the Baal Shem Tov, that the only spiritual guide he ever alluded to was the prophet Ahijah of Shiloh, with whom he was in constant spiritual and visionary contact.)

What's the locus of the undoing, the great work of undoing spiritual and societal cliché? Where does the heavy work of the undoing take place? It takes place significantly in the poet's apprehensions of thought coverings and the formulaic, his koan-work. Where are the centers of formulas and the comforts of shared root generalizations? Where should the poet be? What is the nature of the ideal community within which he may freely and flexibly discover? What is the nature of addiction? "Addicts are desperate," says Jungian analyst Marian Woodman. "They have a fierce energy."

> a. Draw the line around the addict. b. Draw the line around the communicant. c. Show the distinctions between the two drawings. d. Explain.

Buddhism does not embody Christianity's eschatological and apocalyptic historicity. And thus, as Gary Snyder has argued, and as contemporary Buddhist groups such as the Buddhist Peace Fellowship now implicitly affirm, the consciousness of social service and the urgent sense of the need for social change—which are the mercy of Christianity—embody paradigmatic lessons for Buddhist practitioners and communities. (And here I bracket the enormous problems involved in the workings-out of a nondualistic ethics.) Even though Buddhist thought does have its own nirvanic version of Stop the World I Want to Get Off at the End of Time, Buddhist teachings have nonetheless conferred upon contemporary poetics a radiating boon.

In the field of Buddhist teachings, by means of what James Hillman calls "soul-work," we glimpse a way of being-in-poetry that bypasses the temptations both of solipsism and of a complex modern agenda, that which points toward a reconstruction of the reflexive, centripetal, narcissistic dance of the postromantic, which relates more closely to the postmodern than is usually conceived. The particular nature of Buddhist teachings partly manifests for our time through the creative denudations of deconstruction and phenomenology. The prereflective, which from the time of Heraclitus has been the realization-object of numberless poets endlessly releasing enervating language showers upon the parched fields of the self, can't exist as a self-target. The prereflective exists only as the poet experiences the abyss, paradoxically both factitious and unbridgeable, between words and things. The poet, in transit through those parched fields of self, finally learns to depend on neither poems for life nor, out of anger and frustration under the influence of the powerful half-light of the Rimbauds of our tradition, to despise our poems because they're not themselves the world.

The Vajrasattva meditation serves as paradigm for poetry. In greatly simplified presentation it involves the following sequence: the meditator first visualizes, an arrow's length above his head, the figure of a particular bodhisattva seated on top of a lotus with one hundred thousand petals, the stem of which comes down through the top of the meditator's head to a depth of four finger-widths. The visualized body is nonobstructively apparent, a rainbow, diaphanous. Between the bodhisattva and his consort, who is seated upon his thighs, a flat moon disc floats, overlaid by a long mantra written in small, cold, fine white hairs. The meditator's repetition of the mantra causes the words to melt like ice. The white nectar flows through the sexual nexus of the bodhisattva and his consort, passes through the lotus and down its stem into the meditator's head and body. The nectar cleanses as it travels through the crystallizing body of the meditator. The two visualized figures melt into light and dissolve into the meditator.

He becomes the two figures.

At his heart a tiny moon disk, the size of a flat mustard seed, manifests five short mantras in different colors, each emanating rays of light. Like sunlight in darkness, the rays transform and purify the six realms of suffering. The meditator's body dissolves into the letters, which sequentially dissolve into each other and finally disappear into clear space. The nature of these interrelations and of these transformations is the nature of poetry.

TABLET XXIV

no wisdom no ice no forest no segment no foolishness no cave no knowledge

harmony of rabid openness and + + + + + + + + + + + + the cities sigh under the fullness of too much [heavy cream]. I + + + + + + + + +

the ruminant anxiety that the old question
is the new question. among the craftsmen I busy myself
among the veins, identifying ores, laughing
with the tailings. underneath the bed of brilliant metal families
another *underneath,* as well as another *below*
below my anger about the ridiculousness
of trying to remember . . . . such a delight . . . . . . a light
. . . . . + + + this continuous attention a form of plant, emptiness
of wind, speed beyond speed, form of wind, such weary conviction
+ + + as if to walk inside one's own uniform were one's uniform.
the musical cities, born again and again
in the sky which is always the sky, ribbed and partly bodied by
   cloud holes
like sudden bright mines . . . .
inside* their own tones . . . .

   **perhaps 'on the side of.' In fact, conceivably 'outside.' This term*
on occasion refers to its opposite.

the native good, the native star, the native dust, the native prince
of his own ore as if a righteous handmaid of the world's house
had brought the ibex home to all homes . . . . . . what joy if the
   birth-giving veins
and the tailings were all rapt inside an unfixable slow sound of
                                   themselves . . . . no
unlikeness. brilliance in the dead ochre ground, alluvial and alive or
bright mind of the particular in ores . . . . + + + + ... sharing
strains of going and returning with the host
+ + + + + + + in this way to love the clear light as if from the light.
so the origin of the moment of seeing fills my mind every second
+ + + + + + + + + + + fills my moment . . . .
like darkness . . . . . . brilliant ochre ground . . . .
the unextractable ores in the unreachable vein are nevertheless my
   sweetness*

         **'craftsman,'/'host,'/ 'my sweetness,'/ 'my anger.'*
('sweetness' in one questionable archaic locus has been taken
as 'consciousness.') I really find the texture of the narrator's
persona increasingly puzzling and strongly suspect later accretions to ac-
count for characterological inconsistencies and philosophic opacities; the
original from which this Tablet was transcribed has disappeared from the
museum at Ferney; was a palimpsest?

seeing darkness every time for the first time*

> * unusual adverbial coinage, 'infantly'; probably in the abstract
> sense of 'firstly.' Very rarely, 'seldom.'

....
.... that I saw, a reed hut for instance,
a carefully woven black net, four-winged flies, products of
   resinous trees,
say the cypress, giš*, lapis, diorite and firestone .... as if

> * giš, 'wod,' used to determine the names of trees, shrubs and
> objects made of wood; though a determinative, used alone here. The signi-
> fication of giš is extremely intricate; it generally occurs before the names of
> almost every conceivable utensil and implement into whose composition the
> least piece of wood could have entered. Weapons are almost invariably
> designated by giš, although wood could not have entered extensively into
> their composition. Cf. ugiš, 'nerve,' 'light.'

standing on top of the minute point and with it + + + + + + + +
circulation + + + + + + + + + sky-veins, and very slowly with
   many other people

threads

> through the Denkoroku, records of the transmission of the light

The forest floor is white
the sparrow touches
down, finds the bread crust in the snow
bamboo leaves fall only in May and June

his heart beats like a ferryboat
between two islands, endless
dream of docking

why do you apply mathematics
to your pain
as if the turtle in a warm haze of spring
evades its shell

the two fat inmates on the bridge
are hoping for rain
the self-confident guards
try to tell the weather apart
one and one and one and one

although the understory of the woods is white
you apply three, nine, thirty-three
to your pain

do you think they are one and one or perhaps one
like the observant healers
who try to tell the feeling apart

his heart beats between
an endless dream of docking
and the idea of number
does the turtle choose between itself?

no islands—or is it
no continents? in and out
as if an eye
breathed

to be clear about this, with
with no place to be clear from . . .
might as well call yesterday's lentil soup
tomorrow, what's left is
one is left. no words. no book.

having arrived at this no-place
you see how the adjectiveless world
in its practice
can't see itself
as its attributes. such
nonesuch. o bright crust
of snow unseparable
magic show

Larry Smith

Larry Smith grew up in the industrial Ohio Valley. Except for a year as Fulbright Lecturer in Sicily, he has always lived in Ohio, where he is professor of English and Humanities at Firelands College of Bowling Green State University and editor of Bottom Dog Press. His fifth book of poetry is *Ohio Zen Poems: Inside the Garden* (Bottom Dog Press, 1989).

Waves

The way a man carries luggage . . .
hands gripping, arms arched,
his steps bending forward
as if nothing were wrong.

The way a woman waits tables . . .
eyes attentive, quiet smile,
her setting things gently
her reaching to serve.

Whatever it is, it is doing—
not this looking out windows,
not this waiting for trains—
the umbrella out in the rain.

Fall Melon

I cut into the melon / feel it
open in the air / feel cool moisture
on my palm / again I slice / again

the fresh heart broken for you. Vines

forget themselves turn garden brown
in the full fall sun. We eat the ripeness
that we've found, turn the earth again each spring.

In my daughter's hair a leaf.
Trees climb inside us ring for ring.

Zen Garden

Sitting under the magnolia
I unfold the morning's news
across my lap.
The sun blinds the words
as birds talk inside the leaves
of other worlds than these.
Branches bend with dew
as page after page this
paper life falls through.

I turn to watch tomato plants
as they ripen, and a yellow moth
lands inside the green.
We and the plants share the air
become each other's lives.
I let my eyes go shut.
The air is tender here
before machines cut the grass
like this news cuts me.

Is there loving a world I can't understand
that denies this world I see?
I turn back to face the light
so strong I melt into the day
knowing this internal weather
goes on this way forever.

Seeing

The mirror is formless
Original nothingness
On which no dust settles.
              —Eno

The dead gull
beside the dusky road . . .
becomes a corn husk
as I pass.

That huge rock
along the sunny berm . . .
is the dried carcass
of a dead raccoon.

My hands become leaves
turning through sun.

Your lips, petals,
give birth to your tongue.

Like the wind we are turning—
inside as we climb.

Immersion

(*for Alan Watts*)

I step inside the stream of sky
   flowing blood beneath the skin
   texture of water
   liquid skeleton
   the gravity of wind
   within the flame

I think of markings in the jade
   wood grains
   birdsong of leaves
   inside the rain
   the smell of river

Till I hear myself listen, turn
   feel wet soap slipping through my hand.

Gary Snyder

Gary Snyder lived in Japan for many years. He practices in the Linji Ch'an tradition. He has written many books of prose and poetry. For the last twenty years he has been in the northern Sierra Nevada. He teaches at the University of California at Davis every spring.

Riprap

Lay down these words
Before your mind like rocks.
   placed solid, by hands
In choice of place, set
Before the body of the mind
   in space and time:
Solidity of bark, leaf, or wall
   riprap of things:
Cobble of milky way,
   straying planets,
These poems, people,
   lost ponies with
Dragging saddles—
   and rocky sure-foot trails.
The worlds like an endless
   four-dimensional
Game of *Go*.
   ants and pebbles
In the thin loam, each rock a word
   a creek-washed stone
Granite: ingrained

> with torment of fire and weight
Crystal and sediment linked hot
> all change, in thoughts,
As well as things.

Hunting

16.

How rare to be born a human being!
Wash him off with cedar-bark and milkweed
> send the damned doctors home.
Baby, baby, noble baby
Noble-hearted baby

One hand up, one hand down
"I alone am the honored one"
Birth of the Buddha.
And the whole world-system trembled.
"If that baby really said that,
I'd cut him up and throw him to the dogs!"

said Chao-chou the Zen Master. But
Chipmunks, gray squirrels, and
Golden-mantled ground squirrels
> brought him each a nut.
Truth being the sweetest of flavors.

Girls would have in their arms
A wild gazelle or wild wolf-cubs
And give them their white milk,
> those who had new-born infants home
Breasts still full.
Wearing a spotted fawnskin
> sleeping under trees
> bacchantes, drunk
On wine or truth, what you will,
Meaning: compassion.
Agents: man and beast, beasts
Got the buddha-nature
All but
Coyote.

Song of the Taste

Eating the living germs of grasses
Eating the ova of large birds

    the fleshy sweetness packed
    around the sperm of swaying trees

The muscles of the flanks and thighs of
        soft-voiced cows
    the bounce in the lamb's leap
    the swish in the ox's tail

Eating roots grown swoll
        inside the soil

Drawing on life of living
    clustered points of light spun
        out of space
hidden in the grape.

Eating each other's seed
        eating
  ah, each other.

Kissing the lover in the mouth of bread:
        lip to lip.

Without

the silence
of nature
within.

the power within.
the power

without.

the path is whatever passes—no
end in itself.

the end is,
grace—ease—

healing,
not saving.

singing
the proof

the proof of the power within.

For Nothing

Earth a flower
A phlox on the steep
slopes of light
hanging over the vast
solid spaces
small rotten crystals;
salts.

Earth a flower
by a gulf where a raven
flaps by once
a glimmer, a color
forgotten as all
falls away.

A flower
for nothing;
an offer;
no taker;

Snow-trickle, feldspar, dirt.

As for Poets

As for poets
The Earth Poets
Who write small poems,
Need help from no man.

O

The Air Poets
Play out the swiftest gales
And sometimes loll in the eddies.
Poem after poem,
Curling back on the same thrust.

O

At fifty below
Fuel oil won't flow
And propane stays in the tank.
Fire Poets
Burn at absolute zero
Fossil love pumped back up.

O

The first
Water Poet
Stayed down six years.
He was covered with seaweed.
The life in his poem
Left millions of tiny
Different tracks
Criss-crossing through the mud.

O

With the Sun and Moon
In his belly,
The Space Poet
Sleeps.
No end to the sky—
But his poems,
Like wild geese,
Fly off the edge.

O

A Mind Poet
Stays in the house.
The house is empty
And it has no walls.
The poem
Is seen from all sides,
Everywhere,
At once.

Little Songs for Gaia

18.

THE FLICKERS
　sharp clear call
　　THIS!
　　THIS!
　　THIS!
in the cool pine breeze

20.

I am sorry I disturbed you.

I broke into your house last night
To use the library.
There were some things I had to look up;
A large book fell
　　　　and knocked over others.
Afraid you'd wake and find me
and be truly alarmed
　　　　　　　　I left
Without picking up.

I got your name from the mailbox
As I fled, to write you and explain.

Surrounded by Wild Turkeys

Little calls　　as they pass
　through dry forbs and grasses
Under blue oak and gray digger pine
In the warm afternoon of the forest-fire haze;

Twenty or more, long-legged birds
　all alike.

So are we, In our soft calling,
　passing on through.

Our young, which trail after,

Look just like us.

　4 IX 87, for the teachings of the wild turkey flock

Raven's Beak River at the End

Doab of the Tatshenshini river and the Alsek lake, a long spit of
gravel, one clear day after days on the river in the rain, the
    glowing
sandy slopes of Castilleia blooms & little fox tracks in the
    mooseprint swales,
& giant scoops of dirt took out by bears around the lupine
roots, at early light a rim of snowy mountains and the ice
fields slanting back for miles, I find my way

To the boulders
    on the gravel   in the flowers
At the end of the glacier
    two ravens
Sitting on a boulder
    carried by the glacier
Left on the gravel
    resting in the flowers
At the end of the ice age
    show me the way
To a place to sit
    in a hollow on a boulder
Looking east, looking south
    ear in the river
Running just behind me
    nose in the grasses
Vetch roots scooped out
    by the bears in the gravels
Looking up the ice slopes
    ice plains, rock-fall
Brush line, dirt sweeps
    on the ancient river
Blue queen   floating in
    ice lake, ice throne   end of a glacier
Looking north
    up the dancing river
Where it turns into a glacier
    under stairsteps of ice falls
Green streaks of alder
    climb the mountain knuckles
Interlaced with snowfields
    foamy water falling

Salmon weaving river
  bear flower   blue sky singer
As the raven leaves her boulder
  flying over flowers
Raven-sitting high spot
  ear in the river,   eyes on the snowpeaks,
Nose of the morning
  raindrops in the sunshine
Skin of sunlight
  skin of chilly gravel
Mind in the mountains, mind of tumbling water,
  mind running rivers,
Mind of weaving
  flowers in the gravels
At the end of the ice age
  we are the bears, are the ravens, are the salmon
In the gravel
  at the end of an ice age

Growing on the gravels
  at the end of a glacier
Flying off alone
  flying off alone
  flying off alone
Off alone

               Mountains and Rivers Without End
               Tatshenshini/Alsek
               Lake

The Bear Mother

She veils herself
  to speak of eating salmon
Teases me with
"What do you know of my ways"
And kisses me through the mountain

Through and under its layers, its
        gullies, its folds;
Her mouth full of blueberries,
We share.

Brooks Range
VIII:86

At White River Roadhouse in the Yukon

For Gary Holthaus

At White River Roadhouse in the Yukon
A bell rings in the late night:
A lone car on the Alaska highway
Hoping to buy gas at the shut roadhouse.

For a traveler sleeping in a little room
The bell ring is a temple in Japan,
In dream I put on robes and sandals
Chant sutras in the chilly Buddha-hall.

Ten thousand miles of White Spruce taiga.
The roadhouse master wakes to the night bell
Enters the dark of ice and stars,
To sell the car some gas.

Piute Creek

One granite ridge
A tree, would be enough
Or even a rock, a small creek,
A bark shred in a pool.
Hill beyond hill, folded and twisted
Tough trees crammed
In thin stone fractures
A huge moon on it all, is too much.
The mind wanders. A million
Summers, night air still and the rocks
Warm. Sky over endless mountains.
All the junk that goes with being human
Drops away, hard rock wavers
Even the heavy present seems to fail
This bubble of a heart.
Words and books
Like a small creek off a high ledge
Gone in the dry air.

A clear, attentive mind
Has no meaning but that
Which sees is truly seen.
No one loves rock, yet we are here.
Night chills. A flick
In the moonlight
Slips into Juniper shadow:
Back there unseen
Cold proud eyes
Of Cougar or Coyote
Watch me rise and go.

Will Staple

Will Staple is a founding member of what would later become Ring of Bone Zendo. He lives and writes in the northern Sierra Nevada.

Who's a Buddhist?

I suppose the guys wearing the square cloths around their necks are the Buddhists. I'm a sitter, I wear robes in the *zendo,* lead Buddhists and non-Buddhists in *sesshin* and am delighted with my koan practice. There are a limited number of wrong answers to seemingly insoluble riddles, and the insight experience and progressive content of the riddles replicate the experience of "Buddha," the savvy and spirit of the fully illuminated one who touches beings and saves them.

Meaning no disrespect, but don't Buddhists have a purity trip? Buddha's bigger than they are. I don't think this is full realization. There's a trace of difference between themselves and perfection. Coyotes don't. They aren't attached to a limited human viewpoint. They don't give a pussy willow about setting themselves apart.

It's like poetry, you've got to want it so bad you'll give up everything, you'll even, finally, give up your own blindness and shortsightedness, you'll even get out of your own way and give in to the groundlessness of inconceivable being. You've got to want it so bad you'll give up wanting it and do it, nothing else matters, all of me right here, attention focused, awareness increasing to psychedelic intensity and brilliance. It's not a trance state; it's a birthright.

That's where the breath comes in. Gently aware, watch it awake.

When people suppose me to be a Buddhist, I leave them with their suppositions. I did not say, "No, I, Coyote, sweat and sing. The old Indians know me at the sweat, you can ask them if you don't believe me." I give instruction in procedure, method, detailed fine-tuned "how to be a buddha," but I don't know if I ever urged anyone to believe in a

Buddha bigger than their own potential. If I did that, it would be worship, it would be Buddhism, not "being Buddha." I know I'm repeating this differentiation.

You could call me anything, really, and support it with assumptions, suppositions, limited human viewpoints, axes to grind, petty justifications for your own miserable suffering.

I don't mean to be impolite to the Buddhists among you. I admire the prescientific psychology, the perfection of posture, and the koan system. The dharma of truth cannot be limited to a 2,000- or 2,500-year-old "religion." For 800,000 years feelings have been drawn with words into images. *The body unfettered has a health shared with all. This is the savage religion.*

Maybe nonviolence is Buddhist, but I was sure glad I had that frying pan when the bear was trying to come upstairs on the ladder. I don't kill because an old Indian woman told me that to be a poet, I should try to stay on the living side of the line. "I understand." "How?" she asked me. "It's like a sleeping man who, in the middle of the night, reaches behind his head for his pillow," I said. "Yes," she said, "when you have nothing on your mind the animals will try to communicate with you."

Don't lower your head to linger in thought, trying to figure it out with the intellect. When myriad visions appear in profusion, look upon them without being moved: this can be called accomplishment without accomplishment, effortless power; when mind and things are both forgotten, nature is real.

Raven

I knew her down near Sonoma State
smell of fields and trees, in a fixed-up chicken coop
so the windows were a little low
shy to her assured poise
it got hard to breathe near her quiet eyes
      or at least breath harder
the windows were open to cool off
we were sitting on her bed
she had long black hair, black expectant eyes
she was talking quietly
and her voice had a soft musical quality

she was calmly telling me truths about myself
nothing a hand or face or star date would tell her
but with real concern
getting right down to where my blood pounded
my heart to feel my life as I do
calling my shots and telling me who I was.

She looked at me in a way irresistible
a promise of everything satisfying
                religious and erotic
I looked at her in a trance of lust
my eyes sort of crossed and my mouth crooked
she blew in my face
and puffed out her chest
somewhere I saw feathers
and remembered something like this
"we'll do it your way, I want to do it
like you deep down want to do it"
"you're an enchanted creature?" I asked
for the first time suspecting I was in a dream
"yes, coyote" her head made a birdlike gesture
ducking under her hair like a shoulder of wing
"I'm Raven,"
she smiled confidently
"and I'm going to make you rave."

nanao speaking

in desert cave, so light, so strong.   far
from moving graveyard—vast ghost town
visited by millions of weekend tourists
                one last time

Had i the chance; priests
for calm end of survival; faint
when realizing how far is left to walk.

motionless in trance, open-eyed coma,
      no consciousness.   my spirit listening,
leaves me   vacant   to soar   so far—

goodby people civilization roles actors,
goodby future goodby life, there is no life.
only;   Bright silence of the sun.

          Fasting;
completely stop outside . . . try by yourself,
from inside; then you see whole world
(not small part the "agents" display
"we are content cause it doesn't seem worthwhile
to get ahead of anybody"
so suffer the same   limitations as they.)

to cut off all desire; that is biggest desire
    ("possible to disen*chant* yourself
        by indulgence to grow more tired?")

need so strong inner demand
        you can't have desire.
                    cleaning,
cleansing power, desire comes up at first
but such a power   changing to cleansing power—
you become desire itself
then you forget desire, you are nothing.
no life, no future, no like or dislike,
no individuality;
if you have desire
                you have individuality
but if you have no more desire
                you are no more individual.

God is silence, keeps always silence
mt. stream bubbling—carrying down to ocean,
emptiness and eternity same ocean,
emptying to emptiness, giving more—easily,
        learning to give more easy.

Neither the speaker nor the spoken, the seer not the seen nor any discrimination whatsoever

the hopalong cassidy pocket watch hangs at the right time
the old glass in the east, the only window
casts wavering light on the bare board floor

the door bangs
the 5 gallons of leaking water are on the porch
the fly is ignored because it is not a mosquito
the water in the quart jar is good
the smoke rolling is put off
every possession cries to be hung up
the walls crack
the candle burns, the sun rises
the shade lasts
the ant is only a scout and will not find
a dirty bowl.

Mudra

    She who turns you on   in the
right direction, lites you up, makes you
interested, interesting
    any moment of concentration
potency, poignancy, poise.

    up a steep thicket of
manzanita, poison oak, oak
all grown together   sweating
    the deer can get thru
so so can you, always   fair
    even if she's hard, climbing
a rock face   can be done
even if there's only one way
step by step, just.

    the lover who brought you thru
ecstasy seven times one morning
and who was never seen again.

Charles Stein

Charles Stein currently teaches part-time at Bard College and has Buddhist affiliations with the Kalu Rinpoche center, Karme Thubten Choling, the Tsegyalgar Dzogchen Community, and the Kwan Um Zen School. Recent publications include *A Night of Thought* (St. Lazare, 1989) and *The Secret of the Black Chrysanthemum: The Poetic Cosmology of Charles Olson and His Use of the Writings of C. G. Jung* (Clinamen Studies, 1987). He is also editor of *Being = Space × Action: Searches for Freedom of Mind Through Mathematics, Art, and Mysticism.*

I think I began being interested in interfering with my own mind states almost as early in my life as I began wanting to be a writer. That is, before I could write. Swinging pocket watches at the ends of chains to hypnotize myself and others. Attempting to stun the mind into silence by various attitudes.

I began writing poetry at about the same time I began to learn about Buddhist meditation activities—around 1958—first from a TV show where a Burmese boy spoke about the nonexistence of the world, or something like that.

So in general, for me, processes of mind and processes of writing developed concurrently.

I could list Dharma topics and their poetics correlates, but for the most part, as a Buddhist friend remarked, my work is a gloss on *shunyata, sTong-pa*—emptiness:

> *shunyata*—and the notion that a poem has a syntactic space
> *shunyata*—and the notion that a poem's assertions are hypotheticals

shunyata—and the evanescence of meaning, the materiality of language, or the real time subtending the flow of speech
shunyata—and the chasm between the word and its referent
shunyata—and the codependent origination of all linguistic occasions
shunyata—and the imaginative realm where events can shift erratically because radically disjunct from a cosmos of consensual norms while at the same time (and almost in the same utterance) application can occur of a universe of daily fact because those same events are radically inseparable from a cosmos of consensual norms
shunyata—and the incapacity to fix a stable self—hence the multiplicity of voices or identities—this as a fact of the poetry—it speaks with many voices—but also as a subject matter—the self as multiple
shunyata—and the unreliability of objects, their lack of entitativeness

O

In my poems I allow a free disordering of the larger spaces of the poem: there could be various sorts of disjunctions in content, reference, voice. The inner topology of syntactic space should crackle and bruise, but whether or not it has utterly succumbed must seem to await a decision not yet promulgated. This disordering, however, is usually extra-sentential rather than with respect to the intrasentential syntactical matrix. Most of my sentences or fragments sound like someone is actually saying or thinking or writing them.

This is a predilection I have encouraged in myself mainly to preserve the sense that in my poems the disruption of discourse is *not* being performed as a permutation of lexical or syntactical possibilities, concocted from outside the process of the emergence of language in a thinking mind (however much language and the history of poetry determine the range of lexical and syntactic forms, however much these forms determine the possibilities of "thoughts," and however much "thought" and language are therefore "historical").

O

Someone asked me after a week-long retreat in a winter cabin, did I think poetry helped anybody. I said I was sure it must since it certainly does a lot of people harm.

Once, a boy suffering through horrible cures for leukemia told me after a reading that one of my poems had made him laugh for the first time in a year.

The claim that the "ethical responsibility" of the public writer entails responsibility for the implications of the formal character of his or her means has been articulated often enough, but in the context of a Buddhist ethics, what does this mean?

To claim that such responsibility should be understood as an intent toward the enlightenment of all sentient beings is probably harmless, and I avow such an intention.

I also avow thoughts as above, regarding the analogies between disruptive literary events and the perspectives of *shunyata*.

But whatever the analogues between my verbal machinations and my attempts to practice Buddhism, I do not claim my poems project enlightened states of writing, emitted to purify and liberate a public domain. To do so would be to claim attainment of the end of a process currently being undergone. Nevertheless, according to the teachings of (for instance) the Great Perfection, the enlightened state is not only to be attained at the temporal denouement of one's spiritual endeavors. For the practitioner it is considered to inhere through all one's mental, energic, and somatic acts. And not only for the practitioner. It is therefore not impossible that some color of the goal transmit itself even through the writings of one who lays no claim to personal realization.

O

I think I want my mind to be loose. Precise, but loose. Perspicacious, but free from fixity. Indomitable, but without assertion. A quality of something unperturbed, but without relying on any personal quality to construct such a quality. And that the poem should shake loose the fixities of others. Or bind and ground the volatilities. Create perplexities of a genial kind. Suggest the unavoidable disturbances. It should be permissible to be quite disturbed. The famous large field in which a raging bull (blue or otherwise) harmlessly conducts himself.

from theforestforthetrees

I

in the middle of the music   (meaning

this little patch of time I
happen to pass by in

Imagine a space vehicle   manned by Name Alone

I have forgotten the number they gave me
and now my name becomes vague to me

I try to catch it as it passes
in a costly limousine

The clothes I wear won't give me away—
the voices I muster to speak to the master . . .

2

These people are cats
at the door   all   summer
seeking
status   among the   other
cats that
LIVE here   cats that
know that   they belong

and the evening
sky's   hay-colored   light
glowed   in the sheep's coat

3

In a party of friends and acquaintances
suddenly a small
cat comes
close to me and
starts to speak.

It says that I
have been mistaken
about its nature.
Of *course* cats speak.

I try to tell everyone
but obstructions
block our conversation

    O

A long necked cat accuses me.

There is scratching and cat meowls
of a violent and distressing kind:
cats attacking human throats!

I am a Cat Killer
and one of the worst!

(People will know I am crazy
but there's no escape
from cats'
howling, scratching
and speaking in terrible whispers
                    all night
                            everywhere (!

4

The sound "ite" as in "bite"
now.

Bite now.

    O

I threw the black crow claw away, hating evil—
not even wanting
to possess the tainted object

And therefore request
a settlement regarding
the lexical item "BEYOND" vis:

    That posit that acts as a gland
    to secrete our secrets.

      "Beyond the nature of the giraffe
      a beast with just that nature
      lopes towards sundown."

"Beyond the causes that conspired to land us here
a living monument of its own exclusion
flames at the heart of the day."

And no boat exists
    to skim the quiet harbor surface long enough
        to skim the quiet harbor surface long enough

      I have good teeth.

      They shine
            like Mice.

Giant Noises
    hide in the Toad's Sky

5

      That
      dog
      is
      at
      least
      one
      half not
      dog

6

      That
      Ape
      men thought
      to talk
      sign talk to

      thought him-
      self a
      man to
      talk to

7

The cat at the top of the stars has
a serious look in his loungey eyes as
I climb the stairs and confute him.

8

My hat vanished.

When that cat that
sat up looked straight at it

that hat had had it.

9

Moments of mind reflected in moments of language
scorching white paper—
"The Language of Lights"
and the world.

[Your reading so massive so curious—
        white doves spring from your hands]

And did I detect a tremor in the voice of the wise one who
                                        whispered:

        "It does not die"?

The dark halls
pure as space
        horses
                marching across Paradise

and the marks left by their hooves in the muddy turf
were "read" by the sages of that area

        and there was an effort on the part
of some of us to resume
a space in which discussion might
be possible among the learned
persons having mastered after
centuries the methods
appropriate to the text

and our pleasures passed into the manifest universe

Lucien Stryk

Lucien Stryk has published widely in the fields of poetry and Buddhist scholarship. Collections of his poems include *Collected Poems, 1953–1983* (Swallow/Ohio University Press, 1984), *Bells of Lombardy* (Northern Illinois University Press, 1986), and *Of Pen and Ink and Paper Scraps* (Swallow/Ohio University Press, 1989). He has brought out two spoken albums on Folkways Records; a book of interviews, *Encounter with Zen: Writings on Poetry and Zen* (Swallow/Ohio University Press, 1982); and, among other translations, *On Love and Barley: Haiku of Basho* (Penguin, 1985) *Triumph of the Sparrow: Zen Poems of Shinkichi Takahashi* (University of Illinois Press, 1986), and *The Dumpling Field: Haiku of Issa* (Swallow/Ohio University Press, 1991). He is also editor of *World of the Buddha: An Introduction to Buddhist Literature* (Grove Press, 1982). With the late Takashi Ikemoto he translated *Zen Poems of China and Japan: The Crane's Bill* (Grove Press, 1981) and *The Penguin Book of Zen Poetry* (Penguin, 1977), which received the Islands and Continents Translation Award and the Society of Midland Authors Poetry Award. He has received fellowships from the National Endowment for the Arts, the National Translation Center, and the Ford and Rockefeller Foundations. He has held a Fulbright travel/research grant and two visiting lectureships in Japan, and currently holds a Research Professorship at Northern Illinois University, where he teaches Asian literature and poetry.

Death of a Zen Poet:
Shinkichi Takahashi (1901–1987)

It was one of those moments one stands outside one's body, staring at the silhouette, dumbstruck, not wanting to believe words coming in. The phoned message from Japan was that the greatest modern Zen poet had died. I waited for the eulogies, a voice to cry out at the passing of a man who made fresh visions of the world, made wild and powerful music out of anything: shells, knitting, peaches, an airplane passing between his legs, the sweet-sour smell coming from a cemetery of unknown soldiers, the crab of memory crawling up a woman's thigh, a sparrow whose stir can move the universe. A man who showed that things loved or despised were, when all's said and done, as important and unimportant as each other. But all was silence as I looked out, hoping for a cloud of his beloved sparrows bearing his karma wheel around the earth.

I realized that he might prefer it this way. Yet there remain the masterworks, his gift to us, in spite of his mixed feelings on the handing down of insight with mere words. "If we sit in Zen at all," he says in the foreword to *Afterimages,* a collection of his poems, "we must model ourselves on the Bodhidharma, who kept sitting till his buttocks grew rotten. We must have done with all words and letters, and attain Truth itself. As a follower of the tradition of Zen which is above verbalization, I must confess that I feel ashamed of writing poems and having collections of them published. My wish is that through books like this the West will awake to the Buddha's Truth. It is my belief that Buddhism will travel round the world till it will bury its old bones in the ridges of the Himalayas."

Yet, paradoxically, Shinkichi Takahashi was one of Japan's most prolific poets, greatly honored (his *Collected Poems* won the Ministry of Education's Prize for Art), thought by the Japanese to be their only poet who could properly be called a Zen poet, for his practice of the discipline was exceptionally pure. He discovered early in life that unless he grappled with the severest of the doctrine's principles he would not be living, or writing, worthily. Yet, stuffy as this sounds, there was much humor in him, as in all enlightened Zennists:

Afternoon

My hair's falling fast—
this afternoon
I'm off to Asia Minor.

The Pink Sun

White petals on the black earth,
Their scent filling her nostrils.

Breathe out and all things swell—
Breathe in, they shrink.

Let's suppose she suddenly has four legs—
That's far from fantastic.

I'll weld ox hoofs onto her feet—
Sparks of the camellia's sharp red.

Wagging her pretty little tail,
She's absorbed in kitchen work.

Look, she who just last night
Was a crone is girl again,

An alpine rose blooming on her arm.
High on a Himalayan ridge

The great King of Bhutan
Snores in the pinkest sun.

The poet, born in 1901 in a fishing village on Shikoku, smallest of Japan's four main islands, was largely self-educated, but broadly so: writing extensively on many aspects of Japanese culture, he introduced an important series of art books and had a successful career as man of letters. Not bad for one who had dropped out of high school, rushed off to Tokyo in hope of a literary career. There he contracted typhus and, penniless, landed in a charity hospital. His circumstances forced him to return to his village. But one day, fired up by a newspaper article on dadaism, he returned to Tokyo, working as a waiter in a *shiruko* restaurant (*shiruko* is red-bean soup with bits of rice cake) and as a "pantry boy" in a newspaper office.

In 1923 he brought out *Dadaist Shinkichi's Poetry*, the first copy of which was handed him through the bars of a police cell—at this time he was often in trouble for impulsive actions—and he tore it up without so much as a glance. Other collections followed, but by 1928 he knew his life was in dire need of guidance, and like many troubled artists he sought the advice of a Zen master. He could not have chosen better. Shizan Ashikaga, illustrious Rinzai Zen master of the Shogen Temple, was known to be a disciplinarian, one not likely to be impressed by a disciple's literary forays.

At first the toughness of the training proved too much. Pacing the temple corridor, he fell unconscious: when he came to, he was off his head. Later he was to write that this was inevitable, considering how completely different ascetic exercises were from his daily life and with what youthful singlemindedness he had pursued them. He was sent back to his family and virtually locked up in a small (two-mat) room for three long years. During this confinement he wrote many poems, which may have helped him to survive the ordeal and recover.

Back in Tokyo in 1932, Takahashi began attending Master Shizan Ashikaga's lectures on Zen. Shizan once cautioned him, "Attending lectures cuts no ice. Koan exercise (meditation on Zen problems set by a master) is all important." Takahashi became his disciple in 1935. During almost seventeen years of rigorous training he experienced both great hardships and exultations of satori (enlightenment). By 1951, having learned all that he could, he was given in the master's own calligraphy "The Moon-on-Water Hall," his *inka,* or testimony that he had successfully completed the full course of discipline, one of only six or seven over many years so honored by the master.

Takahashi visited Korea and China in 1939 and was deeply impressed by Zennists he met there. He lived chiefly by his writings, and in 1944 began work for a Tokyo newspaper, leaving when its office was bombed out in 1945. He married in 1951 and lived with his wife and their two daughters in great serenity, a life he scarcely could have dreamt of in his turbulent youth.

The poet had distinguished himself in many ways by the time the first translated collection of his poems, *Afterimages,* appeared (simultaneously in the United States and England in 1970) to much acclaim. A reviewer in the *Hudson Review* observed that while other poets, East and West, would appear to descend from time to time into the natural world, Takahashi would emerge from it like a seal from the depths of the sea, his constant element. But it wasn't sea or nature the poet lived in, it was Zen.

Yet that would hardly account for the appeal of his work, especially among fellow poets, throughout the world, with or without interest in Zen. He was foremost an artist. Many aestheticians have spoken of the difficulty of defining art, yet some artists have on occasion chosen to speak out, as did Tolstoy in *What Is Art?* Tolstoy identified three essential ingredients of effective art—individuality, clarity, and sincerity—and to the degree that each, in combination with the others, was present, a work could be ranked on a scale of merely acceptable to necessary. Tolstoy was a moralist in all such matters, never tired of inveighing against aesthetic notions based largely on the pleasure principle, among them "art for art's sake"—life was too serious for such twaddle.

Though as Zennist Takahashi was not inclined to theorize on literary matters, he might well have agreed with Tolstoy. Surely none would question the sincerity (integrity?) of his work, and that it should be individual, as all true Zen art, is perhaps axiomatic. It is the remaining essential in Tolstoy's triad, clarity, that some may claim is critically missing. But as the poet often said, the very nature of the Zen pursuit, the attainment of spiritual awakening, rules out likelihood of easy accessibility to its arts. "When I write poems," he told me, "no allowances can be made. Thought of a poem's difficulty never troubles me, since I never consciously make poems difficult."

A major reason for the difficulty of Zen poems, throughout the fifteen hundred years they have been written, is that many, perhaps the best known and most valued in and out of Zen communities, are those of "mutual understanding" (*agyo* or *toki-no-ge* in Japanese). Such poems are basically koan interpretations, as is the following piece, "Collapse," written by Takahashi early in Zen training:

> Time oozed from my pores,
> Drinking tea
> I tasted the seven seas.
>
> I saw in the mist formed
> Around me
> The fatal chrysanthemum, myself.
>
> Its scent choked, and as I
> Rose, squaring
> My shoulders, the earth collapsed.

This, Takahashi told me, was written in response to a koan his master asked him to meditate on, one often given disciples early in training, "Describe your face before you were begotten by your parents." We observe the poet deep in zazen (formal Zen meditation), experiencing the extraordinary expansions and penetrations sometimes realized by the meditator. Suddenly, in the mist, he sees that face, and is repulsed ("Its scent choked"). He rises, freed from it, ready for anything—old world breaks up, he enters the new.

Though Takahashi was always forthcoming with me about circumstances that may have led to the making of such poems (I was, after all, his translator), he was reluctant to reveal the manner in which they were received by the master, feeling such revelations would be too intimate. That attitude is only natural, perhaps, and besides, Zennists are cautioned to avoid such disclosures. The poet did confide, however, that the following was his versification of the master's response to one of his koan-based poems:

Words

> I don't take your words
> Merely as words.
> Far from it.
>
> I listen
> To what makes you talk—
> Whatever that is—
> And me listen.

It is intriguing to imagine the scene: poet sitting before master for *sanzen* (meeting for discussion of progress with koan), daring to complain that his interpretive poem was being misunderstood. "Words," expressing more than gentle reproach, relates intimately to a special bond, while at the same time it defines perhaps the nature of such talk, in or out of a *zendo.* As one might suppose, there are no correct interpretations. The koan is meant to dislodge, throw off balance, and the adequate poem reveals to what degree the disciple has righted himself. Nothing more nor less. And the more successful the interpretation, the finer the poem as poem.

The poem of mutual understanding, important to Zen since the T'ang dynasty, is a clear gauge of progress in discipline. It is not "poem" until such judgment is made, not by a literary critic but by a qualified master. Most awakening poems are of this type, though hardly planned or anticipated. Only a master, aware of his disciple's needs, lacks, and strengths, knows whether the longed-for breakthrough had been made. The poem tells all, accompanied of course by numerous signs in conduct itself, in speech, walk, work, relationship with others.

The Japanese master Daito (1282–1337), when a disciple, was given by his master the eighth koan of *Hekiganroku,* a Chinese work of great antiquity made up of one hundred Zen problems with commentary. Daito, who gained satori from his struggle with the koan, wrote at least two poems of mutual understanding based on it. Here is the text of the koan and the two most important poems it inspired:

> Attention! Suigan, at the end of the summer, spoke to the assembly and said: "For the whole summer I have lectured to the brethren. Look! Has Suigan any eyebrows?" Hofuko said, "He who does robberies has a heart of deceit." Chokei said, "They grow." Unmon said, "A barrier!"

> Unmon's barrier pulled down, the old
> Path lost. Blue sky's my home,
> My every action beyond man's reach:
> A golden priest, arms folded, has returned.

> At last I've broken Unmon's barrier!
> There's exit everywhere—east, west; north, south.
> In at morning, out at evening; neither host nor guest.
> My every step stirs up a little breeze.

Not all awakening poems are written in response to koan. Often a master, in normal conversation, will unconsciously challenge disciples to grapple with more general things. The subject of Time is much discussed in Zen communities. Takahashi once told me that the following lines came about that way.

Time

Time like a lake breeze
Touched his face.
All thought left his mind.

One morning the sun, menacing,
Rose from behind a mountain,
Singeing—like hope—the trees.

Fully awakened, he lit his pipe
And assumed the sun-inhaling pose:
Time poured down—like rain, like fruit.

He glanced back and saw a ship
Moving toward the past. In one hand
He gripped the sail of eternity,

And stuffed the universe into his eyes.

The American poet Richard Ronan, in his M.A. thesis "Process and Mastery in Bashō and Wallace Stevens," dealt most convincingly with this and other Takahashi poems. He wrote:

> The "lake breeze" is an allusion to the Hindu concept of *nirvana*, literally to be "blown away," a concept from which the Japanese *satori*, enlightenment, is derived. Reaching *nirvana/ satori*, one's relativity is necessarily blown away, leaving only one's essential nature, which is identical to that of the Void, the Buddhist Absolute. Having conquered the sun of Time, the speaker inhales it, absurdly smoking his pipe. He consumes the universe by seeing it for the first time as it is. "Devouring time" is devoured by the poet's *satori* conquest of the relative.

The conquest of the relative, the leap from the conditioned to an unconditioned plateau of being, is the extraordinary goal of Zen, and it is the reigning paradox of Zen art that work so private, of "mutual understanding," should have such broad appeal. In order for the Zennist to take the leap, he must attain a state of no-mind (*wu-hsin* in Chinese)— "All thought left his mind" in Takahashi's "time"—an essential precondition of *muga*, the full identification of observer and observed. The aesthetic term *zenkan* (pure seeing) has application to all Zen arts, and what it implies about the practitioner is startling: somehow he has won through, crushed the hungering ego, which in the unenlightened bars realization. The true Zen artist, of whatever medium, is a man risen from that smoldering.

Among modern poets, East and West, Shinkichi Takahashi was distinguished largely through the practice of *zenkan,* identifying effortlessly with all he observed, through which he ennobled not only his art but life itself. Like all awakened Zennists he found no separation between art and life, knowing the achievement of no-mind led not only to right art but to right living. He rarely used such general terms, but on occasion would explain what the practice of *zenkan* had meant to him. As artist, he had engaged for years in intense, unobstructed observation. Things moving, stationary, each no more appropriate than another, no circumstance more nor less favorable. He always cautioned, as he himself had been, against dualism, assuring that little by little one learns to know true seeing from false, that it was possible to reach the unconditioned. The world, he claimed, is always pure—we, with our dripping mind-stuff, foul it.

So puzzling to most of us, yet in the West some, Paul Valéry for one, without reference to Zen or other disciplines, turned in horror from the shifting mind, all a-wobble, twisted this way and that, filled with anxieties. Such men have spoken out of the need to subdue mind, crush ego, but where have they offered the way to make that possible? We don't appreciate how wise we are, speaking of troubles being "only in the mind," for born and heavily nourished there, they become giants that slay. When emptied of them, pointed properly, mind's no longer a destructive agent: it is the only light we need. Zen has been saying this for fifteen hundred years, never more effectively than through its poets, among whom in our lifetime Shinkichi Takahashi was the most profound.

I last saw the poet in the summer of 1985. He had insisted on postponing entering the hospital so that we might meet at his home in Tokyo. Ten years had passed since our last meeting, in the very same room. Though much changed, so weak he could not stand, there was the same vitality in his voice, the old sparkle in his eyes. In the past we had met chiefly to discuss his poems, pieces I was attempting with Takashi Ikemoto's help to render into English. Now we laughed together with his gentle wife, remembering old moments. When a common friend took out a camera, he begged him not to waste the film on him but instead photograph his *inka* framed on the wall. Suddenly he looked up, smiled at me, said, "You have seen me on the path of life. Now I am on the path of death." As he spoke, lines from his poem "Life Infinite" flashed through my mind:

> Beyond words, this no-thingness within,
> Which I've become. So to remain
>
> Only one thing's needed: Zen sitting.
> I think, breathe with my whole body—

Marvelous. The joy's so pure,
It's beyond lovemaking, anything.

I can see, live anywhere, everywhere.
I need nothing, not even life.

Shinkichi Takahashi was a remarkable poet. Few in our time have encompassed so much, left such a bracing legacy. How he achieved so much will, I am confident, engage the minds and talents of future scholars, but this I will claim for him: he found early in life what his life most needed, lived it, and wrote it as no other could.

The poet died the night of June 4, 1987. I could only lift my head with gratitude for having known him, and now offer to his memory a few words:

June 5, 1987

While I wash dishes to
Gregorian chants, what
started out a ho-hum
day—the usual round

of doodles, chores,
anxieties—explodes
with a bright swallowtail
joyriding by the window,

looping where by whitest
columbines a robin, head
cocked to love sounds,
watches as a squirrel

near the old pear tree
quivers astride his mate.
The phone rings, bringing
word Shinkichi Takahashi

died last night.
     And so
the world goes on. Now
the squirrels scamper

through the branches,
making leaves dance
like the poet's sparrows
wing-stroking an elegy in air.

Translating Zen Poems

(*I. M. Takashi Ikemoto*)

The sliding doors open in
the house hugging the mountainside where my children sled

in sandpapered orange-crates,
downswoop into our garden under
snow-glazed cypress, walnut,

fig, persimmon trees, mowing
dried stalks of tall eulalia
grass along the way. Inside,

we sit crosslegged, flushed
with hibachi embers, before
the plum-black Sado vase,

under your gift, the Taiga
scroll plum-blossoming out of
season. Over green tea and sweet

bean cake, I watch you shuffling
pages where I've englished
sparrows, temple gardens, fish,

time, universe—waiting
your word.
          Now, thumbing through

years of those poems, I see you,
old friend, in flickering
light of sunset over snow-roofs

of this midwest town, recall
a moment under a mountain, when we
knew a master's words need never die.

Misty Morning

The bluejay leaps in/out
vague rakings of the long ago.

Brief photos skelter by,
so many squirrel generations

back in time. Our children
once again are those small

armfuls we might dream would
stay. Our son, racing me

up the mountain path (I let
him sprint ahead), to reach

the Shinto Shrine. Joyfully
there he tries to capture

bubbles of reflected light
between his hands. The memory

turns. I'm sledding with our
girl, warmed by her spirit.

Down she tumbles, laughing,
auburn hair like flame against

the snow. Deep in this sacred
album mists rise, fall about

the trees that are, that were—
cover the distance of our

paths, now that the years
have made us what we are.

Latest News

The Hubbard Glacier, 80 miles
long, 360 feet tall,
is splitting from Alaska,

threatening ocean levels,
sending tremors through
the markets of the world.

Seas will flush out factories,
centuries of masterworks,
blueprints for doom into

the sludge. Igloo and mansion,
barrack and doss-house will
make a new Atlantis, moldy

with warheads, yo-yos, monuments
stockpiling barnacles,
leaving no trace. Sanctuaries

are tipped off to go under,
sending waves of walrus, polar
bear and sprat over seawalls.

Meanwhile as the glacier surges
14 yards a day, ticker-tapes
snake onto desks of speculators,

land values of mountains swell
their dreams. From the Rockies,
Alps, the Urals up to Katmandu,

who knows—if cities, forests,
valleys disappear—Mount Ararat
might come into its own again?

Willows

(*for Taigan Takayama, Zen master*)

I was walking where the willows
ring the pond, meaning to reflect
on each, as never before, all
twenty-seven, examine twig by twig,
leaf by pointed leaf, those delicate
tents of greens and browns. I'd

tried before, but always wound up
at my leafless bole of spine, dead
ego stick, with its ambitions,
bothers, indignations. Times
I'd reach the fifth tree before
faltering, once the seventeenth.

Then, startled by grinding teeth,
sharp nails in the palm, turn back,
try again. Hoping this time to
focus on each bough, twig, leaf,
cast out all doubts that brought
me to the willows. This time

it would be different, could see
leaves shower from the farthest
tree, crown my head, bless my eyes,
when I awakened to the fact—
mind drifting to the trees ahead.
I was at fault again, stumbling to

the flap of duck, goose, a limping
footstep on the path behind,
sun-flash on the pond. Such excuse,
easy to find, whether by willows
or bristling stations of a life.
Once more, I'm off. This time

all's still. Alone, no one to blame
distractions on but self. Turn in
my tracks, back to the starting point.
Clench, unclench my hands, breathe in,
move off telling the leaves like
rosary-beads, willow to willow. Mind

clear, eye seeing all, and nothing.
By the fifth, leaves open to me,
touch my face. My gaze, in wonderment,
brushes the water. By the seventh,
know I've failed. Weeks now, I've been
practicing on my bushes, over, over again.

Nathaniel Tarn

Nathaniel Tarn was born in Paris and educated around the world. He moved back to the United States in 1967. He has published some twenty books of poetry, most recently *Lyrics for the Bride of God* (New Directions, 1975), *The House of Leaves* (Black Sparrow, 1976), and *Seeing America First* (Coffee House, 1989). As a translator, he is mainly known for his work on Pablo Neruda, his versions from Segalen, and a *Rabinal Achi* from the Maya in Jerome Rothenberg's *Shaking the Pumpkin*. His *Views from the Weaving Mountain: Selected Essays in Poetics and Anthropology* has just been published by the University of New Mexico Press. He founded and directed Cape Editions and Cape Goliard Press, and continues to hold many editorial and consulting positions here and abroad. A professional anthropologist, he is a specialist in the Highland Maya and is also known for his work in Buddhist Southeast Asia, especially in Burma. He has held fellowships from the Ford and Rockefeller foundations, and was awarded the Guinness Prize for Poetry and the Commonwealth of Pennsylvania Literature Award. In 1988 he received the Rockefeller Foundation Residence in Poetry at Bellagio.

Before the Snake

Sitting, facing the sun, eyes closed. I can hear the sun. I can hear the bird life all around for miles. It flies through us and around us, it takes up all space, as if we were not there, as if we had never interrupted this place. The birds move dioramically through our heads, from ear to ear. What are they doing, singing in this luminous fall. It is marvelous to be so alone, the two of us, in this garden desert. Forgotten, but remembering ourselves as no one will ever remember us. The space between the trees, the bare ground-sand between them, you can see the land's skin which is so much home. We cannot buy or sell this marvelous day. I can hear the sun and, within the sun, the wind which comes out of the world's lungs from immeasurable depth; we catch only a distant echo. Beyond the birds there are persons carrying their names like great weights. Just think: carrying X your whole life, or Y, or Z. Carrying all that A and B and C about with you, having to be A all the time, B or C. Here you can be the sun, the pine, the bird. You can be the breathing. I can tell you, I think this may be Eden. I think it is.

Retreat Toward the Spring

While they sit and walk in alternation, their glance cast down, the only stirring from the external world he'll allow himself is a flare from her olive skirt. Noises of the alley outside: sunday loafers passing, excited talk, a radio at full tilt, far off a siren, ambulance sounding so sweet for a change, as if pain were singing in joy far away young and affectionate. Alternation of silence and chanting, the harmonizing sometimes very loud. Then: swift cataract of silence within whose pool only a bird warbles, as in a world only he crowds. The dead watch them in silence: from their planets, are in such close touch, so intimate, woven into all life: they know them all so well (the living) there is no reason ever to manifest. Need to come to that which will come to you so flying and so *entirely?* As knees cramp, pain spreads up the spine, as the silent forms almost break with aching, breath coming shorter, turning to sobs almost, an exquisite smell of roast veal wafts down from the outer street into the door of the monastery. It is five o'clock.

The Poet Who No Longer Made Use of Words

"Then it is the same as sitting?" he had stressed with that accented use of the word sitting. "Yes" the other assented. "As if the whole holy session were like a gliding, and you the pilot" extending arms for wings for a moment, "holding up the ship straight through the glide, knowing now if pushed downwing whichever way, such art of straightening the soar as"—"*Ja* but the feel you have with the machine, it is so direct—nothing is speculation and so you will find the place blesses your sleep

and you will zero in there each time from habit."
Fascinated, he ate the—what was it, quiche with
a salad while the other held: "in my car, driving
down the street, I know it, I know it, wherever I
knock on doors out of intuition no less, wherever
I sit down to talk with people, break speech with
them and—sometimes they will open and let me in
and sometimes they will close in front of me like
flowers dying but in any case, there is the rank,
reference, power: I'm looked after" said the poet
who'd vacated words to go into the homeless life.

Entering Into This

for J.R., in no way differently.

Granted that
        life is
irremediably *dukkha:*
        dis-comfort, dis-satisfaction,
Dis, in this life above ground
    which is mostly shadow, in which light
must be introduced, dab at a time:
      fingertip, brush of eyelid, chest hair,
aura round the generation machine in its upstanding
        jus/tice—and finally that light
so hard won is shaded, stroke by stroke, by the same
    pencil in its pride of darkness,
drawing you down to Dis in this life . . .
        Whoever promised
all floors were different: "in my mansion, many rooms"
but did anyone say, this room, that, will be a garden?
did anyone promise? Did one say tulips? roses? maple
just before snow: the ultimate in fire? Or ever say
snow—whose white defeats those strokes for blind days?
        Then, if you, yes, I thought if you would, grant
such a premise, we could rest from hope in the definite,
        you and I—this hope knowledge would be ours
WHOLE—after the escalation. And no more climb. The
mountains are, last enough if last is any point to make,
while the world's flowers take our eyes on down
    to the canyons arush with crazy april waters—
    Where we see the great wall move at us, take us,
and we wait for it, standing stock still.

from The Beautiful Contradictions

EIGHT

It happened once   in an unwilling but fascinated way
some aberration of the collector's instinct having overtaken me
that I was responsible for the destruction of a fragment of history
a fingernail dislodging a minute particle from a fresco
some one thousand five hundred years old at the very least
the particle   as I should have expected   falling away in powder
There were six monks who had come down from the mountains at
     the time
as monks had probably been coming for one thousand five hundred
     years
they waited for the tourists to leave each cave
and then went in to bow to every one of the Buddhas
with great piousness and no concern at all for their aesthetic value

There were a great many Buddhas there   small and large
though not as many as there are persons or blades of grass not to be
     saved
sand-grains   water-traces   light-particles   not to be saved
and taken into an inexistent Nirvāna by an inexistent Bodhisattva
that is if you understand the great armor of the Prajñāpāramitā
Then the six monks returning walked round the tourist buses
took the proceeds   bought with wide smiles a plateful of fish
which they ate with wide smiles as they might have eaten a seventh
     monk
I do not believe that I have ever been so moved in my life by any
     men
or felt that I was so close to the origins of compassion
or to the skin of patience I had scratched by misrule

The destruction of history by not setting down the history you
     know
by refusing to be a witness to your times is a crime against the earth
in this I have done some wrong by failing the history of the Sangha
refusing to write the history of one section for busyness
though that section *were* located in a relatively insignificant culture
a suburb of Asia   very ugly into the bargain   not to mention pre-
     tentious
no limb of the great East I dreamed   my childhood bride
yet inalienably part of the field of merit in which we sow our deeds
Somewhere in the billowing robe between Sarnath and Kyōto

among the incalculable elements of stuff in that time-quenching
    garment
the smallest gash bears witness   the smallest rent unrepaired

It is made worse by the knowledge that much of the Sangha is dead
    or dying
the Sangha of the four quarters flourishes only among museums
the mystic East you love is as good as pickled
new people are being heaped on new people   and being chosen
most urgently by history without concern are lineage
from Vladivostok to Sinkiang the settlers for squatting
all along the twenty-six-thousand-mile border   give or take a mile
the provinces   the counties   the heavenly shires the Russians took
as imperialist in their time as the worst of the breed
are being contested   maps out   banners up   the tribes drinking tea
now with one side   now with the other

The musics are being composed   the slogans set to music
to teach us hate for what we had come to love
painfully slowly because it is at the other end of the earth
and love is very hard to bear when it has so far to go
as you know when you weep for Aberfan   a little less for Vietnam
What good have the Waleys   Pounds   Perses   and Segalens been
Chavannes   Granets   Steins   and Groussets been
who have given their lives to the study of the middle earth
or Fenellosa   whom some of you admire as a critic
if there be some   writers at that   I know
to drink willingly until two a.m. arguing the East never matched

Saint Thomas Aquinas or Dante or other equally respectable persons
there being in such a case nothing like a relevant East
not to mention all the Chinese   Japanese   Indians   *et al*
who have tried to tell their people about Aquinas   Dante   you
if it is all to begin again at the drop of a treaty on a larger scale
and for that matter why did I have to remain in exile
years in the West   years in the East
if we are to be taught again laboriously the habits of hate
if all that mingles in the end will be our plasma
There is no worthier subject for poetry in our time
than the fear that the races should rise and rend each other

our mother the earth should forget herself   her milk run dry

John Tarrant

John Tarrant is a Roshi in the Harada-Yasutani line of koan Zen, one of
the Dharma heirs of Robert Aitken. Originally from Tasmania, he now
lives in Santa Rosa, California, where he writes and follows his trade of
psychotherapy in depth. He is married with a young daughter. He holds
Zen retreats regularly in Perth and Sydney, Australia, and directs the California Diamond Sangha in Santa Rosa and Berkeley.

Zen, Poetry, and the Great Dream Buddha

Zen and poetry: two things that have no use because they are two mon-
sters, creatures outside the comfortable course of days. Any connection
is neither obvious nor soothing. Both of them answer, with an effec-
tiveness that varies from day to day, the longing to describe, to appre-
hend, and to embody the marvel of the world: its beauty, its pain, and its
contradictions. They are also ends. They exist by their own justification
as practices, full of human effort. Thus, whatever else they are in the way
of craft, struggle, and revelation, they are ways of being, forms of life.

   This essay is an entertainment in that it chases a possibility: the con-
junction between poetry and Zen is explored by connecting poetry with
the Buddhist division of the world into the three bodies of the buddha.
These bodies in turn are given a characteristically Western reading, one
that notes their resonance with the old Mediterranean partition of being
into spirit, soul, and body. I am aware that such a reading puts the
Buddhist concepts under a certain distorting pressure. There are other,
more orthodox approaches to Buddhist doctrine. I have chosen my
course in order to link, at least implicitly, the elegant liveliness of Zen
with the tradition of European literature, and thereby to emphasize that
Zen is a civilizing as well as liberating path; one that offers not only
courage and joy but self-knowledge and respect for the beauty that appears in the small corners of a life.

Perhaps we can begin by asking about one of these particulars, about location. "What is the place of poetry, what is its domain and ground? And how does this connect with Zen?"

The first and most personal response is that these two things, Zen and poetry, are linked through attention. There is a discipline in both. This discipline refers to work. It refers to the necessity of form that contains, directs, and displays transformations. It refers to a trust in balance: on the one hand the poet or Zen student identifies so intensely with the object—the koan or the poem—that everything else is dark and there is no longer even an observer; on the other hand, and at the same time, there is the more equable knowledge that the center of the universe is located in all pieces of ground.

More generally, in its inclusiveness poetry relates to the Mahayana, the great vehicle of the bodhisattva. There is a willingness to include pain, love, and hatred not merely as stages of a journey but as themselves portions of a great wholeness. Given this readiness, our experience does not need to be transcended in order to have depth. The numinous appears in the ordinary, just as Aphrodite appears in a cheerleader. Our attachments and griefs are a move towards totality, while our serenity, which appears without warning, rests in totality.

Poetry needs to locate itself, and an intense sense of region can be very helpful. I think of Gary Snyder and of Antonio Machado. But what about poets who are nomads? Well, the locus of the poem can also be the interior life, as it is for Rainer Maria Rilke. But I should like to locate poetry in a map of Zen, the way the medieval cartographers located mists and dragons at the edge of the known seas.

One of the many ways in which Buddhism divides up the world is in terms of the three bodies of the Buddha: *dharmakaya, sambhogakaya,* and *nirmanakaya.* The *dharmakaya* is the main referent of the experience of Zen. It is the place of dazzling clarity, of insight beyond space and time and utterly present. In this body of the Buddha, all are equal, equivalent, and sacred. The Sanskrit word *shunyata,* usually translated as emptiness, pertains to the *dharmakaya.* It refers to the place beyond categories that is empty or mysterious, the place without form from which all form comes, spring with its flowers, autumn with its gales. Most poetry has some tinge of the *dharmakaya* and some poets spend a lot of time here. Basho has an utter equanimity with his own loneliness, with plum blossoms, with horses pissing, and with his own impending death, not because these events have meaning—meaning does not interest him—but merely because they *are.* And because they are, or we might say *it is,* each of these events involving the horse, the man, and the blossoming tree contains the other and all possible universes in its tiny compass. One doesn't feel a great human affection for Basho, not because human affection is banished, but because its place is exactly that of everything else, of the tree and of the horse; it too fills the universe and has no special place. Wallace Stevens is another poet like this. He refers particularly to the way ideas and feeling contaminate our grasp of the *is*ness of things, masking the *dharmakaya*.

The *nirmanakaya* is the body of form. This body is you and me and bear and kangaroo and the cheerleader and the city of San Francisco and the sea beating on the cliffs of Tasmania, if all these are taken as phenomenon—that is, if the city is taken as an assemblage of buildings and roads and bridges and not as the city of light or as the city watched over by Assisi and Don Quixote. The *nirmanakaya* is particular and somehow naive. When, in a poem called "A Man Doesn't Have Time" (translated by Chana Bloch), Yehuda Amichai says that while the soul is experienced, the "body remains forever an amateur," I think he is talking about this domain. The body is always surprised when it bumps into something. Issa is a poet with a tender regard for this body of the Buddha. The universe is, from this point of view, rather fragmented, composed of brilliant colors but without an obvious organization.

When there is a set of two—like form and no-form, or body and spirit—it tends to generate a third in the middle. This third doesn't at first make sense because it can be understood only from its own locus. In terms of the general map of Buddhism the third is the *sambhogakaya*. The *sambhogakaya* is mysterious because the world of form with its transparent naïveté cannot encompass it and the *dharmakaya*, which is simultaneously present everywhere, has no need for it. Traditionally this body is considered as a body of bliss that buddhas acquire as a consequence of their merit and discipline. So it seems as if something shamanic has appeared. Well, this is true, but in Zen the body of bliss is the common one; the strangeness is hidden in the now: night with its stars, the longing of the lover, and the sound of cars driving off.

Because it is touched by mystery this body of the Buddha also functions as a projective test. Different things are read into it. I take it to refer to the domain of myth, story, dreams, meditation visions, and the archetypes. That is, it is the locus of meaning and of experience, of what we undergo. This is a highly charged realm. It has its own point of view, which in the West is called soul or psyche—here understood as a process rather than a structure. This realm of experience is important to the Mahayana because it is here that the bodhisattva works with the suffering of beings.

I think of this body of the Buddha as being the main locus, the native earth, of poetry. Poetry belongs here even if it's away a lot, traveling in other lands. Rilke, for example, talks a lot about the *dharmakaya,* but from the point of view of this mediate realm. The weight and feeling for sorrow in his poetry mark it as of this place. Poetry makes expeditions into other territory, but this seems to be its true home.

The melancholy and longing that is such a pronounced and international poetic tradition (the *Man'yoshu* and the troubadours of Provence come to mind) is a portion of the territory of *sambhogakaya*. I think it is a large portion because access to what is deeply unknown is through what we have turned away from, through suffering, through error and foolishness, through boundary situations. The path opens, in other words, through an acquaintance with greed, hatred, and ignorance. Poetry and koan work gather and transform this thick material.

There are two senses in which *sambhogakaya* is not truly personal. The first is that it relates to myth and so works simultaneously with the personal and beyond it. In mythic experience it is the story that is dreamed onwards and to which the individual conforms. The second is that, when we examine our consciousness minutely as, say, Joyce did in *Ulysses,* we find that there isn't an absolute self beyond our search for it. Tou-shuai designed a koan to explore the subtleties of this point. It goes, "People go through abandoned, grassy places only to search for the nature of the self. Now, where is that nature?"

The intimate, tender not-knowing that appears in the inner life of the Zen student is an emergent form of the openness, the cloudiness of this realm. In the *dharmakaya* there are no opposites; our middle realm contains the opposites and some of their tension. The core of this world is its *both-and* quality. *Sambhogakaya* seems both numinous and intensely personal. Issa has a poignant haiku written on the death of his daughter:

> The world of dew
> is the world of dew
> and yet, and yet . . .

The Mahayana is built out of that "and yet." We never quite give up the personal, since if we did there would be nothing at all. We recognize how insubstantial things are, and yet our sorrow has its own integrity. There is a kind of loyalty that we owe to the world's pain and loveliness, and to the truth that pain and loveliness cannot be disentangled.

Soul is always in love with the things of the world and with the productions of time. Its whole tendency is to be unsatisfied, incomplete, full of longing. This is not only a description of the poet and the reader but of the bodhisattva who puts off her own entire serenity and yearns, helplessly, for the enlightenment of every creature.

It is the power of the *dharmakaya* that brings equanimity to this longing and saves it from narrowness. The *dharmakaya* is not interested in meaning or even in self-knowledge. From the point of view of *sambhogakaya, dharmakaya* is spirit; that is, when it tries to include *dharmakaya*, spirit phenomena occur—visions, synchronicity, and that sort of thing. From the same middle realm, *nirmanakaya* is body, a concept both more organized and more ambiguous than the *nirmanakaya*'s fragmented but clear perspective.

One of the features of *sambhogakaya* that derives from its mediate and transitional nature is the instability of the landscape. It is the domain of those fleeting, unstable, and haunting experiences that seem both to be located in the body and to transcend the bounds of the body. The consciousness that pertains to these experiences is called by various names— the subtle body, the dream body, *kundalini*.

In this realm too is the feeling and awareness of presence that lovers and friends may have with each other, that Zen teachers may have with students, and that poets may have with a muse. To the *dharmakaya* belongs the characteristic Zen experience of meeting the ancient masters face to face. In the middle realm a different kind of meeting occurs; it has to do with the willingness to include pain and love of the world in one moment. Presence is one term for this openness to what is. Presence gives meetings, whether with an animal, a person, or a landscape, a sense of depth. Writing attended by this openness is sometimes called poetry, writing that lacks it is verse, a craft activity. Because it recognizes and allows wounds, presence is a healing field wherever it occurs, in a poem or in a meeting.

At the beginning of koan practice some teachers discourage students from writing. I think this is because the teacher is tending the fire that pain lit. Everything that is not tied down the teacher steals. Everything that is not fire is taken away. The teacher's primary interest is in having the student meet the *dharmakaya*. If she doesn't meet her original face then there is no Zen. The teacher contains, surrounds the student so that she sits with the pain instead of avoiding and dissipating it. The student must struggle without aid, in the midst of dark pain. There is just darkness. Anything might become poetry or revelation, but events are still composed of fragments—suffering and endurance and courage and waiting. They have not yet achieved the fierce reality of true speech. So she sits, walks, talks with the koan, finally identifying with it. At the place where all roads end nothing is of much use. At this point, finally she meets herself, and the meeting is full of light. I don't think it matters whether or not a student stops writing for a while in training. The important thing is the same in meditation as it is in poetry—not to have a back door. And the mythological truth is that the student at first is not a poet because she is herself in a poem, caught up in its great processes.

It is after satori that koans reveal themselves as a great language for discussing with clarity the movements of the universe both subtle and broad. I think no other language as accurate or illuminating. Poems occur throughout the long curriculum of koan study and over and over again are taken up as koans. Poetry is indispensable to completeness in Zen. When I think of its rigor in dealing with truth, its concision, its multiplicity of direction, and its beauty, it seems easy to argue that the koan is a poetic form. Here are two examples to speak for themselves, both from the great Sung dynasty collection *The Blue Cliff Record,* first published by Yuan Wu in 1128. These versions are closely based on an unpublished translation by Yamada Koun Roshi and Robert Aitken Roshi.

CASE 54

Yun-men asked a monk, "Where have you come from?"
The monk said, "Hsi Ch'an."
Yun-men said, "What does Hsi Ch'an have to say these days?"
The monk stretched out his arms.
Yun-men slapped him.
The monk said, "There is something else."
Yun-men stretched out his arms.
The monk was silent.
Yun-men slapped him.

CASE 82

A monk asked Ta Lung, "This physical body perishes. What is the everlasting body of the Dharma?"
Ta Lung said, "The mountain flowers are blooming like brocade; in the valley, the river is as blue as indigo."

I think Zen cultivates the virtues of the soul as well as of the spirit, and hence the virtues pertaining to the ground of poetry, in a number of subtle and sometimes hidden ways. The frustration inherent in koan work is both agonizing and deepening. While the koan work clarifies the *dharmakaya,* the great myths of student and teacher, of hidden wisdom being revealed, and of the soul's journey are also inevitably pursued. The primary feature of this journey is the inclusion of the excluded. Specifically this always means the inclusion of pain. In the realm of the *sambhogakaya* the inclusion of pain means that it is suffered for its own sake, with the acceptance that it is sacred. The meaning of the experience is that it too is at the center of the universe.

The watermark of the Mahayana is this willingness to include what we are inclined to refuse or deny. So, if yesterday I was wise and clear and today am lost again, caught in my familiar sense of weakness and failure, *both* these things can be true. There is a funny and helpful koan on this subject that goes, "The clearly enlightened one falls into a well." Dark and light do not cancel each other. A poem full of despair can engender a sweetness. Poetry and Zen change the shapes of things deep down, not just the surface effects.

The uneasiness and cloudiness that surround the joining of poetry and Zen is further evidence that it is a matter of the *sambhogakaya*. Clarity and certainty are of the *dharmakaya*; in the middle realm we struggle along and learn by our failure and our vulnerability. The strength of this point of view is that it moves with the forces in the world. Nothing is refused as unsuitable material. Cancer, divorce, imprisonment, strange quirks and attachments—in this realm the awareness ruminates on our human disasters, turning away from nothing, until, gradually, movement appears.

It seems to me that it is in this middle realm that the mythopoesis that will make Zen native in the West goes on. And what Zen brings to poetry is important too—a sense of the sacred relatedness of living creatures and the ground we walk on, a sense that precise expression opens paths in the world, and a sense that speech can be true simultaneously in all the realms of the Buddha. By this last I mean true in all the realms of experience. So a poem reveals the everlasting light from which things are always springing into being and in which nothing is ever lost, shows the simple fact of the thing itself, and embodies the middle realm, the dream that holds both what is timeless and what is dying.

The Marriage Bundle

There is one heart
but many birds
for the heart is where we are joined
and the birds are joy.

Abalone is endless presence,
the spiral shell is ancient layers
and the white shell, truth.
The dangerous bear gives roots,
                loyalty, and the branching

ancestral line.
Blue corn is nurturing
and the turquoise—
sky and waters in the dry arroyo—
turquoise is spirit
and plenty, two things
not always paired,
but because difficult, not always joined,
making a question that goes on
like a road to hold us:
the plenty of the living rock,
and the listening we return to—
which is lapis lazuli—wisdom.
The shell leaf is change
without which none of this can be mastered,
and the green mastery is a slow letting go.
Hematite is the future, heavy and dark
with what we must greet,
Red garnet is constant, peridot
is harmony and yellow
agate is fertility.

Each danger is necessary,
each choice will never be made again,
each joy is piercing
            and can never be replaced.

The great sky comes near. The snow
finds out the dear twig, the small
            green needle and the shoots of spring,

and all of this makes up a marriage bundle,
all of this makes up a kind of steadiness.
It goes on past our knowing
and only then is it enough:
It is more than we intended.

> *Pecos River*
> *Season of shoots and snow, 1987*

The Restoration of the World

There's a blessed fidelity in things.
Graceless things grow lovely with good uses.
Hour after hour of zazen in a brick fortress
in the hills; and this place,
where we have been so cold, changes us.

We give things souls when we pour our lives into them.
In their true, original lives,
the chair, the fence, and the stones thrust up
out of a profound silence.

Two shorn sheep graze
facing the low sun.
Green, gold and blue, two rosellas cross the paddock.
Wings squeak in the air.

They touch me, as if the woman I love
had touched my bare skin.

Spell to Be Recited for Banishing Loneliness

Like a good Zen student Mephistopheles
says "Myself am hell."
So all the old accounts are mistaken.
We need to translate,
the meanings are turned around:
for his screams, read "delight,"
and for the tortures he undergoes,
read "he does not shut out
any part of himself."

I make a flower arrangement
of frangipani like a froth of stars
and a black eucalypt twig.
I don't care why I am lonely;
it's the taste of copper dust and the ringing of hammers,
the feeling of being so huge

that I don't know what's inside.

For despair, read
"when I stare and stare at a flower
it's bigger than me,"
and for grief, read
"the gentleness of my hands brings out of things
the light that is inside them."

Why the Gods Screw Things Up

For them, everything they are not
fills them with longing.
The Bunraku puppeteers
are three men
with one heart.
It's the heart of the old woman
who, as a girl,
rejected her lovers.
It's the heart of the general
upset about killing a boy;
killing has never disturbed him before,
but this boy, this boy's pain
has forced into his mouth
the new, metallic taste of grief.

We can hear their feet on the boards,
and see their faces,
dimly through the black gauze,
but they are invisible
because they have made
the heron spirit dazzling.

She shakes the snow from her umbrella,
and is suddenly exposed,
a girl like a plum twig,
under the white and pink,
a promise in winter.

Each puppeteer longs for life then,
not to be her,
for he is already this,

but to answer her,
to know by her small, surprised steps,
that he's the one
she's been waiting for,
and now
he can weep.

Flute

Flute—a simple remedy
of which the herb is sound.

My eye is a planet with another motion,
with its orbits and burials;
each dawn I forget
where I came from.

The river, the hugging mist,
the shroud of the body unwrapped
at the beginning of the world
recently completed with already memories,
fossils, foreign advisors,
Radio Independence.

I joined the courtship of a bird;
he built a bower
and danced with a flower in his beak,
blue petals were the color of his satin feathers
and his beady eye.

I saw the amorphous monuments
and fungus gardens of the termites,
the polyps building their houses
with their bones.

I watched the anthropologist continue.
He studied the shanties, made of sticks
and corrugated iron,
tottering out into the bay.
I watched the starved dreams caught
like bats

in the people's hair.

I was secretary to the natural order of all things.
Animals approached me.
My companions died.

I watched the small ants bring them
into their holes.

Time's music ate me free of myself
and I live in a flute now,
in ecstasy.

Anne Waldman

Anne Waldman, a poet, performer, teacher, translator, and editor, has published twenty books of poetry, most recently *Skin Meat Bones* (Coffee House, 1985), *Helping The Dreamer: New & Selected Poems* (Coffee House, 1989), and *Lokapala* (Rocky Ledge Editions, 1991). As reader-performer, she has worked collaboratively with numerous musicians, dancers, and composers. She toured as poet-in-residence with Bob Dylan's Rolling Thunder Review, and, until 1978, was Director of The Poetry Project at St. Mark's Church In-the-Bowery in New York. She has recently edited an anthology from The Poetry Project entitled *Out of This World*. Her research on oral traditions has taken her to India, Nepal, and Bali, and she has recently lectured and presented her own work in Czechoslovakia, London, Germany, Austria, Switzerland, and the Netherlands. Cofounder, with Allen Ginsberg, of the Jack Kerouac School of Disembodied Poetics at the Naropa Institute in Boulder, Colorado, she currently designs and directs the Institute's Department of Writing and Poetics. She is also on the adjunct faculty of The Institute of American Indian Arts in Sante Fe, New Mexico.

Gender and the Wisdom Body: Secular/Sexual Musings

Artemis

I pray you are always above me
Imperial Ruler Of The Stars
with your silver new-moon-bow,
arrows swift as science

You strike trees dead
fell a wild hind
& finally a city of unjust men
(I dreamt last night of warring
Jerusalem)

Chaste sprite, spicy nymph,
wounding witch, any guise you wish
No hesitation, Dakini of Incantation
Command your spike deep in my heart

So I may ride, hunt, speak, shine
mid-wife your sting.

As a woman poet seeking Muse, I touch the woman in the man in myself. In his fine foreword to Edward H. Schafer's *The Divine Women: Dragon Ladies and Rain Maidens* (North Point Press, 1980), an excellent study of the permutations of imagery in T'ang poetry, Gary Snyder points out the difficulties for women writers in the poet/Muse relationship. This relationship is seen from the male side only, as we've been living for several thousands of years in cultures—both Eastern and Western—dominated by men. For women practicing Dharma, there is some of the same ambiguity as well, since the Dharma as official codified "text" has also been dominated by men. In the relative sense therefore, I need to join the woman principle (*prajna*) in the man in me with the man principle (*upaya*) in me.

In Geshe Kelsang Gyatso's commentary on Shantideva's *Guide to the Bodhisattva's Way of Life,* he reminds us that although Shantideva emphasizes the bondage of sexual longing through focusing on man's longing for women, and uses as antidote ghoulish images of woman's body (that "bag of filth"), specifically Shantideva was addressing monks. Yet how are women to sit comfortably with invocations of women's foul odors, her face unveiled by vultures, her "zombie-like body moving about like a wailing corpse controlled by momentary impulses," the disgusting saliva from her mouth? Why, even a soft pillow is more desirable. Surely Shantideva is not implying that one sex is by nature unclean while the other is pure!

Gyatso wisely suggests that we "make whatever changes might be necessary—in viewpoint, gender, and so forth—for a more personal interpretation to the material." I deem this highly sensible advice (Buddhist scholars and interpreters, please take note), although in the long run it doesn't make prospects for enlightenment any brighter if we, as women, are presumably attached to "hairy (male) bags of water." And perhaps it's best to react with a shade of humor when Shantideva says, "May all the females throughout the universe who so desire be reborn in a male form" (Gyatso's paraphrase). "Who so desire" keeps it open. After all, is it really all that so desirable these days? Although in many (particularly Third World) countries I've visited, oppression of women is visciously rampant, I've rarely met a woman who said she'd rather have been born a man. Perhaps the karma is shifting in favor of being born in a woman's body, at least in some parts of the world where women's rights have made substantive gains. Does it work that way, mysterious karma? The point for women, I think, is to see the gender issue in its proper (albeit degraded) cultural context and not lay every blame on men, thereby abdicating responsibility to fight for some changes themselves. Or feeling, wrongly so, that there's no place for women in the so-called dharma "hierarchy." After all, we were probably lording it over men at some point between the Upper Paleolithic and Bronze Ages. And some evidence suggests that men were kept out of the goddess temples for a long, long time.

At a "Women in the Dharma" gathering held over Mother's Day weekend at Karma Triyana Dharmachakra in Woodstock, New York, several years ago, a question was raised after Bhikshuni Pema Chödrön's talk, which touched on the subject of anger. A woman, in a mixed group of men and women (although there were many more women present), said she had a difficult time with her anger—almost hatred—toward men in general. They had demeaned her in relationships and in the workplace. Furthermore, how could one not feel rage and scorn at the way women were treated, for example, in Muslim and African countries? We joined in her indignation as she spoke. Pema Chödrön asked her if she herself thought that women were in some way inferior, because it seemed that her anger might have a different quality if she weren't "buying into" that assumption. It was a subtle point and seemed genuinely well taken by the woman, who lingered with this suggestion to examine her own mind. Pema cautioned everyone present against blaming others. "Drive all blames into one" (i.e., oneself) is Atisha's classic Mahayana slogan.

Another young woman, mother of two sons, boys who in spite of her attentiveness were still developing what she considered sexist attitudes toward girls, asked if this behavior is irrevocable, are boys naturally like that? Then her real question emerged: when are the external forms—the domination by men, as she perceives it, in the "Buddhist set-up" going to change? I mentioned my own experience with the Naropa Institute (essentially run by women on the executive, faculty, and administrative levels) and Shambhala Training, both of which are organizations that manifest "feminine principle," or atmosphere. The Zen Mountain Monastery in Mt. Tremper has also been highly supportive of women in both its administrative hierarchy and arts programs. My point was that there's a definite opening and invitation for women in many dharma scenes to cut through the poverty of some kind of dualistic attitude and "get involved." There is particularly the need for women artists, poets, musicians, composers, writers, dancers, to bring their skills to the Buddhist community. I see my own commitment as part of the bodhisattva vow to restore balance and equilibrium to a calamitous world. It is a political commitment as well. In one poem I proclaim: "I'm coming up out of the tomb, Men of War / Get ready, big boys, get ready!" There's no time to wait for some kind of external confirmation. From the point of view of ultimate reality, you won't get any confirmation on the Buddhist path in any case.

Earlier in the day during the same gathering, Thrangu Rinpoche had given an explication of the two principles of *prajna* and *upaya,* speaking of how they are used in practice, and the need to join them together psychologically and actively in our own lives. He said he believed in equality but he also saw people in the name of equality not manifesting those two principles, which are clearly distinct. Although some women present said later they felt he wasn't addressing their questions, he seemed on one level to be taking the discussion higher, cutting through the pervading sense of women's poverty. His basic message was to "keep practicing," whoever you are.

The exchanges at the conference included a funny moment when a Westerner who had recently taken monk's vows was questioning the traditional rights of nuns in relation to monks and used the word *secular* in his query. Thrangu Rinpoche replied, through a Tibetan translator, that he couldn't address the question because he wouldn't know anything about *sexual* experience, being celibate himself. There was some hilarity at this and the translator, not understanding the word *secular,* asked the monk for a clearer word at which point the monk, quite innocently, blurted out "Lay!" That, of course, brought the house down. This charming confusion seemed to penetrate further our conceptual way of discussing, and even thinking about, questions of gender. It was doubly sweet, or perhaps ironic, that the men speaking so playfully were both celibate and seemed to have come to terms with feminine principle in themselves.

Meetings With Remarkable Women: Buddhist Teachers in America (Shambhala Publications, 1988) is a revelatory book because it takes a clear, unsentimental look at the strides that have been made within the various Buddhist (primarily Zen and Tibetan Buddhist) scenes. There's a penetrating strength and humor in these very particular portraits. Because of the current state of the world we live in, I have a sense that these women, too, are working with the women in the men in themselves and experience the double effort of that. What becomes clear is the choicelessness of their Dharma connection—whether born in Hitler's Germany (Toni Packer and Gesshin Prabhasa Dharma Roshi), or born a musical prodigy in Canada (Maurine Stuart Roshi), or coming to Dharma as a political radical on a Fulbright grant studying nationalism in Third World countries (Joanna Macy). All these women struggled with the external forms to realize their karmic connection to the path, to be ordinarily and truly and remarkably themselves, and to "shine like stars."

On the poetry side, *The Penguin Book of Women Poets* (Penguin 1986) is a fortifying collection, as it documents on every possible aspect of women's experience—erotic, worldly, oppressed, spiritual, ecstatic, transformative—through the ages from ancient Egypt to the present. The great Chinese poet Ts'ai Yen (circa 200 B.C.E.), captured by the barbarian Huns, cries out in "Eighteen Verses Sung to a Tartar Reed Thistle,"

> Earth was pitiless.
> It brought me to birth in such a time.
> War was everywhere. Every road was dangerous

and later in the poem:

> Men here are as savage as giant vipers,
> and strut about in armour, snapping their bows.
> As I sing the second stanza I almost break the lutestrings
> Will broken, heart broken, I sing to myself.

This torn lyric parallels the war-wracked situations of today, created by the "strut" of male aggression. Kassia, the ninth-century Byzantine Greek abbess of a convent exclaims: "A nun's life—free as a bird." Veronica Franca, a sixteenth-century Italian courtesan who founded a hospice for "fallen" women, rages: "No more words! To the field, to arms." And the contemporary Turkish writer Gulten Akin writes:

> Living with people, as they live
> Inhaling the air they breathe
> Breathing knowledge into them

Perhaps as women practitioners, or poets, or both, we need to breathe more knowledge, more *prajna* into the world to restore the balance.

The Muse who hovers about my own poetry has taken many forms over the years. She is frequently hermaphroditic, an androgynous shape-shifter. She often manifests as a pure field of energy. Sometimes she is like the *Jnanasattva* in Tibetan Buddhist practice, the "wisdom body" who descends to confirm or "untrip" the projected visualization, which is called the *Samayasattva,* the "coming together" or "sacred vow" being. These are the two levels in Vajrayana Buddhist practice one works with constantly. The *Jnanasattva* is basically the practitioner's own sanity, which possesses the *Samayasattva* projection, or aspiration. What you have only imagined becomes real. Likewise, the Muse not only inspires me, but enters into the ritual of "making the poem." She is invited in. She always meets me halfway. I seem to have no difficulty approaching her as a source. I seek out female deities. I identify with the *Dakinis* or "sky walkers." From some point of view, every woman is the *Dakini*. I've had dreams about Padmasambhava's consort, Yeshe Tsogyal, who has appeared as a kind of quintessential Muse figure. In one dream she shows herself as hag-shaman-doctor bending over my reclining nude body, which she studies as a map. With her twig she circumscribes and mumbles a mantra over my *yoni,* which expands into a vivid, sonorous ocean, teeming with activity and light. In another dream she is "just another tortilla lady" cooking bread in her oven in a dusty pueblo. The air resounds with the music of crickets. She takes her intricately woven shawl and unravels it in front of my eyes. It turns into the night sky—the glorious celestial firmament with twinkling planets and stars—and then beyond that into the whole universe. I reel with this vision. She constantly drives or directs me further into particulars to see the larger complexities of primal energy fields and sources.

This Muse-hag reminds me always of the vastness, the profundity of outlook and the uncompromising outrageousness manifested in the Vajrayana teachings. In a discussion of Anuyoga tantra, Chögyam Trungpa Rinpoche was asked if one is influenced in one's relationship to practice by whether one is male or female, since there seemed to be an aspect of working with passion at this point. His answer was clearly that your karma shapes your body but that your body's shape is not the fundamental thing. There *is* basic feminity and masculinity and Anuyoga tantra relates with fundamental types, independent of body types. He also said that the world is infinite and not divided only into two types. There are billions of types of sexual experiences! I remember something popping in me on a cellular level upon hearing this good news.

At a "Dharma and Poetics" seminar at Green Gulch Farm Zen Center in California, Gary Snyder commented that perhaps now, with the availability of the Vajrayana path, which seems to work the most provocatively of all the Buddhist traditions with female energy, women seeking liberation could realize their power fully and passionately. I instantly visualized Vajrayogini with her three eyes, skull bone necklace, and tiger skin 'round her waist, stomping on the corpse of ego. Yet one needs favorable conditions to hear and practice the Dharma in any *kalpa,* and especially in our particularly dark and violent *Kali Yuga.* The practice of Buddhism, similar to a practice of poetry, although seemingly marginal and demanding, is from some point of view, a luxury. From another point of view, it's indispensable.

Women in many places still need to hear the "good news," just as they did over two thousand years ago. Here is my own version of one of the *Therigatha* ("Psalms of the Buddhist Nuns") songs from the Pali Canon, circa 80 B.C.E., based on a much earlier oral tradition:

Sumangala's Mother Speaks

I'm free!
Free from kitchen drudgery
I'm no longer dirty among my cooking pots
(My pot smelled like an old water snake!)
And I'm through with my brutal husband
and his tedious sunshade weaving
I pop lust and hate with a sizzling sound—zap!
I sit at the foot of a tree and think
"O happiness! this is it!"
I meditate upon this as happiness.

Makeup on Empty Space

I am putting makeup on empty space
all patinas convening on empty space
rouge blushing on empty space
I am putting makeup on empty space
pasting eyelashes on empty space
painting the eyebrows on empty space
piling creams on empty space
painting the phenomenal world
I am hanging ornaments on empty space
gold clips, lacquer combs, plastic hairpins on empty space
I am sticking wire pins into empty space
I pour words over empty space, enthrall the empty space
packing, stuffing, jamming empty space
spinning necklaces around empty space
Fancy this, imagine this: painting the phenomenal world
bangles on wrists
pendants hung on empty space
I am putting my memory into empty space
undressing you

hanging the wrinkled clothes on a nail
hanging the green coat on a nail
dancing in the evening it ended with dancing in the evening
I am still thinking about putting makeup on empty space
I want to scare you: the hanging night, the drifting night,
the moaning night, daughter of troubled sleep I want to scare you
I bind as far as cold day goes
I bind the power of 20 husky men
I bind the seductive colorful women, all of them
I bind the massive rock
I bind the hanging night, the drifting night, the
moaning night, daughter of troubled sleep
I am binding my debts, I magnetize the phone bill
bind the root of my sharp pointed tongue
I cup my hands in water, splash water on empty space
water drunk by empty space
Look what thoughts will do   Look what words will do
from nothing to the face
from nothing to the root of the tongue
from nothing to speaking of empty space
I bind the ash tree
I bind the yew
I bind the willow
I bind uranium
I bind the uneconomical unrenewable energy of uranium
dash uranium to empty space
I bind the color red I seduce the color red to empty space
I put the sunset in empty space
I take the blue of his eyes and make an offering to empty space
renewable blue
I take the green of everything coming to life, it grows &
climbs into empty space
I put the white of the snow at the foot of empty space
I clasp the yellow of the cat's eyes sitting in the
black space I clasp them to my heart, empty space
I want the brown of this floor to rise up into empty space
Take the floor apart to find the brown,
bind it up again under spell of empty space
I want to take this old wall apart I am rich in my mind thinking
of this, I am thinking of putting makeup on empty space
Everything crumbles around empty space
the thin dry weed crumbles, the milkweed is blown
   into empty space

I bind the stars reflected in your eye
from nothing to these typing fingers
from nothing to the legs of the elk
from nothing to the neck of the deer
from nothing to porcelain teeth
from nothing to the fine stand of pine in the forest
I kept it going when I put the water on
when I let the water run
sweeping together in empty space
There is a better way to say empty space
Turn yourself inside out and you might disappear
you have a new definition in empty space
What I like about impermanence is the clash
of my big body with empty space
I am putting the floor back together again
I am rebuilding the wall
I am slapping mortar on bricks
I am fastening the machine together with delicate wire
There is no eternal thread, maybe there is thread of pure gold
I am starting to sing inside about the empty space
there is some new detail every time
I am taping the picture I love so well on the wall:
moonless black night beyond country plaid curtains
everything illuminated out of empty space
I hang the black linen dress on my body
the hanging night, the drifting night, the moaning night
daughter of troubled sleep
This occurs to me
I hang up a mirror to catch stars, everything occurs to me out in the
night in my skull of empty space
I go outside in starry ice
I build up the house again in memory of empty space
This occurs to me about empty space
that it is nevered to be mentioned again
Fancy this
imagine this
painting the phenomenal world
There's talk of dressing the body with strange adornments
to remind you of a vow to empty space
There's talk of the discourse in your mind like a silkworm
I wish to venture into a not chiseled place
I pour sand on the ground
Objects and vehicles emerge from the fog

the canyon is dangerous tonight
suddenly there are warning lights
The patrol is helpful in the manner of guiding
there is talk of slowing down
there is talk of a feminine deity
I bind her with a briar
I bind with the tooth of a tiger
I bind with my quartz crystal
I magnetize the worlds
I cover myself with jewels
I drink amrita
there is some new detail every time
there is a spangle on her shoe
there is a stud on her boot
the tires are studded for the difficult climb
I put my hands to my face
I am putting makeup on empty space
I wanted to scare you with the night that scared me
the drifting night, the moaning night
Someone was always intruding to make you forget empty space
you put it all on
you paint your nails
you put on scarves
all the time adorning empty space
Whatever-your-name-is I tell you "empty space"
with your fictions with dancing come around to it
with your funny way of singing come around to it
with your smiling come to it
with your enormous retinue & accumulation come around to it
with your extras come round to it
with your good fortune, with your lazy fortune come round to it
when you look most like a bird, that is the time to come around to it
when you are cheating, come to it
when you are in your anguished head
when you are not sensible
when you are insisting on the
praise from many tongues
It begins with the root of the tongue
it begins with the root of the heart
there is a spinal cord of wind
singing & moaning in empty space

Helping the Dreamer

It seems you've been misled through
the wrong instrument which would have you
wind tears around trees, would have you
devote your head to biology, the history
and cost of reproduction in *Daphnia pulex,*
would have you gibbering of night things
glassy water of the bay, unmitigated blackness,
sleek fur, a sharp hoot, butane lamps

The air full of music now, those runnels
speak to me, human and mechanical images
meshed together, speak to me gliding
around a room crosshatched with your desire,
speak in low smoke tones, monosyllabic,
dry, the repeated pattern of flowers
on wallpaper, speak a language I'll
understand (smiling lips and eyes)

Speak to master your shuddering, and
the surface looks you in the eye
which is how it seems, some kind of
ecstasy instead of taut anger which
dissolves into the indelible feeling that
you've always lived to be in this moment
stretched out between serenity and turmoil
this world you pounce on with your heart

Which has been loitering and hidden
in the havoc of the same instrument which
operates like an anemone in the first
touch of an idea, say, that you live
in a lair of fear and quick-panting
That your body could be mentally prepared
for any ride, that life is a maze-room,
the busy clicking of a computer, that

It's all over your head, petulant and sombre,
That it rides you, the dreamer, bitterly
disappointed in the weather, in the

gawky shapes of friends who haunt you,
biorhythms in a tangle, refusing to be
relegated to anyone's pocket, returning
the jeers, your footsteps quicken to get you
out of here, out of your brute nature

A difficult technique, stuff in the blood
stream, coursing to seep its aureole
into the sky in front of you, the sky a
forehead of the fathers, a large reflection
of whoever they may be in any mythical sense
while you are set up as Mother Earth
The colors conspire to make you glow and
your crepe-soled boots set up a reverberating

Echo though the landscape which is only
your projection anyway, newborn mountains
steaming from the sea, old-born negotiations
of civilizations about who can and can't reside here
Here with your white skin, your tinny voice,
telepathic gifts, inspired by the climb in
horror and astonishment, seeing how everything
works and co-exists, laboratories of

Discretion and secrecy, true believers
in shadow-power, believing in the solidity
of gadgets that do the appointed jobs,
axis of belief structures falling apart
accepting caprice as natural door into
the unknown, and slithering back inside
to the heart which would now like to
relax in soft upholstery, a contradictory parallel

To life as you experience it out here
on the wild hill. Hold back and let the
clothes speak, tight at groin, let the
buildings you left below speak of their
being so square at edges, let the
architects speak of their maniacal designs

to control and imprison space, making it
lucrative in a false version of comfort

Let more places open up with the names of
initials. B.C.'s, J.R.'s, J.J.'s, M.O.'s
as if it's hip to be in shorthand and
"cute" while out on the pond the shifting
ice groans its name of mutability and promise
The geese are also handsome in the light
honking their presence out of sorts or in tandem
while I'm sorting the crumpled papers

which speak of worshiping Ninni–zaza
Akkadian goddess whose eyes were clouded
by love, who was replaced by Saint Simeon
centuries later and then the world gets
married again to yet again another male saint, how
if these words could be hammered back by
an alien planet, what would we make of them?
What are the dimmest memories of solar systems?

Anomalies of man and woman power, as the new/old
comet appears in the sky in the region
of Jupiter before the watchful eye of the
perpetual "watcher" who remains arrogant
till he blisters under the hot sun and is
left to comment on all this as some kind of
irritable miraculous mistake, not being able
to understand that the plateau ahead

would be just right for getting
around with relatives, anyone who has ever
been part of you, next to you, that it *is* hospitable
this great warm earth, that it's all here:
the stormy sky, the fragrant trees, the
tenacious lichen, while elsewhere a woman
in all artifice dyes her hair black underneath
to convey secret mourning for a lost lover

Both, both. Both the way you want it,
and the way it is. Both staying and leaving.
Both memory and no memory, both things that
can tell lies and things that don't know how,
both acquiescing and resisting, both familiar
and strange. Both sheer and thick, both
separated and together, walking and standing still
Both audible and silent, both flat and round

And you are never not linked up with how
you perceive it all and how it really is,
all the messages of the sublunary sphere
at a time fueled by the iron fist of profit-
and-gain, what makes it all run, a time
which seems to be smiling nonetheless
as if to say perhaps the moon's in the
wrong corner of the sky, look up and see

Philip Whalen

Philip Whalen was born in Portland, Oregon, and educated at Reed College. He has written a number of works, including *On Bear's Head, The Diamond Noodle, Enough Said: Poems, 1974–1979*, and *Grey Fox*. He is an ordained Zen Buddhist priest.

About Writing and Meditation

I thought that I'd write books and make money enough from them to travel abroad and to have a private life of reading and study and music. I developed a habit of writing and I've written a great deal, but I've got very little money for it.

With meditation I supposed that one could acquire magical powers. Then I learned that it would produce enlightenment. Much later, I found out that Dogen is somewhere on the right track when he tells us that the practice of zazen is the practice of enlightenment. Certainly there's no money in it. Now I have a meditation habit.

Jack Kerouac said that writing is a habit like taking dope. It's a pleasure to write. I usually write everything in longhand. I like the feel of the pen working on the paper.

In my experience these two habits are at once mutually destructive and yet similar in kind. I write for the excitement of doing it. I don't think of an audience; I think of the words that I'm using, trying to select the right ones. In zazen I sit to satisfy my sitting habit. It does no more than that. But while sitting, I don't grab onto ideas or memories or verbal phrases. I simply watch them all go by. They don't get written; they don't (or anyway, very seldom) trip the relay on my writing machinery. Considering that I've spent more days in the past fifteen years sitting zazen than I have spent in writing, it's little wonder that I've produced few books during that time.

I became a poet by accident. I never intended to be a poet. I still don't know what it's all about. If I wrote poetry at all, it's because I could finish it at the end of the page. Maybe it would run halfway down the next page, but it would come to a stop. What I wanted to do with writing was to write novels and make money like anybody else. And now I find myself in this ridiculous industry of writing these incomprehensible doodles, and why anybody's reading them I can't understand.

As far as meditation is concerned I'm a professional. I've been a professional since 1973. And that's my job. I find it very difficult to sell. And that's interesting; that's another job I have, to sell you on this idea that it's good to sit. Maybe that's where the poetry comes into all this, that it has to be an articulation of my practice and an encouragement to you to enter into Buddhist practice. To get yourselves trapped into it I hope. And then try to figure out how to get out of it. It's harder to get out of Buddhist practice than it is to get out of writing poetry.

I write very little nowadays. There is a journal in which I write things like "the sun is shining" or "Michael McClure was in town and we had a nice time" or "the flowers are blooming." And so I don't have much to say because I talk all the time. I have to give lectures, I participate in seminars, and I have not much chance to wander up and down a hillside picking flowers and picking my nose and scratching my balls and whatnot. And thinking of hearing, having a chance to hear what's going on around me, or hearing people in restaurants or on a bus. There are no restaurants in Santa Fe worth sitting in, there are no buses at all. So I don't hear anymore, hardly at all, unless I travel. I was recently in New York and around, and now I'm here at Green Gulch Farm, and it's interesting to hear what's going on outside. While somebody was talking there was a robin outside raising hell. But that doesn't mean anything. I mean I'm not about to write a poem on the subject of so-and-so talking, while a robin outside was raising hell.

And so I'm here under false pretenses. You must deal with that however you can. I'm quite willing to talk to people and explain things to them if they have questions. Or I might be sitting doltishly looking out the window. So it will be necessary for you, if you want something from me, to try to get it by asking questions. I'm not about to offer anything, I don't have anything to offer. I'm sorry—that's the "emptiness" part.

I think there's a great deal of misunderstanding about what emptiness is, the idea that emptiness is something that happens under a bell jar when you exhaust all the air from it. That's not quite where it's at as far as I understand it. The emptiness is the thing we're full of, and everything that you're seeing here is empty. Literally the word is *shunya,* something that's swollen up; it's not, as often translated, "void." It's packed, it's full of everything. Just as in Shingon Buddhism, the theory that everything we see and experience is Mahavairochana Buddha, the great unmanifest is what we're actually living and seeing in. Wallace Stevens said, "We live in an old chaos of the sun." Well we're living in a live chaos of Mahavairochana Buddha. What are you gonna do with it? How are you gonna handle that?

My Buddhist name is Zenshin Ryufu, which is very impressive. The reason that you have a name like that is that you keep forgetting it and it makes you wonder about why you got it and why it's for you, because it's a very exalted idea. *Zenshin* means "meditation mind" and it's also a Japanese pun. It means something like "complete mind." There's also a zenshin essay by Dogen. *Ryufu* is two Chinese characters that literally mean "dragon wind," but in Chinese literature I found out it means "imperial influence" (the dragon stands for the Chinese emperor). It's pretty complicated, and you wonder, well what does that have to do with me? Four words—Zen-Mind-Dragon-Wind. What in the world, what connection does that have with this individual who has received this name and is ordained as a monk? So that is a problem that becomes more or less clear as you continue being a monk—what your name is. And of course names and poetry all come together. Gertrude Stein says poetry is calling the name of something. That's what we do all the time, actually—call ourselves. There's the story of the Zen master who every day would call his own name. He'd say, "Zuigan!" And he'd say, "Yes!" "Zuigan! Don't be misled by other people!" Of course the other people were Zuigan too.

I like the idea somebody mentioned of erratic practice. It immediately reminded me of rocks that were left around when the glaciers receded. A lot of times setting out in a field there are no other rocks. It's a very strange appearance. You can't account for the rock's position unless you remember the glacier that carried the rock there and then went away. Zazen is slow but leaves erratic boulders.

I have a number of fancy titles at the Dharmasangha in Santa Fe. But when push comes to shove it means that I'm the person who goes down and does the opening ceremony in the zendo every morning and sits two periods. And then I go down again at 5:30 in the evening and sit again with whoever shows up. And the rest of the time I study. We have two seminars a week with Baker Roshi on the koans in the *Shoyoruko* as translated by Thomas Cleary. I've also been studying with Baker Roshi closely for the last three years with the intention at last of trying to become a Buddhist teacher, to help get this show on the road, which is still very precarious in this country. The chances as I see it of Buddhism simply becoming something that people do on Sunday just like Methodism or Catholicism are very strong. But I hope that there will continue to be centers in the country like Tassajara, or Shasta Abbey, or Mt. Baldy. There will be these hidden spots around the country where people can hide out and do more serious, concentrated practice, to keep the door open for everybody to get the chance to try it out, find out what it's like to not do anything except follow a particular schedule and do a lot of sitting and a lot of physical work. This is something that I think is necessary in order for human beings to go on being human beings. So far all we've been able to invent in the United States is the business of building small cabins in the woods and going there to hide out, then come back and write a book about it.

That practice, that sort of individual, hermit, erratic practice, is something that's really important. The danger of Zen Centers or monasteries is that people will take them seriously as being real. We should find our own practice; we might start out in an official place, but we should discover somehow that we don't need official institutions. It's exactly like Lew Welch says in his poem about the rock out there, the Wobbly Rock, "Somebody showed it to me and I found it myself." The quote isn't exact. Lew was an erratic Zen practitioner who was a great poet.

The real tension, I think, is between official poetry, the kind that we're taught in school and is kept in libraries, and the kind we really believe in—what we are writing and what our friends write. The same thing holds for meditation: what we discover for ourselves and learn. At some point you can forget it and go off and make a pot of spaghetti. We used to do go down to Muir Beach years ago to gather mussels off the rocks. We'd build a bonfire, put seaweed on the fire to steam the mussels. We'd eat them, then jump up and down in the waves and have fun. That was . . . enough. Probably enough. Or too much. Oh, I guess Blake said it, "Enough, or too much." That's all.

All About Art & Life

a compulsion to make
          marks on paper

whatever good or bad

                "& as for meaning
                let them alone to mean
                themselves"

or that I'm ill
out of adjustment
not relating with real situation in living

room I just left below
    i.e. two other people, friends of mine
    reading books

a shock out of the eye-corner
Dome & cornices of Sherith Israel
    blue sky & fog streaks
    (reminiscences of Corot, Piranesi)

                to mean themselves
                Adam & Eve & Pinch-Me

walks out of silence, monotony
many colors dangling & sparkling

       (TINKLE?)

there.   You know.   Uh-huh

               we kill ourselves making it

PICTURE: a wood-engraving by Bewick
                   GIANT WOOLY COW

PICTURE: children, their faces concealed
                   by their hats which are heads which are
                   flowers

PICTURE: Leonardo: *Madonna & Child, with*
                   S. Giovanbattista

PICTURE: Ladies in marble palace with fountains
                   located high in Canadian Rockies a peacock
                   light the color of burning incense

PICTURE:.   a room, & through the door a hallway with
                   a small round or octagonal window

PICTURE: 2 Bedouins praying in sand/ocean a camel
                   with square quizzing-glass on head

PICTURE: All of us when we were young before you

were born

2 PICTURES: Battle scenes (medieval-type) in high plaster
                  relief curved glass not lens, no sound

LARGE PICTURE: C. S. Price: Indian women who might be
                  mountains picking huckleberries in moun-
                  tains that might be Indian women

PICTURE: 5 Persimmons (Chinese)

52 PICTURES: (Mexican provenance) playing-cards, each
                  one different, repellent & instructive

PICTURE: 360 degrees: the world is outdoors it is both
                  inaccessible & unobtainable
                  we belong to it

. . . most of your problems will disappear if you sit
still (privately, *i.e.* in solitude) 1 hour per day
without going to sleep (do not speak, hum or whistle
the while) . . .

The orders of architecture we are to suppose symbols of the
human intellect & inspiration (in this case, severe Romano-Judaic)

"a symbol doesn't MEAN
    anything
    it IS
    something . . . relationship of that kind doesn't exist
    except in the old philosophy whose vocabulary
    you insist on using . . ."

              MANIFESTS itself
whether I write or not
    we call it good, bad, indifferent as
    we feel ourselves exalted or brought down
it has its own name but never answers
never at home
              & we want a stage for our scene

(wow)
as if Shakespeare
                    LIED

---

all of us end up

                    Zero for Conduct

You bet.

              Why bother to say I detest liver
                              & adore magnolia flowers
              Liver keeps its flavor the blossoms
                    drop off
                                    & reappear, whoever
              cares, counts, contends

I said to the kitten rolling the glass
      "Kitty, you're stupid"
Thoughtlessly: the cat's growing
      exercising & I merely talking to hear my head rattle

What opinion do you hold on Antinomianism?
It makes me nervous trying to remember what it was
& which side of the argument Milton took
      also rattles
              Not I love or hate:

              WHAT IS IT I'M SEEING?

                    &

              WHO'S LOOKING?

It comes to us straight & flat
My cookie-cutter head makes shapes of it

              CHONK: "scary!"
              CHONK: "lovely!"
              CHONK: "ouch!"

                    but any of us is worth more
                    than it
                    except that moment

> it walks out of me, through me

& you ask, Where does it come from
Where did I go

Some people got head like a jello mold
It pours in & takes one shape only
Or instantly becomes another flavor
> raspberry to vanilla
> strawberry to vanilla
> orange to vanilla, etc.

Some legendary living ones can take it or leave it alone
They go on planting potatoes, writing poems, whatever they do
Without hangups
Minimum bother to themselves & all the rest of the world
And anyone observing them a little may
> turn all the way
> ON

Meanwhile, psychologists test us
> & get a bell-shaped curve
They know something or other I could tell them any time

All this is merely
> GRAMMAR

The building I sit in
A manifestation of desire, hope, fear
As I in my own person, all the world I see . . .

Water drops from tap to sink
Naturally the tap's defective or not completely "OFF"
Naturally I hear: My ears do what they're made for

> (a momentary reflection—will my brain
> suffer a certain amount of water erosion
> while I sleep?—)
&
> OUT

28:viii:59—9:ix:59

Opening the Mountain, Tamalpais: 22:x:65

Hot sunny morning, Allen and Gary, here they come, we are ready. Sutras in creek-bed, chants and lustrations, bed of Redwood Creek John Muir's Woods.

First Shrine: Oak tree grows out of rock
                     Field of Lazuli Buntings, crow song

Second Shrine: Trail crosses fire road at hilltop
                     Address to the Ocean,
                     Siva music addressed to the peaks

Third Shrine: Rock Springs music for Sarasvati
                     Remember tea with Mike and JoAnn years ago
                     Fresh water in late dry season

Fourth Shrine: Rifle Camp lunch, natural history:
                     Allen: "What do wasps do?"
                     Gary: "Mess around."

Fifth Shrine: Collier Spring, Great Dharani & Tara music

Sixth Shrine: Inspiration Point, Gatha of Vajra Intellectual
                     Heat Lightning

TO THE SUMMIT: North Side Trail, scramble up vertical North
                     Knee WHERE IS THE MOUNTAIN?

Seventh Shrine the Mountain top: Prajnaparamita Sutra, as many
                     others as could be remembered in music & song

Eighth Shrine, The parking lot, Mountain Home
                     Sunset Amida going West
                     O Gopala, &c Devaki Nandi na Gopala
                     with a Tibetan encore for Tara,
                     Song against disaster.

RETURN TO CREEKBED, MUIR WOODS: Final pronouncement of the
Sutras

> We marched around the mountain, west to east
> top to bottom—from sea-level (chanting dark stream bed
> Muir Woods) to bright summit sun victory of gods and
> buddhas, conversion of demons, liberation of all sentient
> beings in all worlds past present and future.

Japanese Tea Garden Golden Gate Park in Spring

1.
I come to look at the cherryblossoms
>> for the last time

2.
Look up through flower branching Deva world
>> (happy ignorance)

3.
These blossoms will be gone in a week
I'll be gone long before.

That is to say, the cherry trees will blossom every year but I'll
disappear for good, one of these days. There. That's all about the
absolute permanence of the most impossibly fragile delicate and
fleeting objects. By objects, I mean this man who is writing this, the
stars, baked ham, as well as the cherryblossoms. This doesn't explain anything.

2:iv:65

John Wolff

John Wolff was born in Sioux City, Iowa, and has lived mainly in the West and Midwest. He is the author of *Complaints from the West-River Country* and *Möbius Landscapes*. Recently returned from a year in the People's Republic of China, he lives and teaches in Pocatello, Idaho.

The Governors of Zuni (A Photograph)

Politics like water
takes the path of least resistance.
All my life I've been trying to tell you
and now I see their still torsos
those governors of Zuni
pressed like leaves in the book of my imagination
severe and abstracted almost archetypal
as though to tell you
how each of us sits in his own shadow
letting the walls treat us like rats.

So those governors they sat still as trees in July
eight limbs hung dead at their sides
while politics like water washed over them.
And because we were once wrong
ignored their sympathy for nature
we can never be right for this world
its only sun must turn and lever down
on lodgepole rafters cold adobe without us.
Nor allowed to be right ever after
we stepped out to the edge of the world

deluded with self-potential
and a faith that we were new.

Again the desert appears within us.
Paths cross in wastelands
drifting toward empire's end.
We stagger from moment to moment
alone in sandy places in dry
the countryside hills blooming with spines
and desert cities green with the wasted Colorado.
We recognize this place like all of them.
We have been here
oh we have always been here
though once we tried to leave
before each frontier became the vista of our return.

Nursery Song for Two Sons

My son rides rocking horse
my other son rides the ocean
of his mother in darkness.
He is blind and numb
but he hears voices
wandering where he is planted.
His root is blood
his branch reaches air
though he is drowned
divine in the heart
that beats every measure of his life
wave in wave.

Outside
voices inscribe the lipless dark
with futile hopes.

In this story
no one may dismount
but rage toward the line of battle
and revolution
born.

We are perhaps unique rememberers
of our mothers' wombs
driven vainly to duplicate them
like no other species
the world that is light in our original dark.

I say my son rides tirelessly
a blue steed with yellow saddle.
He knows fresh horses
must come to him in life.
But the ride cannot stop
and the war fields stretch away
invincibly.

Möbius Landscape

Hard to hide
my love for it
it runs down Argue Road
a bend and a hill
the green is verdurous
the trees are full
and heavy
with leaves rolled in the heat
exposing the gray egg sacs
of insects left to be born
in spring months
when the larvae flourish
consume the leaf
as we consume
the branch where we've been hung
and in that leaf
digest the souls of our dead
the chlorophyllic echo
of predecessors
who fly themselves toward decay
like the sun does in its bloodbath
tonight so left
with the green cicada's song
a voltage of the trees
a moment when all the generations sing.

Butterfly Effect

You watched as men in tall hats
rode beautifully to the focal point
and then stopped propping themselves
on the necks of their horses
blowing smoke
as the vast undulations of Wyoming
carried them away again
the dun earth drummed by animals.
You could not speak to the photograph
even though they waved and smiled at you
from a distance of a hundred years.
They rode into mists of your whispers
twenty miles deep
goes the picture of their eternity.

But I tell you it does not take much
to change things permanently deeply.
Only a moment ago I was here alone
watching the sun burn a path through afternoon
quiet birds preening on poles.
They say "a special sensitivity to original conditions"
will infinitely ripple through the world
without diminution
as though those strong dark horses
stealing over cirrus plains
and what aspect of minuscule men feeling confident
would blow up the world to radioactive confetti
or pass dinner to their children at the tables of dusk
or stand amid acres of sage
sniffing and retaining nothing
of quiet silos' buried missiles.

No we put down our lives indelibly
impossible to say what effect
a billion years could bring.
But bring it it will
as though mere seeing daydreaming thoughts
would blow against the pavilions of belief
as though it were peace that is the thought of peace
what sputtering fabric of the real

runs to palsy because I simply am.
It is not possible to close the book upon that stark Wyoming
where antebellum riders rein cattle out
on edgeless pages of legacy.

Everything lasts.
I said it lasts.
We plow
and the margin of the west
is no thicker than a blade of grass.

About the Editors

KENT JOHNSON is a member of the faculty of Highland Community College in Freeport, Illinois, where he teaches English and Spanish. His writing has appeared in the *American Poetry Review, Grand Street, Michigan Quarterly Review,* and *Sulfur.* He is editor of *Third Wave: The New Russian Poetry.*

CRAIG PAULENICH is an Assistant Professor of English and Writing Coordinator at Kent State University, Salem Campus. He was the recipient of the Academy of American Poets Award at the University of Pittsburgh in 1982. His poems have appeared in *The Georgia Review, Kansas Review, South Carolina Review, Southern Poetry Review, Tar River Poetry,* and *Windhorse.*

Credits

Index of Titles

Index of First Lines